Lecture Notes in Computer Scien

Commenced Publication in 1973
Founding and Former Series Editors:
Gerhard Goos, Juris Hartmanis, and Jan van Leeuwen

Hitomi Murakami   Hideyuki Nakashima
Hideyuki Tokuda   Michiaki Yasumura

Ubiquitous Computing Systems

Second International Symposium, UCS 2004
Tokyo, Japan, November 8-9, 2004
Revised Selected Papers

 Springer

Volume Editors

Hitomi Murakami
KDDI, IT Developement Division
GARDEN AIR TOWER, 3-10-10, Iidabashi, Chiyoda-ku
Tokyo 102-8460, Japan
E-mail: hi-murakami@kddi.com

Hideyuki Nakashima
Future University - Hakodate
116-2 Kameda-Nakanocho, Hakodate, Hokkaido, 041-8655, Japan
E-mail: h.nakashima@fun.ac.jp

Hideyuki Tokuda
Keio University
Faculty of Environmental Information
5322 Endo, Fujisawa, Kanagawa 252-8520, Japan
E-mail: hxt@sfc.keio.ac.jp

Michiaki Yasumura
Keio University
5322 Endo, Fujisawa, Kanagawa, 252-8520, Japan
E-mail: yasumura@sfc.keio.ac.jp

Library of Congress Control Number: 2005929501

CR Subject Classification (1998): C.2, C.3, C.5.3, D.2, D.4, H.4, H.5, K.4, J.7

ISSN   0302-9743
ISBN-10   3-540-27893-1 Springer Berlin Heidelberg New York
ISBN-13   978-3-540-27893-1 Springer Berlin Heidelberg New York

Springer is a part of Springer Science+Business Media

springeronline.com

© Springer-Verlag Berlin Heidelberg 2005
Printed in Germany

Typesetting: Camera-ready by author, data conversion by Scientific Publishing Services, Chennai, India
Printed on acid-free paper   SPIN: 11526858   06/3142   5 4 3 2 1 0

Preface

This book is a collection of papers presented at UCS 2004, held on November 8–9 in Tokyo. UCS is a series of international symposia sponsored by the special interest group Ubiquitous Computing Systems of the Information Processing Society of Japan. The first UCS was held on November 17, 2003 in Kyoto. It was held as an invitation-based symposium. UCS 2004 was the second of the series, and the first submission-based conference.

UCS focuses on the emerging research area of ubiquitous computing systems. This emergence is an outcome of the rapid evolution in smart appliances and devices, as well as tremendous advances in wireless networks and mobile computing. In the last few years, various applications of information technology have been changing our everyday life rapidly and to a large extent. The best example is the use of mobile phones. By getting new sensing devices, cameras, their application field is no longer limited to communication but covers data communications including Internet access, and data and program up-/downloading, and so on.

The symposium offered the opportunity for in-depth exploration of the most recent research and development findings in the field of ubiquitous computing. The submitted papers presented at UCS 2004 suggest such a direction to at future technologies, including mobile ad hoc networks, sensor networks and context-aware technologies.

Reflecting the growth of the research field, we received 50 submissions from 15 countries ranging all over the world, from which we accepted 20 papers resulting in a 40% acceptance ratio. Each paper was reviewed by at least three PC members and all review comments were examined carefully by PC co-chairs to finalize the decision. In this book, we have 18 normal papers, plus 2 papers from invited speakers.

We also carefully selected two invited talks. The first one was titled "The Pervasive Sensor" by Kristof Van Laerhoven, Lancaster University, UK. The second one was titled "From Everyday Things to Everyday Memories: Two Kinds of Interactions with Objects in A House" by Hisao Nojima, Seijo University, Japan. The first talk was on the basic-level technology of ubiquitous computing, and the second was on a possible application of ubiquitous computing technologies.

May 2005   Hideyuki Tokuda and Hitomi Murakami

           Hideyuki Nakashima and Michiaki Yasumura

Organization

UCS 2004 was organized by the Ubiquitous Computing System Group of the Information Processing Society of Japan (IPSJ) in cooperation with IPSJ-SIGHI, IPSJ-SIGMBL, the Human Interface Society, the URON group of IEICE, the Ubiquitous Networking Forum, and the Japan Society for Software Science and Technology.

General Co-chairs

Hideyuki Tokuda   Keio University, Japan
Hitomi Murakami   KDDI, Japan

Program Co-chairs

Hideyuki Nakashima   Future University—Hakodate, Japan
Michiaki Yasumura   Keio University, Japan

Posters/Demonstrations Chair

Yasuto Nakanishi   TUAT, Japan

Publicity Co-chairs

Michael Beigl   University of Karlsruhe, Germany
Jalal Al-Muhtadi   University of Illinois at Urbana-Champaign, USA
Hiroyuki Morikawa   University of Tokyo, Japan

Treasurer

Yoshito Tobe   Tokyo Denki University, Japan

Local Arrangements

Hiroaki Higaki   Tokyo Denki University, Japan
Masayuki Iwai   Keio University, Japan
Masana Murase   IBM, Japan
Kazunori Takashio   Keio University, Japan

Web Master

Mika Minematsu   Keio University, Japan

System Management

Tadashi Yanagihara   Keio University, Japan

Publications

Koichi Kurumatani   AIST, Japan
Kenji Sasaki   Tokyo Denki University, Japan
Akio Sashima   AIST, Japan

Secretariat

Masayoshi Ohashi   KDDI, Japan

Technical Program Committee Members

Michael Beigl   University of Karlsruhe, Germany
Miwako Doi   Toshiba Corporation, Japan
Masaaki Fukumoto   NTT DoCoMo, Japan
Motohisa Funabashi   Hitachi, Japan
Hans-Werner Gellersen   Lancaster University, UK
Kôiti Hasida   AIST, Japan
Lars Erik Holmquist   Viktoria Institute, Sweden
Hiroki Horiuchi   KDDI R&D Labs, Japan
Antonio Krueger   DFKI, Germany
Koichi Kurumatani   AIST, Japan
Marc Langheinrich   ETH, Switzerland
Toshiyuki Masui   AIST, Japan
Hiroyuki Morikawa   University of Tokyo, Japan
Tatsuo Nakajima   Waseda University, Japan
Kumiyo Nakakoji   University of Tokyo, Japan
Jin Nakazawa   Keio University, Japan
Masayoshi Ohashi   KDDI, Japan
Jun Rekimoto   Sony C.S. Labs, Japan
Ichiro Satoh   NII, Japan
Bernt Schiele   ETH, Switzerland
Itiro Siio   Tamagawa University, Japan
Frank Stajano   University of Cambridge, UK
Kazunori Takashio   Keio University, Japan
Youichi Takebayashi   Shizuoka University, Japan
Steven Willmott   Universitat Politècnica de Catalunya, Spain

Reviewers

Yuji Ayatsuka	Sony CSL, Japan
Jörg Baus	Saarland University, Germany
Michael Beigl	University of Karlsruhe, Germany
Juergen Bohn	ETH Zurich, Switzerland
Boris Brandherm	Saarland University, Germany
Christian Decker	University of Karlsruhe, Germany
Miwako Doi	Toshiba, Japan
Masaaki Fukumoto	NTT DoCoMo Multimedia Laboratories, Japan
Motohisa Funabashi	Hitachi, Japan
Hans Gellersen	Lancaster University, UK
Kôiti Hasida	AIST, Japan
Paul Havinga	University of Twente, The Netherlands
Dominik Heckmann	Saarland University, Germany
Lars Erik Holmquist	Viktoria Institute, Sweden
Masaru Honjo	KDDI Corporation, Japan
Hiroki Horiuchi	KDDI R&D Labs, Japan
Kiyoshi Izumi	AIST, Japan
Michimune Kohno	Sony CSL, Japan
Albert Krohn	University of Karlsruhe, Germany
Antonio Krüger	Saarland University, Germany
Koichi Kurumatani	AIST, Japan
Marc Langheinrich	ETH Zurich, Switzerland
Toshiyuki Masui	AIST, Japan
Yutaka Matsuo	AIST, Japan
Daisuke Morikawa	KDDI Corporation, Japan
Hiroyuki Morikawa	University of Tokyo, Japan
Tatsuo Nakajima	Waseda University, Japan
Kumiyo Nakakoji	University of Tokyo, Japan
Jin Nakazawa	Keio University, Japan
Masayoshi Ohashi	KDDI Corporation, Japan
Jun Rekimoto	Sony Computer Science Laboratory, Japan
Michael Rohs	ETH Zurich, Switzerland
Akio Sashima	AIST, Japan
Ichiro Satoh	National Institute of Informatics, Japan
Bernt Schiele	TU Darmstadt, Germany
Takahiro Shiga	Toyota Central R&D Labs Inc., Japan
Itiro Siio	Tamagawa University, Japan
Frank Stajano	University of Cambridge, UK
Shigeru Tajima	Sony CSL, Japan
Kazunori Takashio	Keio University, Japan
Yoichi Takebayashi	Shizuoka University, Japan
Yoshito Tobe	Tokyo Denki University, Japan
Steven Willmott	Universitat Politècnica de Catalunya, Spain
Akira Yamaguchi	KDDI Corporation, Japan
Tomohisa Yamashita	AIST, Japan
Hidetoshi Yokota	KDDI R&D Labs, Japan
Tobias Zimmer	University of Karlsruhe, Germany

Sponsoring Institutions

Crossbow Technology
Ubigraph
OS Technology
J-Techno

Table of Contents

Systems

Context Awareness

Sensors and Tags

The Pervasive Sensor

Kristof Van Laerhoven

Lancaster University,
United Kingdom
http://www.comp.lancs.ac.uk/~kristof

Abstract. Forget processing power, memory, or the size of computers for a
moment: Sensors, and the data they provide, are as important as any of these
factors in realising ubiquitous and pervasive computing. Sensors have already
become influential components in newer applications, but their data needs to be
used more intelligently if we want to unlock their true potential. This requires
improved ways to design and integrate sensors in computer systems, and
interpret their signals.

1 Introduction

Most dictionaries agree on the fact that sensors are devices that are capable of
detecting and responding to physical stimuli such as movement, light or heat. The
more perceptive reader will observe that this definition is not very specific:
Identifying the sensors in a system is often fairly straightforward, but trying to track
down examples of the first human-made sensors with this definition for instance is
much harder. Similarly, the difficulty in exactly identifying the parts in a system that
belong to one sensor, underlines the vagueness of what a sensor really constitutes.

This introduction will begin with challenging a few preconceptions one might have
about sensors and the process of sensing and measuring, before moving on to stress
the importance of sensors in the future of computing.

1.1 What Does a Sensor Look Like?

Show an engineer a photodiode, and chances are that he or she will identify it as a
(light) sensor, or at least would not object to someone else calling it a sensor. Saying
that a bird in a cage is a sensor might seem a lot more challenging, but given the
definition above it would be possible to treat it as such: 19th century miners would
carry along 'cages' with them to detect the presence of carbon monoxide or methane,
deadly mine gases which humans cannot detect until it is too late. The canary in the
cage, on the other hand, is more sensitive to these gases and drops dead minutes
before humans will. Few will challenge the idea of a thermometer being a sensor, but
convincing people that their pet canary is really a sophisticated toxic gases sensor is
usually a bit harder.

Using a wide enough interpretation, almost anything fits in the definition of a
sensor: In fact, even humans can be considered as sensors.

H. Murakami et al. (Eds.): UCS 2004, LNCS 3598, pp. 1–9, 2005.

1.2 The Eye of the Beholder

The observation of, and response to, the state of the sensor plays a crucial role as well. The shape and colour of clouds, the way insects fly, or the arrangement of a Galileo's thermometer[1] may be interpreted as just pleasant things to look at by some people, but are tell-tale signs for weather forecasting to others. Instruments to measure the outside temperature during a cold winter, or devices to alert miners when dangerous gasses are present, are useless until they are observed properly by someone who monitors the sensor's output and takes actions accordingly.

1.3 One-Way Bridge from Real to Digital

The sensor can also be regarded as a way to capture information from the real world and reflect it in the virtual or digital world. It is the ideal mechanism to integrate new information into an application, and sensing methods for many applications are evolving from a typical scenario where the human provides all input to the application, to one where this becomes more and more automated.

Healthcare monitoring applications, for example, used to rely on information that the doctors would manually enter in the system after doing the measurements themselves. Nowadays, this process has advanced to a stage where medical sensing devices are constantly observing the patient's state.

To focus on this automated sensing, the remainder of this extended abstract will restrict its use of the word sensor to the devices that detect physical phenomena without the help of a human.

1.4 Taking the Human Out of the Loop

Historically, sensors were primarily there to directly suit the user, and the user would be very involved in the process of sensing (e.g., tapping on a needle based barometer), interpreting the sensed (e.g., reading the amount of water in a rain meter), and taking action based on what was sensed (e.g., slowing down the car after noticing you are going too fast on the speedometer). Recent trends, however, -and ubiquitous computing is part of this as well- seem to minimise this human factor, and sometimes even remove it altogether from the process. Being able to build devices that interpret sensor data and act on it without disturbing the user, means that sensors would enable all these ubiquitous computing elements to live without strict user supervision, making them truly unnoticeable.

1.5 The Impact of Sensors

Sensors are increasingly being integrated and embedded in user interfaces to give the user a more intuitive, more sensitive, or more appropriate way to interact with computers. At the same time, sensors are also being used as replacements for user interactions altogether, in cases where the sensing is trivial, or where mistakes are

---

[1] Galileo's thermometer is made of suspended weights in a sealed glass cylinder containing a clear liquid. If this liquid changes temperature, it changes density and the suspended weights rise and fall. The weights' positions can thus be interpreted as a temperature measurement.

limited and not critical. The sensors are therefore crucial components in the visions of ubiquitous and pervasive computing, and advancing research into sensors and how one can take advantage of their data is valuable even beyond these fields.

A few challenges summarize the key areas: 'Embedding and Interfacing Sensors' considers the practical issues of adding and networking a sensor component to an object or application, 'Learning from Sensed Data' points out the difficulty of replacing the human perception with algorithms, and 'Sensor Fusion' lists some prospects and problems when trying to combine sensors' output.

2 Embedding and Interfacing Sensors

Knowing the right sensor and algorithm that process the sensed data is not enough to guarantee the system will work; this section will begin with another requirement.

2.1 Considering the Physical Properties of Sensors

The location and orientation of a sensor can play a vital role. To show what the impact can be of *where and how* a sensor is attached, consider this scenario in the area of body-worn motion sensors: A student wants to build a wearable system that monitors his posture and activities throughout the day, and as an easy start he sets out to just detect at what times in the day he is sitting down, and at what times he is standing upright. Knowing a bit about sensors, he believes that an orientation sensor just above the knee would be sufficient: it would give a relatively horizontal reading when sitting down, and the sensor would give a vertical reading when standing upright. Figure 1 illustrates the reasoning behind this.

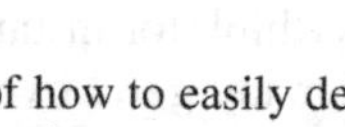

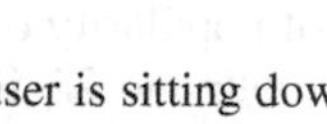

QuickTimeô and a
TIFF (LZW) decompressor
are needed to see this picture.

QuickTimeô and a
TIFF (LZW) decompressor
are needed to see this picture.

Fig. 1. Example of how to easily detect whether the user is sitting down or standing upright by attaching an orientation sensor to the upper leg. It seems to be a sound approach

Figure 2 shows how the weaknesses of this approach become obvious when following the student trying his system out: To wind down after the efforts of building his wearable sensor, he visits his local pub. Standing at the bar, he habitually places his foot on a higher position, which results in the sensor being oriented almost horizontally and logging the student, mistakenly, as 'sitting down' (Figure 2a).

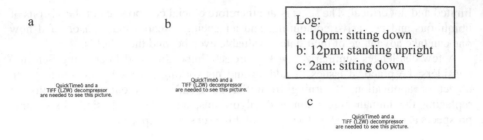

a   b

Log:
a: 10pm: sitting down
b: 12pm: standing upright
c: 2am: sitting down

QuickTimeô and a
TIFF (LZW) decompressor
are needed to see this picture.

QuickTimeô and a
TIFF (LZW) decompressor
are needed to see this picture.

c

QuickTimeô and a
TIFF (LZW) decompressor
are needed to see this picture.

Fig. 2. A few examples of how the system from Figure 1 fails to correctly recognize 'sitting down' and 'standing upright' throughout the student's evening

Similar mistakes can also happen the other way around: the student might be sitting on an elevated surface, leaving his leg dangling downwards far enough for the system to register this as 'standing upright' (Figure 2b). Even worse, poses that are neither 'sitting down' nor 'standing upright' could also be wrongly detected as one or the other: lying down (Figure 2c) for instance has the upper leg in a horizontal position, making the system register 'sitting down'.

It is important to stress here that these errors happen regardless of the quality of the sensor or the algorithms that treat the sensed data: increasing the sensor's sensitivity or using better machine learning techniques will not help.

This scenario shows not only how crucial the location, the orientation, and the position of sensors are, it also points at the importance of *combining sensors*. Adding a sensor on the other leg would improve the system dramatically (though errors can still occur). This leads to another challenge: how to transport the data from multiple, distributed sensors.

2.2 Networking Sensors

The sensed data needs in many cases to be processed elsewhere or merged with other sensed data from different locations. The first practical issue becomes then to transport and perhaps send the data over a network. Also, having multiple sensors is often just the first problem; some applications require sensor nodes in a network to be insertable or removable in an ad-hoc fashion, or they require the nodes to do both sensing and routing of neighbouring nodes' data.

Many common standards exist for these cases, with especially body-wide wireless networks gaining a lot of popularity over the last years (think for instance of the IEEE 802.15 standards, Bluetooth and ZigBee). There exist many good overviews of these types of networks (see for instance [13] or [14]), but a different, non-wireless method of networking will be discussed next, to widen the spectrum of sensor networking possibilities.

Pin&Play is based on the vision that layered surfaces can be used as a network for objects, such as sensor nodes, that become attached to these surfaces. It is very similar to the Pushpin initiative from Lifton and Paradiso [6], but has a simpler, bus-type structure with a master-slave type of architecture. Even tiny devices can be attached by means of pin adaptors and a surface with layers of conductive sheets (see Figure 3), to gain power and networking capabilities with the freedom of being plugged in any place or in any orientation.

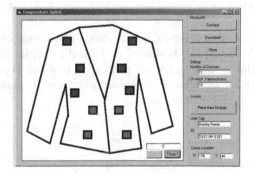

Fig. 3. The components of Pin&Play: top: the node with pin connector, bottom-left: the surface structure (using conductive textile), and bottom-right: an application using clothing as the surface and temperature measuring pins that have been attached ad hoc to the clothing [12] [9]

This network is far more appealing from an engineering point of view, since it doesn't require the network nodes to have batteries or wireless communication modules. Everything is handled via a 'master' that provides the power to the entire network and regulates network traffic, the nodes just need to be pinned in the surface to switch them on and introduce them into the network. The use of off-the-shelf components and a well-supported network protocol resulted in robust and small prototypes that are cheap, easy to (re)produce and yet more than powerful enough for many applications (see Figure 3). The network can handle hundreds of devices in a small, though two dimensional, space, which is especially attractive in the augmentation of small and mobile sensing applications. The main disadvantage for use of this networking technology in sensor networks, however, is the low bandwidth (at best 16300 bits per second). The network has in its current state also no way of finding out where a node is in the network, unlike many wireless solutions.

Pin&Play is nevertheless a great alternative to traditional wired and wireless networks, especially for dense topologies and applications where nodes rest on a common surface and where sensors' simplicity and size are more important than their transmitting speed (e.g., [11]).

3 Learning from Sensed Data

Many applications in ubiquitous and pervasive computing do not use the sensors' output directly. Instead, they classify the sensed information into concepts that are more useful to the application. These mappings between the raw sensor data and classes of interest can be straightforward (e.g., thermometer values that get classified in 'warm' and 'cold', or a passive infrared detector's values that are transformed to 'motion' and 'no motion'). These mappings are for many applications a lot more complicated, however; think for instance of a microphone for which its audio signal can be transformed into syllables or words in speech recognition, or a camera for which its images can be mapped to objects in image analysis. This more complex mapping of sensor data to high-level concepts has notably in the field of human-computer interaction frequently been marked as *context awareness*, where information from sensors is used and classified to give a description of the user's context.

The more complex classification algorithms usually work by building an internal world model that is shaped by typical examples in a so-called training phase. This is similar to finding typical properties in a few representative pictures of the number seven for a character recognition algorithm, to make it afterwards able to recognize all new instances of seven.

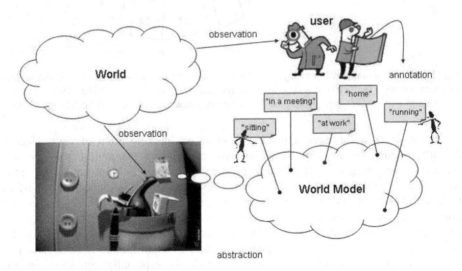

Fig. 4. Diagram of incremental learning: both user and system observe the same world, which is modeled and abstracted by the system and annotated by the user

An interesting and highly flexible type of classification of sensor data goes a step further: *incremental learning* keeps the system's world model flexible, so that new contexts can be taught to the system at any time. It works by 'showing' the new context to the system repeatedly, similar to the way speech recognition can be optimised by letting the user repeat a few phrases. Figure 4 shows a diagram of such a system where both user and system perceive the world, using respectively senses and sensors, and where the system maintains a flexible internal world model that the user is then able to annotate with her concepts.

4 Sensor Fusion

The traditional sensing system usually has one or a few sensors, and is combined with an algorithm that is specific to that architecture. There exists an alternative architecture, however, which is more distributed in nature: it is based on a large number of small and simple sensors. This direction was taken in research at MERL [5], Philips [4], the TEA project [3], or more recently MIT [1] and [7], but is still rather new and unexplored. The combination of many simple sensors that individually give information on just a small aspect of the context, results in a total picture that might be richer than the one-smart-sensor approach. The distinction between both approaches is depicted in Figure 5.

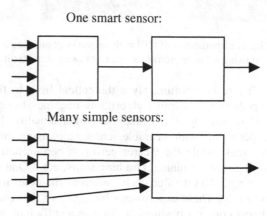

Fig. 5. Two sensor architecture approaches

4.1 Many Sensors

Most of the benefits of using multiple sensors were mentioned in previous research (see for instance [5]):

- **Cheap**. The small simple sensors require generally less resources and cost less than for instance cameras and GPS systems. An extremely large amount of simple sensors could of course invalidate this.
- **Robust**. Since the sensors we use are small, they can smoothly be distributed over a larger area, which makes the sensing system less prone to errors. In case a sensor gets blocked or damaged, other sensors will still capture context-relevant information due to the redundancy in the sensors.
- **Distributed**. The size also allows the sensors to be integrated into clothing much easier, and the high number allows them to increase the sensed area.
- **Flexible**. The richness and complexity of the identifiable contexts is directly linked to the amount, position and kind of sensors. Adding, moving, or improving sensors hence increases the performance of the system.

4.2 Simpler Sensors

The real bottleneck in this method is the software algorithm that has to combine and analyze all the data. Research described in [8] defines the choices one has to make in finding a suitable algorithm and argues for using neural networks to first cluster the sensed data.

Fig. 6. Experiments of [10] with networks containing a large amount of motion sensors: the left two using 40 accelerometers, the right two using 90 tilt switches

There is unfortunately a theoretical limit to the number of sensors one can fuse together: the adaptive algorithms become slower and less effective as sensors get added, due to the Curse of Dimensionality [2]. Figure 6 shows snapshots of experiments with wearable sensor suits using motion sensors that are distributed on the legs, while the wearer performs certain activities of interest (such as walking, sitting down, running, climbing stairs, etc.). One suit uses 40 accelerometers attached (giving a 10 bit value each), whereas the other uses 90 much simpler tilt switches (1 bit each). These experiments have shown that even simple binary sensors are able to detect complex postures, as long as a sufficient amount of them is distributed. This is important because these simpler sensors require far less resources.

5 Summary

This extended abstract argues that sensors are key components in the vision of ubiquitous computing. The traditional sensor is defined vaguely already, but the new breed of sensors and sensing applications will require even more investigation. Placing and designing sensors optimally and organising them in networks, creating algorithms that are able to learn what is being sensed, and combining sensed data, are issues that will require more attention.

Acknowledgements

Thanks go out to the organisers and all participants of UCS 2004, Tokyo, for providing a most stimulating environment with plenty of questions, remarks, and quality research that shaped this extended abstract.

References

1. Bao, L., and Intille, S. S. "Activity Recognition From User-Annotated Acceleration Data" In Proceedings of Pervasive 2004, Lecture Notes in Computer Science. Springer Verlag, Vienna, Austria. 2004.

2. R. Bellman, Adaptive Control Processes. Princeton University Press. 1961.
3. Esprit Project 26900. Technology for Enabling Awareness (TEA). http://www.teco.edu/tea, 1999.
4. Farringdon, J., Moore, A., N. Tilbury, J. Church and P. Biemond "Wearable Sensor Badge & Sensor Jacket for Context Awareness". In Proceedings of the Third International Symposium on Wearable Computers (ISWC'99), San Francisco, pp.107-113.
5. Golding, A. R. , and N. Lesh, "Indoor navigation using a diverse set of cheap, wearable sensors". In Proceedings of the third International Symposium on Wearable Computers, 1999, pp. 29-36. 1999.
6. Lifton, J., Paradiso, J. "Pushpin Computing System Overview: A Platform for Distributed, Embedded, Ubiquitous Sensor Networks" In Proc. Of Pervasive Computing, LNCS 2414, Springer Verlag. 2002. pp. 139-151.
7. Tapia, E. M., Intille, S. S. and Larson K. "Activity Recognition in the Home Using Simple and Ubiquitous Sensors". In Proceedings of Pervasive 2004, Lecture Notes in Computer Science. Springer Verlag, Vienna, Austria. 2004.
8. Van Laerhoven, K., Aidoo, K. and S. Lowette. "Real-time analysis of Data from Many Sensors with Neural Networks". In Proc. of the fifth International Symposium on Wearable Computers, ISWC 2001, Zurich, Switzerland, IEEE Press, 2001, pp. 115-123.
9. Van Laerhoven, K., A. Schmidt and H.-W. Gellersen. "Pin&Play: Networking Objects through Pins". In Proceedings of Ubicomp 2002, G. Boriello and L.E. Holmquist (Eds). Lecture Notes in Computer Science; Vol. 2498, Goteborg, Sweden. Springer Verlag, September 2002, pp.219 - 229.
10. Van Laerhoven, K., and H.-W. Gellersen. "Spine versus Porcupine: a Study in Distributed Wearable Activity Recognition". In Proceedings of the eighth International Symposium on Wearable Computers, ISWC 2004, Arlington, VA. IEEE Press, 2004, pp. 142-150.
11. Van Laerhoven, K., Villar, N., and H.-W. Gellersen. "A Layered Approach to Wearable Textile Networks". In Proceedings of the IEE Eurowearable 2003; IEE Press. Birmingham, UK, pp. 61-67.
12. Van Laerhoven, K., Villar, N., Schmidt, A., H.-W. Gellersen, M. Hakansson, and L. E. Holmquist. "Pin&Play: The Surface as Network Medium" In IEEE Communications, April 2003, Vol.41 No.4., ISSN:0163-6804, IEEE Press, pp. 90-96.
13. ZigBee Alliance: http://www.zigbee.org
14. Bluetooth SIG: http://www.bluetooth.com/

From Everyday Things to Everyday Memories: Two Kinds of Interactions with Objects in a House

Hisao Nojima

Seijo University,
6-1-20, Seijo, Setagaya-ku, Tokyo, Japan, 157-8511
nojima@nozy.org
http://www.nozy.org/

Abstract. How many "things" do we have in our house? More than eighty years ago, Wajiro Kon conducted a study to answer the question. In this paper, I introduced the works of Kon and his followers, including the ecological study of life commodities by CDI (Communication Design Institute) and the database of things in a Korean house from the exhibition of "Seoul Style 2002" by National Museum of Ethnology.

By using the Seoul Style 2002 database, I proposed two important aspects of the study of things and people, that are (1) detailed description of human activities in relation to their physical interaction with things, and (2) our emotional interaction with things.

1   Introduction

We are surrounded by many things. We interact with them daily and these things shape our activities, and they are the sources of our personal memories, or what we call OMOIDE in Japanese. UbiComp research needs to cover both physical and emotional interaction with things.

In this paper, I will talk about the research history of "things" in a house, and how to connect the research findings to the analysis of our physical activities in our house, which is relevant to UbiComp research. Finally, I would like to emotional aspects of things in our house.

2   Research on "Things" in a House

To support our activities in a house, we need to know those involved in the scene, people and things. There are many pieces of research on people and their activities in a house, but there are few studies on things themselves.

Researchers in UbiComp often talk possibilities of adding small RFID tags to all objects in a house and what kind of services would become available based on the tag supported environments. However, as far as I know, few of them know how many tags we need to install them on every object in a house. To know the answer, we need to know the number of objects "things" in a house.

H. Murakami et al. (Eds.): UCS 2004, LNCS 3598, pp. 10–19, 2005.

2.1   Research Tradition

To understand how we interact with everyday things, we need to know what kind of things we possess around us. "Material World" by Peter Menzel is one such endeavor, in which he took photos of average families all over the world with what they had in their homes[1]. This project took place in 1994, the United Nations International Year of the Family.

The Japanese tradition of "everyday things" research began about 1925, when Wajiro Kon established "Kogengaku" (Modernology), which studied modern life with an analogy of archeology. He compiled lists of things in Japanese homes, clothing of ordinary people, and other possessions. Kon's successors have made several exhaustive surveys of things in homes in the 1970s to 1990s. Based on the exhibition of the National Museum of Ethnology in 2002, Sato (in [2]) published a complete list of things in a Korean home as a database.

The idea behind these projects is that, from the things we have and use, we can see the person, the family, the life, and the society[1, 3].

2.2   Kon Wajiro and His Successors

There is a research tradition of counting things in a house in Japan. For about eighty years a go, Wajiro KON, who founded a new research area called "KO-GENGAKU (Modernology)", compiled an exhaustive list of every object in a house of a honeymoon couple[4]. He also did some surveys on the belongings of university students, and their clothing and others. Based on these surveys and other observations, Kon established KOGENGAKU, which was the investigation of people's daily activities and their life styles.

It may seem strange, but there were few orthodox successors of Kon and his KOGENGAKU in the academic area, but the tradition was well accepted by people in the field of marketing. From 1975 to 1992, CDI (Communication Design Institute) conducted four surveys of goods in a house. They used questionnaires of list of items and asked the respondents whether they had each item. Questionnaire in 1975 consisted of two thousand kinds items, and one in 1992 consisted of more than four thousand kinds. As shown in the increase in the number of kinds of items, we have come to have more and more things in our house. The surveys by CDI gave us quite useful information on our knowledge on things in our house, but as they counted not the number of things but the kinds of them, they could not be considered as exhaustive lists of things in our house.

2.3   Database of Things in a House from "Seoul Style 2002"

There appeared an another derivation from Kon and CDI research, "Seoul Style database", the exhaustive database of every object in a house in Seoul, Korea. Sato collected every belongings of a Korean family for an exhibition of National Museum of Ethnology, Japan on 2002.

The exhibition of "Seoul Style 2002: Life as it is – with the Lee family" [5] was hosted by the National Museum of Ethology, Japan in 2002. It was an exhibition of all the things of the Lee family, a family living in Seoul, Korea.

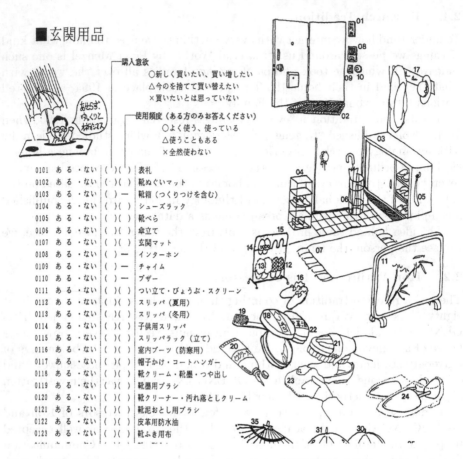

Fig. 1. A page from the Illustrated Questionnaire of CDI: List of things at an entrance of a home[6]

Objects included all the furniture, clothing, pay slips, toys, text books, school reports, photos, letters, and others. They include virtually everything that the family had in the end of the year 2001 except for a few items. After the exhibition has ended, the database is still being developed[7].

We used the database because there are no such database that has complete list of objects in a house, and there are various video and other documents of lives of the families recorded for the exhibition.

3   Analysis of Physical Interaction Processes with Things

Research of human activities with objects are so far done in the area where there are definite flow of work or in the area of fixed kind of merchandise are circulated[8]. Structures of houses differ from these of offices, and they vary

Fig. 2. List of commodities in a kitchen[7]

quite a lot. In the various environment, various kind of people, from infants to the elderly, live with various purposes of their own. As the result, kind of activities observed in houses become quite diverse.

We considered it important to make it clear how people living in a house are surrounded by objects and how they utilize them to realize ubiquitous environment especially configured for houses.

3.1   Analysis of "Seoul Style 2002" Database

Houses are built with kitchens, living rooms, bath rooms, bed rooms, and others. It is not apparent, however, how inhabitants of the house conduct their activities in the house.

In this paper, we first analyze a database of objects collected for the exhibition of "Seoul Style 2002: Life as it is – with the Lee family"[5]. The database is created by Koji Sato, a co-organizer of the exhibition, and it is the exhaustive list of every object in the Lee family, a family living in Seoul, Korea. Using the database as an example of a house and objects in the house, we report what kind of objects there are in a house, how they are located in the house, and how they are shared by its inhabitants.

Then, we propose a framework how to analyze human interaction with the objects in the house. In order to do that, we need how to describe interactions between people and objects. We used video data of family members living in a house, and analyzed in detail to understand how they interact with objects in their daily activities.

3.2   Analysis of Database of Exhaustive List of Things in a House

Overview of the Database. The exhibition of "Seoul Style 2002: Life as it is – with the Lee family"[5] was hosted by the National Museum of Ethology, Japan in 2002. It was an exhibition of all the things of the Lee family, a family living in Seoul, Korea. Objects included all the furniture, clothing, pay slips, toys, text books, school reports, photos, letters, and others. They include virtually everything that the family had in the end of the year 2001 except for a few items. After the exhibition has ended, the database is still being developed[7].

We used the database because there are no such database that has complete list of objects in a house, and there are various video and other documents of lives of the families recorded for the exhibition.

Profile of the Lee Family. Profile of the Lee family is listed in Table.1 and the layout of their apartment house is shown in Fig.3. The most parts of the research and database creation was done between March, 2000 and the end of 2003.

Table 1. Survey of Lee's house

Research Items	Summary
Members	Father, Mother, Grand Mother, Boy, Girl
House	Apartment in Seoul(Fig.3)
Items	Name of Item, Quantity, Location, User, Frequency of use, Year of use, How obtained, When, Price, Interaction with it

Number of Objects in a House. We will show the overall result of the analysis of the database. We counted number of items in the house. The rule of counting was: if there are identical objects and a person cannot discriminate them, we counted them as one kind, but if we can identify each of them, we counted them as separate kinds. For example, if there are three dish plates with the same design, we counted them as three items and one kind.

The total number of objects in the house amounted to 13,553, and there are 7,329 kinds[9]. Fig.2 is an example of all items in their kitchen.

Distributions of Objects by Different Users. Each object has its ownership. They are owned by a person, by several persons, or by the whole families. They also located at various places in the house. By cross tabulating the ownership and locations, we can infer people's activities and functions of rooms.

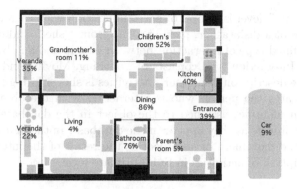

Fig. 3. Distribution of shared objects in each room

In the database of Seoul Style 2002, how objects are owned and used are recorded, so we can examine how objects used by the whole families are located in the house.

The result is shown in Fig.3. As shown in the figure, the dining room is considered as a public (shared) room, and the father and mother's room is used as a private space.

3.3   Analysis of Interaction Between People and Objects

Framework for Description of Interaction. Our next attempt in this paper is to examine the possibilities of creating a framework to describe human interaction with objects. We used the database of the objects in the Lee's family and video recordings of a daily lives of each of family members taken for the exhibition. We first analyzed mother's video tape. It is a record of her daily life activities from the wakeup to the sleep. Many activities, such as preparing for the breakfast, sending her children to schools, social activities, and others[7]. We based our analysis on the GOMS model[10] and the theory of categorization[11] and we categorized human activities as follows. We focused our analysis on human activities in relation to objects as it is difficult to analyze human actions in general. Our analysis is based on the movement of an object as a unit.

We defined a "Unit Task" as a kind of activity which we usually take as one activity, such as taking a breakfast or going shopping. A Unit Task is consists of several parts, which we named "Super Ordinate" after Rosch[11]. Super Ordinates for taking a breakfast include such actions as preparing for the breakfast, serving, eating, and clearing a table.

One Super Ordinate category consists of several "Basic Level" activities. They are sequences of actions, such as taking dishes from a shelf, placing chop sticks on the table, and others. Basic Level categories are, as described in Rosch[11], basic unit of human activities[1].

---

[1] Basic level is often used when one asks something to other person, such as "Please take dishes from the shelf ?, " and "Please place chop sticks on the table."

"Sub Ordinate" level is a level of each interaction with each object, such as opening a door of a dishwasher, picking a cup from a shelf, and others.

We also defined type of interaction between people and an object in Interaction category. Interaction type consists of Touching, Moving and Wearing.

An example description of mother's activities is shown in Fig.2. In the figure, "Person" indicates the person who is interacting with the object ("Object"). "Record" is an identifier assigned to the object in the database. "Position" is the location of objects as they appear in the database. In the figure, gray meshed cells indicate the movement of an object as the result of the interaction. White cells are description of activities in Sub Ordinate level.

Table 2. Example of Activity Database: Mother opens the fridge door, takes some dishes and closes the door

Unit Task	Super Ordinate	Basic Level	Sub Ordinate	Inter Action	Person	Object	ID	Position Before		Position After	
Breakfast	Prepare breakfast	take dish and kimuchi		move	mother	dish	J0035	fridge	K-2	draining board	k-8-1-1
				move	mother	container	J0254	fridge	K-2	draining board	k-8-1-1
			open fridge	touch	mother	fridge door	J0561	fridge	K-2	fridge	k-2
			take dish from fridge	with mother	mother	dish	J0035	fridge	K-2	mother	-
			take container from fridge	with mother	mother	container	J0254	fridge	K-2	mother	-
			dish on top of container	with mother	mother	container	J0254	mother	-	mother	-
			close fridge door	touch	mother	fridge door	J0561	fridge	K-2	fridge	K-2
			move to draining board	move	mother	-	-	fridge	K-2	draining board	K-8-1-1

3.4   Structure of Objects in a House

In this paper, we analyzed how objects in a house are located and hierarchically organized based on Seoul Style 2002 database. According to the results, Physical Layers to access to the objects are rather small. This means that a house is organized so that inhabitants can have an easy access to an object. On the contrary, the trade-off of the smallness of the Physical Layers, there are many, actually 2,300, objects that can be accessed within one hop. Ideally, a member of the Lee family need to memorize 2,300 locations to directly access to the object. It may be, however, difficult considering the load on memory to memorize all of them. People utilize various heuristics, such as structuring items to remember, search strategy and others.

Advance of the ubiquitous technology, especially those of tags, made it (at least theoretically) possible to identify all the objects in a house. By using such tags, we will be able to investigate how we memorize objects and their locations in our daily lives.

4   Personal Memories from Personal Things

By using the database of things, we can analyze our daily activities and interactions with things in our house. Still, it is difficult to understand the meaning
of things; that is, what a thing means to us. For example, in the Seoul Style
database as described above, there are seventeen hand-towels in the Lee's house.
How do we identify them ? The towels can be considered as 17 copies of a towel,
or it can be 17 different instances of a towel.

After doing some interviews to the mother of the Lee family, Sato found
that each hand towel had different background how they were obtained (e.g. at
a party of a politician, cerebration party of grandmother, PTA meeting of an
elementary school, and opening party of a shop, et al.), and the mother could
talk stories of each towel[7].

Fig. 4. Shoes made by a Japanese shoemaker

Even old weary looking shoes, as shown in Fig.4 can have a story. One of my
informants told me the following story on his old shoes:

> These shoes are the one of my OMOIDEs. The reason why I think it
> important for my personal memory is as follows. This spring, I was wan-
> dering around in Europe, when I found my shoes went wear and tear.
> When I was in Brugge in Belgium, I happened to find the shoes in a
> shop, which were made by MIHARA Yasuhiro, a Japanese shoemaker. I
> had not spoken to any Japanese for a long time, so I was a bit hungry
> with things Japanese. I met the shoes when I was such a mood. I was so
> moved to meet Japan in such a place, I bought the shoes by my credit
> card. This was my first experience of using the card. I enjoy wearing the
> shoes, although the shoes have some troubles; they stink....

We are surrounded by many things, and on most of which, we have some
stories related to them, and if we are asked, we can come up with a story on
each of the things.

We are currently working on a project to understand such collections of personal memories, or "Omoide", many of which are trivial but important pieces of
information for *me*.

We believe it is important to combine the two approaches to understand the nature of our lives, and what the everyday things and personal memories attached to them really mean to us. Thus, we focus our research on the home, in which we have many things and memories[2], and where ubiquitous technology can show its possibilities.

5   Future Work Based on the Analysis

In this paper, we tried to analyze how people interact with objects using the Seoul Style 2002 database in which there are complete list of objects in a house. In this section, we describe our future plan derived from this analysis.

5.1   Activity Modeling

We recorded and analyzed the interaction processes all by hands. It will be possible by using RFID tags and other technologies, we will be able to automatically record all the actions, interactions, movement of objects, location of actors, and others. By using these data, we will be able to construct a human model of activities to describe human interaction with objects. The model will be useful in inferring human behavior (interaction with people and objects) in a certain situation. Moreover, if we can time data for each interaction with an object, we can estimate the total amount of time for a Unit Task, as in a Keystroke level model in GOMS model family[10].

5.2   Support for Finding Something Lost

If all the interactions between people and objects are recorded and their processes are modeled, then we will be able to understand how we lose things and will will be given advice where to search the lost things. The above mentioned support is often used as one of the possible applications in ubiquitous environment, to really actualize the service, we need to collect human interaction with objects as described in this paper.

6   Conclusion

In this paper, we investigated the possibilities of coming ubiquitous society, that is, if we can identify all the objects (and people) in a house, then what kind of possibilities are available to us. For that purpose, we used the database of Seoul Style 2002, in which all objects were tagged (by hand), and human activities were recorded (by video). Based on the data, we could relate human activities and objects in a house. These detailed mapping of actions and objects in a house is necessary for considering future possible services in the ubiquitous environment.

Finally, the importance and the necessity of further investigation on human emotional relationship with things are discussed.

Acknowledgment

I am grateful to my fellows, Professor Koji Sato (National Museum of Ethnology) and Noriko Shingaki (Seijo University) for their help and encouragements.

References

1. Menzel, P.: Material World: A Global Family Portrait. Sierra Club Books, San Francisco, CA (1994)
2. Nojima, H., Harada, E., eds.: Cognitive Science at Home. Shin-Yo-Sha, Tokyo (2004) (in Japanese).
3. Tsuzuki, K.: Tokyo Style. Kyoto Shoin, Kyoto, Japan (1997)
4. Kon, W.: Introduction to Modernology (KOGENGAKU NYUMON). Chikuma Shobo, Tokyo (1987) (in Japanese).
5. Asakura, T., Sato, K., eds.: Seoul Style 2002: Life as it is – with the Lee family. Senri Bunka Zaidan, Osaka, Japan (2002) (in Japanese).
6. Syohinkagaku Kenkyuusyo and CDI: Ecological Study of Commodities of Houses III. Syohinkagaku Kenkyuusyo, Tokyo, Japan (1993) (in Japanese).
7. Sato, K.: http://www.minpaku.ac.jp/menu/database.html: Database of commodities in a Korean family: from "Seoul Style 2002: Life as it is – with the Lee family" (2005)
8. Malone, T.W.: How do people organize their desks?: Implications for the design of office information systems. ACM Transactions on Information Systems **1** (1983) 99–112
9. Shingaki, N., Nojima, H., Sato, K., Kitabata, M., Onozawa, A.: How many objects are there around us?: Towards the support of human-objects interaction in the ubiquitous environment. Journal of Japanese Human Interface Society **7** (2005)
10. Card, S., Moran, T., Newell, A.: The Psychology of Human-Computer Interaction. Lawrence Erlbaum Associates, Hillsdale, NJ (1983)
11. Rosch, E., Lloyd, B.: Cognition and Categorization. Lawrence Erlbaum Associates, Hillsdale, NJ (1978)

Design, Implementation and Evaluations of a Direction Based Service System for Both Indoor and Outdoor

Yohei Iwasaki[1], Nobuo Kawaguchi[1,2], and Yasuyoshi Inagaki[3]

[1] Graduate School of Information Science, Nagoya University, Japan
[2] Information Technology Center, Nagoya University, Japan
[3] Faculty of Information Science and Technology, Aichi Prefectural University, Japan

Abstract. This paper describes a design, implementation and evaluations of a direction based service system named Azim, which utilizes both a position and a direction of a user. In this system, a user's position is estimated by having the user point to and measure azimuths of several markers or objects whose positions are already known. Because the system does not require any other accurate position sensors nor positive beacons, it can be deployed cost-effectively. We have implemented a prototype system using a direction sensor that combines a magnetic compass and accelerometer. We have conducted experiments both indoor and outdoor, and exemplified that positioning accuracy by the proposed method is precise enough for a direction based service.

1 Introduction

As cell phones and other kinds of mobile terminals have become prevalent, and GPS modules have fallen in price, we are seeing an increasing range of location based services, such as ActiveCampus[1], PlaceLab[2], Mobile Info Search[3] and SpaceTag[4]. Global Positioning System (GPS) based methods are common for acquiring positioning information[5], but this approach has some drawbacks: the devices often do not work in street canyons between tall buildings, indoors, and other environments where signals from the GPS satellites cannot reach, and it can take some time until the GPS sensor can be used after power is first applied (cold-start). For indoor environments, a number of position measurement techniques have been developed such as the Active Bat[6] location system that uses ultrasound times-of-flight to ultrasonic receivers whose positions are known, but this system can be fairly costly to deploy the ultrasonic receivers everywhere. In short, today there is no method of position measurement that is both affordable and can be used across a wide range of environments, both indoor and outdoor.

We have already proposed a *direction based services*[7], which are more advanced location based services based on both location and direction of a user. This paper describes a design, implementation and evaluations of a direction based service system named *Azim*, which uses a position estimation method based on azimuth data. In this system, a user's position is estimated when the

H. Murakami et al. (Eds.): UCS 2004, LNCS 3598, pp. 20–36, 2005.

user points to and measures azimuths of several markers whose positions are known. Because the system does not require any other position sensors nor positive beacons, it can be cost-effectively deployed. Since measuring the azimuths of markers is accompanied by some degree of error, we model an error of azimuth measurement, and calculate the user's likely position as a probability distribution, which can consider the error of direction measurement and the pre-obtained field information such as obstacles and magnetic field disturbance. This method also has an advantage for those who are concerned for their privacy, because the position is never acquired without the user's intention. Since not only the user's position but also azimuths are acquired in this approach, the positions and azimuths can be used to develop more advanced location based services, which we named direction based services. We propose an instance of the direction based service in which the system identifies an object pointed to by a user. In addition, the proposed system utilizes wireless LAN to support these advanced services. In order to test the feasibility of our approach, we have constructed a prototype system based on a direction sensor that combines a magnetic compass with an accelerometer. The position estimation accuracy was evaluated in experiments on the prototype system, and we exemplified the usefulness of the proposed system.

The rest of this paper will be organized as follows: In Section 2 we present a direction based service system named Azim that combines the azimuth based position estimation with a wireless LAN. Section 3 details an Azim prototype system implemented with a direction sensor that combines a magnetic compass with an accelerator, and Section 4 discusses experiments to assess the performance of the prototype system. Section 5 surveys some other studies that are related to this research, and Section 6 concludes the paper and highlights a number of issues for the future.

2   Azim: Direction Based Service System

In this section we present *Azim* system that supports a direction based service which is an advanced service based on both the location and the direction of a user. This system has the ability to acquire a user's position employing the azimuth based position estimation. Taking the example of a direction based service, this system also has the ability to estimate the objects pointed to by the user, and provide services relating to those specified objects.

2.1   Azimuth Based Position Estimation

We first propose a method based on measuring several azimuth data to estimate a position. For simplicity, we assume that the position coordinate system is a two-dimensional plane. In this approach, markers whose positions are known are placed in various locations throughout an area, and a user's position is acquired by having the user point to several markers and measuring the azimuths. As illustrated in Fig.1, the azimuth is the absolute angle of horizontal deviation from north as an origin, and is measured by a mobile terminal with a built-in

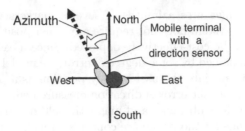

Fig. 1. Azimuth acquired by a direction sensor

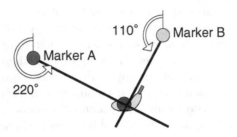

Fig. 2. Position estimation based on azimuth data from several markers

direction sensor. Fig.2 shows that the user's position is at the intersection of half-lines drawn from the markers. Since the direction measurements are accompanied by a certain degree of error, the direction measurement error is modeled in our approach, and the user's position is calculated as a probability distribution, which is detailed in Section 2.7.

When acquiring a position with this method, the system has to know which markers the user is pointing to. For this purpose, we distinguish the markers by color (or shape etc.), so all the user has to do is to push a color-coded button to narrow down the markers being pointed to (in this paper, we will only consider the color-coding scheme). To make the system available in wide area, several markers may be coded with the same color. To deploy the same colored markers, these markers should be distinguished by other environmental information such as rough position information obtained by identifying wireless LAN base stations (see Section 2.4). Since the markers are passive and do not require any equipment, the system can be deployed at low cost. Existing landmarks, buildings, or other everyday objects can also be used as markers. In this case, the user selects the name or type of an object instead of a color.

2.2 Direction Sensor

There are direction sensors available for measuring absolute azimuth from north as an origin, such as devices that combine a magnetic compass with an accelerometer (The north means the magnetic north here, not a true north on the map). With a magnetic compass capable of measuring geomagnetic direction and an accelerometer capable of measuring gravitational force direction, one can acquire

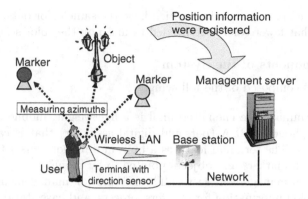

Fig. 3. Azim: direction based service system

the direction (i.e., the pitch, roll, and yaw) of a device, without any other special equipment. Two available devices with these capabilities are the *3DM* manufactured by Microstrain Inc.[8], and the *3D motion sensor* manufactured by NEC Tokin Corp.[9].

2.3   Typical Usage Model

Fig.3 is a schematic representation of the system architecture. The user first measures his own position by pointing to several markers and inputting the marker colors. Then, the user points to an object, thereby enabling the user to receive various application services relating to the specified object. Typical application services might include remote operation of a device that is pointed to, or displaying information on the user's terminal screen about an object that is pointed to. From the same position, the user can also point to other objects. If the user moves and changes his position, the user performs another measurement to determine the new position. However, once a user obtains an absolute position by pointing to the markers, other tracking methods[10] may be used to track the user's position for a short period of time using sensors in the terminal.

2.4   Network Environment

In the last few years we have seen the rapid spread of public wireless LAN services such as hot spots, and use of wireless LANs in residential and office environments. Our method employs a wireless LAN to support communication between the user's mobile terminal and an information management server.

In wireless LAN, the system can know the identity of the base station which the client terminal is connecting to. The base station identity provides rough position information, because the system can know that the user is within the signal reception range, which is about 50-to-100-meter radius when no obstacles. Applying the position distribution calculation procedure described in [7], the prior probability and position space integral range can be confined to this signal reception range. Also only makers that can be seen in the signal reception range can be specified by a user. Accordingly, the system can identify the specified marker if there are other markers which have the same color outside this range. This means that fewer colors are needed to make up the color scheme.

2.5   Components of the System

The system is composed of the following.

- Client terminal: The client terminal is a lightweight, mobile terminal such as a cell phone or PDA (personal digital assistant) that is carried around by the user. The terminal features a built-in direction sensor that measures azimuths to markers and objects pointed to by the user.
- Information management server: The information management server manages location information for markers, objects, and base stations. The server also calculates a user's position distribution, and identifies the object pointed to by the user.
- Base station: The base station of wireless LAN. The client terminal can acquire the identifier (MAC address, etc.) of the base station it is connecting to.
- Marker: An object or landmark that the user points to in order to measure his position. Markers are differentiated by color (or some other means), which the user inputs when pointing to a marker. Existing landmarks or buildings can substitute for markers.
- Objects: An object is one that a user might point to, including a device or piece of equipment, a shop, a landmark, and so on.

2.6   Available Regions

Let us next consider how this system might be used over a wide area. Since users cannot point to markers or objects that are beyond their field of view, we must consider the available region over which a marker or object can be used. It is also necessary to consider the base station signal reception range. Therefore we define the available regions of markers, objects, and base stations. By defining the available regions of markers and objects, we can specify which markers and objects can be seen from a particular position, thus enabling the system to make specific calculations of the marker selection model and object selection model in [7]. The available region of a base station means the signal reception range of the base station, and as noted earlier in Section 2.4, this is used to roughly determine a user's position.

Fig.4 illustrates an example of available regions. The available regions should be defined by considering obstacles and distances to objects, since the user cannot point to the object when an obstacle exists between the user and the object, or when the object is too far from the user.

By knowing the base station identity that a client terminal is connecting to, we know that the user is currently within the available region of that base station. It is only when the available regions of the base station and a marker overlap that the marker can be regarded as a specified marker. For example, consider the point A through D in Fig.4 as markers. The user cannot point

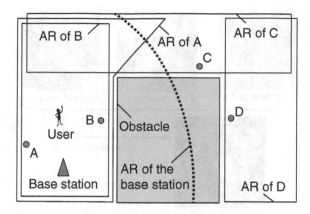

Fig. 4. Available region (AR) example

to marker D even if he is somewhere within the available region of the base station. Considering the marker color scheme, if the markers whose available region overlaps the available region of the base station are assigned a unique color, the system can identify the specified marker.

Let us next assume that the user's position has been calculated. It is only when the available region of an object overlaps with the probable position of the user (i.e., high probability area of position distribution) that the user is able to point to that object. This way, the objects which cannot be seen from the user are never estimated as candidates for specified objects. For example, consider the point A through D in Fig.4 as objects. Only objects A and B whose available regions overlap with the user's position can become specified objects.

2.7 Probabilistic Approach for Azimuth Based Position Estimation

Direction measurements by a user include a certain degree of error, which caused by user's pointing operation itself, or geomagnetic field disturbance by metallic objects. So calculating the intersection of the half-lines is insufficient, because no accuracy information is acquired, and sometimes no intersection. Thus the system calculates probabilistic distribution of a user's position.

The detail calculation formulas are in [7]. We describe only the concept here due to lack of space. The calculation of the position distribution can utilize the following various location based information. First, obstacles influence such as off-limits areas where a user cannot exist, and the occlusions of invisible objects or markers (see Section 2.6). Second, rough position information by wireless-LAN base stations (see Section 2.4). Third, by using pre-obtained magnetic field distribution, robust measurements can be achieved even in geomagnetic disturbance environment.

Fig.5 shows examples of calculations when directions to two markers are measured and a user's position is estimated. In this example, the user is in the center of a square area, and he points first to a marker that is 45 degrees to the left and second to a marker that is 45 degrees to the right.

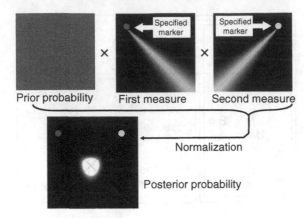

Fig. 5. Calculation of position distribution

By calculating the user's position as a probability distribution, the system can identify the specified object in a probabilistic manner with that position distribution and the target direction.

3   Implementation

We have implemented a prototype of the direction based service system described in Section 2. For the azimuth measurements, we employed the *3DM* direction sensor manufactured by Microstrain Inc.[8] that combines a three-axis magnetic compass with a three-axis accelerometer. For the software development, we used Java 2 Platform SDK 1.4 and *cogma* [11] middleware that supports interworking between network equipment. An IEEE 802.11b-compliant wireless LAN was used for the network environment. In the current version, the available regions of markers, objects, and base stations are not considered.

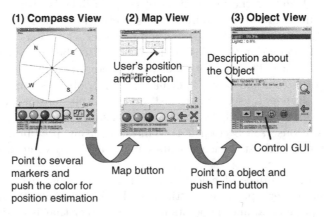

Fig. 6. Screenshots of the client terminal

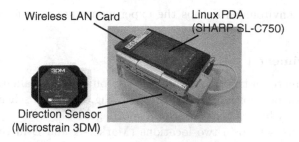

Fig. 7. LocPointer: portable client terminal using a Linux PDA

Client terminals communicate with an information management server over the wireless network. Fig.6 shows several screenshots of the client terminal. The current pointing azimuth is displayed in the compass view like Fig.6(1). A user points to the direction of a marker and presses the button for that marker's color, then repeats this operation several times to estimate the current position. The user can confirm his position on the map view like Fig.6(2). Then the user points to the direction of an object and presses the Find button (hand lens button), then the system identifies the specified object, and displays candidates on the screen as illustrated in Fig.6(3). The specified object with the highest probability is automatically selected, but the user can manually select another candidate. Once a specified object has been selected, the various application services associated with that object can be accessed. We have developed the following two application services.

- Universal Remote-controller Service: A user can remotely control a device via a GUI on the client terminal display. The implementation code of the GUI is dynamically loaded from the specified device, by using code mobility function of the cogma[11] middleware.
- Device Connecting Service: A user can request a connection between two distant devices by directly pointing to them. The user can remotely push the button interface of Touch-and-Connect[12] on the client terminal display.

Using the procedure outlined in Section 2.7, the information management server calculates the user's position distribution and identifies the specified object. The user's position distribution is calculated as a 128×128 two-dimensional array. A normal distribution with a standard deviation of 5 degrees is used as the azimuth measurement model[7].

The client terminal software can also work on J2ME environment. As illustrated in Fig.7, we have developed a portable client terminal using Linux PDA (SHARP SL-C750) called *LocPointer*.

4   Evaluation

Experiments were carried out on the prototype system to evaluate the validity of the proposed method. We expect that our method will be effective across a wide range of environments, thus the experiments are conducted both indoor and outdoor.

4.1   Experiment 1 (Outdoor)

First, we conducted a trial in an outdoor environment to evaluate the accuracy of the proposed position estimation method. Fig.8 shows a schematic overview of the trial site, which is the corner of a sports ground.

Markers were set up in two locations (Marker-A and B in the figure). The distance between the two markers was 30 meters. The proposed method was used to estimate the positions of 14 different points scattered in the vicinity of the markers. We pointed at each of the two makers and measured the azimuths by the LocPointer (described in Section 3). Six measurements were conducted for each point.

The experimental result is summarized in Fig.8. The solid black symbols with numbers show the correct positions of the measurement points. The outline open symbols represent the estimated positions (six estimates). Since the user's position is calculated as a probability distribution in our approach, the estimated position is the center of gravity of the distribution. We adopted different shaped symbols (triangles, squares, circles) in the figure, just to make the results easier to distinguish. Measurement results for the same point are represented using the same symbol shape.

We found that the positions estimated by our method diverged from the correct positions by 1.9 meters on average (80 percent of measurements are within 2.8 meters). We think that this positioning accuracy is precise enough for the direction based service where a user specifies objects by pointing in outdoor environments. We would also note that, since the estimation accuracy is basically proportional to the distance between markers, for situations requiring greater accuracy, a higher degree of position estimation accuracy could be achieved by deploying the markers more densely.

However, at the points on the line between two markers, such as point 13 and 14 in the Fig.8, the estimation accuracy is relatively bad. If the relative angle between the two specified markers is close to a right angle (90 degrees), the estimation accuracy is relatively good. Thus it is a good idea to deploy more than two markers on the service field, and a user can select desirable two markers, or simply measure azimuths of all markers.

By measuring azimuths of more than two markers, the positioning accuracy and robustness improve. Fig.9 shows estimated positions when the subject points to the three markers (Marker-A, B and C in the figure). In this case, the estimated positions diverged from the correct positions by 0.78 meters on average (80 percent of measurements are within 1.1 meters). Note that positioning accuracy is stable on all the positions even between the markers.

4.2   Experiment 2 (Indoor)

Second, a trial were conducted in an indoor environment, which is our test bed room for the ubiquitous computing environment named Cogma Room. In the

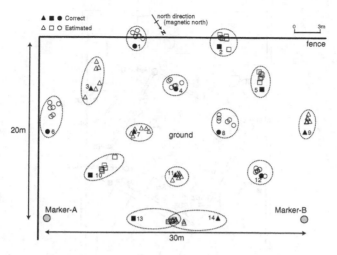

Fig. 8. Estimated positions (outdoor; 2 markers)

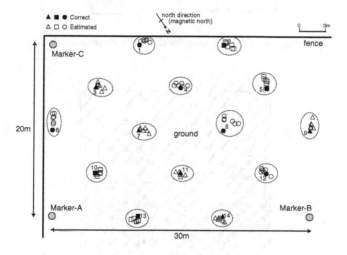

Fig. 9. Estimated positions (outdoor; 3 markers)

room, there are four markers (Marker A – D) and eleven display devices (LCD1 – LCD9, Screen, PDP) as shown in Fig.10. We assumed the direction based service where a user points to one of the displays to show a picture.

Generally indoor environments especially concrete buldings are prone to have geomagnetic disturbance. To correct a azimuth measurement disparities, we obtained a spatial distribution of magnetic field by sampling a magnetic vector in some points in the room. Fig.11 shows the interpolated magnetic field information (abbreviated as MFI later), where the magnetic vector directions are disturbed in the range of 40 degrees. The interpolated magnetic vector in an arbitrarily point was calculated by the weighted mean for the sampled vectors,

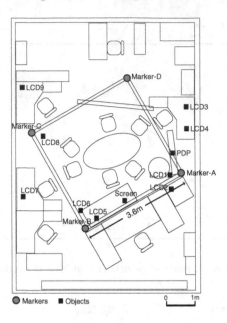

Fig. 10. Objects map in the indoor environment

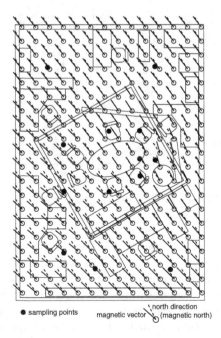

Fig. 11. Pre-obtained magnetic field information (MFI)

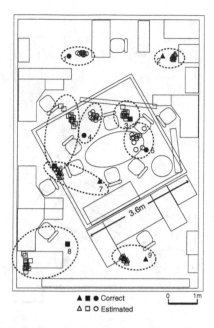

Fig. 12. Estimated positions without the MFI

where the weight is dis^{-3}; dis is the distance to the sampling point. This pre-obtained MFI is used to correct the azimuth measurement (see Section 2.7 and [7]). To evaluate the advantage by using the MFI, we compared the two estimations — *without the MFI* in which magnetic vectors are assumed to parallel to the magnetic north direction anywhere, and *using the MFI*.

We conducted a trial at nine points in the room, Point 1 – 9 in the Fig.12. In each point, the position estimation based on the proposed method is conducted eleven times by pointing to two markers with the LocPointer. The used two markers are Marker A and B in Point 3, 4, 6, 9; B and C in Point 5, 8; C and D in Point 1, 7; D and A in Point 2.

The estimated positions without the MFI are shown in Fig.12. Just like the experiment 1, the solid black symbols show the correct position of the measurement points, and the outline open symbols represent the estimated positions (eleven estimates). The estimated positions diverged from the correct positions by 0.85 meters on average (80 percent of measurements are within 1.51 meters). On the other hand, the estimated positions using the MFI are shown in the Fig.13. The estimated positions diverged from the correct positions by 0.35 meters on average (80 percent of measurements are within 0.60 meters). The two estimations are based on the same measurement data. These results means that the accuracy of the estimated positions are improved by using the MFI. Thus the proposed position estimation method is also useful even in the indoor environment by using the MFI.

We also evaluated the usefulness of the direction based service. After each position measurement, the subject points to one of the display devices shown in

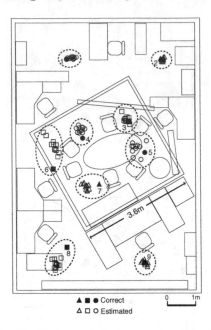

Fig. 13. Estimated positions using the MFI

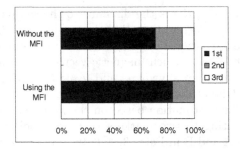

Fig. 14. Order of the specified object in the estimated list

Fig.10. The system estimates the specified display using the position distribution and the display direction (see [7]). The result of the estimation is a list of the estimated objects in order of high probability. The measurements are conducted only on Point 3–7, because the displays are out of sight on the other points. Fig.14 shows the proportion of the order of the specified object in the estimated list. Using the MFI, the specified object is on the top of the estimated list in the 84 percent of the measurements, whereas 71 percent without the MFI. The result means that the proposed method is precise enough for the direction based service assumed here. We expect that the result improves using three-dimentional information such as the altitudes of objects and an elevation angle (pitch) of the pointing device, because some of the objects are overlaped in a azimuth angle but not overlapped in a elevation angle. We will consider that in our future work.

5   Related Research

In the following we will differentiate this research from other related researches in several aspects.

5.1   Position Acquisition Technologies

GPS-based methods of position acquisition are now widely available[5]. In outdoor environments where there is unobstructed line-of-sight, positioning accuracy to within 10 meters can be obtained by GPS. However, GPS is often ineffective in street canyons between tall buildings, indoors, and other environments where signals from the GPS satellite cannot reach, and in environments where waves are reflected. Another shortcoming of GPS is that it can take some time until the sensor can be used after power is first turned on (cold-start).

One technology that has been used in the measurement of cell phone positions is Assisted-GPS[13], where the base station catches the GPS satellites and provides this information to cell phones to cut the time for cold-start. Another location measurement technique for indoor environments is the Active-BAT location system[6] that uses ultrasound times-of-flight to ultrasonic receivers whose position is known. The major drawback of both these systems is that they tend to be quite costly to deploy the system for wide areas.

Another approach that has been suggested for position measuring uses the RF signal strength from (or to) several wireless LAN base stations[14][2]. In our proposal, this approach can also be used to improve the accuracy of the pre-obtain rough position information (about 10 meters) instead of just using the identification of a base station (about 100 meters). Therefore, the number of marker colors can be reduced, or the markers can be deployed more densely.

However, especially for indoor environments, radio waves are spatially and temporally disturbed by the effects of reflection and absorption by obstacles. Reference [15] describes a scheme in which RF signal strength from several wireless LAN base station is measured in advance for various points in the system service area, and this data is used to obtain the spatial distributions of RF signal strength for the area. This achieves position measurements that are robust against fluctuating RF signals. As described in Section 4, we can use a similar approach in which a robust position measurement is achieved even when geomagnetic fluctuations exist, by obtaining the spatial distribution of magnetic fields of a service area in advance.

Let us briefly highlight the key advantages of the proposed position estimation method in comparison with the existing position measurement methods.

– **Cost Effective for Deployment:** Compared to schemes that require special equipment deployed on the environment side, our method only involves a deployment of markers, and because the markers do not require power or other operating costs, the environment side costs are minimal. In fact, if landmarks and other existing structures are used for markers, then no dedicated markers need to be deployed at all. Our system is cost effective even when it works over a wireless LAN, since wireless LAN base stations are inexpensive and already widely deployed [2].

- **Available Anywhere:** By using a magnetic compass and obtaining magnetic field distributions in advance, our approach works very well over an extensive range of environments, both indoor and outdoor.
- **Low-cost Client Terminal:** For the direction based service, since both the user's position and azimuth data are obtained from only direction sensor without any other position sensors, which means that the client terminal can be implemented at a low cost.
- **Quick Start-up:** One advantage of our approach compared to GPS systems is that position data can be obtained immediately as soon as the mobile terminal is turned on.
- **Privacy:** As long as the user does not intentionally measure his own position, the user's position remains unknown to the system. While this might seem like a shortcoming in some situations, it is actually an advantage for those who are concerned for their privacy because it prevents the user's movements from being tracked.

5.2   Location Based Services

Several location based services are proposed. In the SpaceTag system[4], information can be accessed only from limited locations and limited time period. The kokono Search service of the Mobile Info Search[3] provides "location-oriented robot-based search", in which WWW documents that contain location information such as an address are automatically collected, and a user can search these documents based on a location. In the Follow-me Application service[6], the system determines the locations of users with supersonic sensors, and the display which is the closest to the user is selected automatically as a workspace.

The main advantage of our proposed system is that our system utilizes not only the location but also the direction of a user, which provides more advanced and flexible service. With only location data, the user can get information about *where he is*. More finely with direction data, the user can get about *what he sees* or *what he points to*. We have also planned a direction based search service, where the user can get about *which direction the desired service exists* by sweeping around with the client terminal. When the service exists in the direction, the terminal informs by sound or vibration.

6   Conclusions

This paper describes a design, implementation and evaluations of a direction based service system named Azim, which based on both location and direction of a user. In Azim, the user's position is estimated by having the user point to and measure azimuths of several markers whose positions are already known. Azim uses a wireless LAN for supporting these services. Finally, a prototype system was implemented using a direction sensor that combines a magnetic compass and a accelerometer, and we exemplified the usefulness of our approach through experiments in both indoor and outdoor environment. Using two markers outdoors whose interval was 30 meters, the positioning error was 1.9 meters on average. When using three markers, the error was 0.78 meters on average. And using two markers indoors whose interval was 3.6 meters, the error was 0.85 meters on average without MFI (magnetic field information), which improved to 0.35 meters using MFI.

There are a number of areas that need further study. First, further study is required for an easy method for learning the MFI (see Section 4.2). For example, using another positioning method, such as using only relative azimuths, in the beginning phase. And the magnetic field information grows with daily use.

Second, although we assumed that the position coordinate system was a two-dimensional plane for simplicity, our approach could be easily adapted to three-dimensional space by using both the azimuth and angle of elevation (pitch angle) obtained from the direction sensor.

References

1. W. G. Griswold, P. Shanahan, S. W. Brown, R. Boyer, M. Ratto, R. B. Shapiro, and T. M. Truong, "ActiveCampus - Experiments in Community-Oriented Ubiquitous Computing", Technical Report CS2003-0750, Computer Science and Engineering, UC San Diego, 2003.
2. Bill N. Schilit, Anthony LaMarca, Gaetano Borriello, William G. Griswold, David McDonald, Edward Lazowska, Anand Balachandran, Jason Hong, and Vaughn Iverson, "Challenge: ubiquitous location-aware computing and the "place lab" initiative," Proceedings of the 1st ACM international workshop on Wireless mobile applications and services on WLAN hotspots (WMASH'03), pp.29–35, 2003.
3. Katsumi Takahashi, Nobuyuki Miura, Seiji Yokoji, and Ken-ichi Shima, "Mobile Info Search: Information Integration for Location-Aware Computing, " Journal of the Information Processing Society of Japan, Vol.41, No.4, pp.1192–1201, 2000.
4. H. Tarumi, K.Morishita, M.Nakao, and Y.Kambayashi, "SpaceTag: An Overlaid Virtual System and its Application," International Conference on Multimedia Computing and Systems (ICMCS'99), Vol.1, pp. 207-212, 1999.
5. Rashmi Bajaj, Samantha Lalinda Ranaweera, and Dharma P. Agrawal, "GPS: Location-Tracking Technology, " IEEE Computer, Vol. 35, No. 4, pp. 92–94, 2002.
6. Andy Harter, Andy Hopper, Pete Steggles, Andy Ward, and Paul Webster, "The anatomy of context-aware application," Proceedings of the fifth annual ACM/IEEE international conference on Mobile computing and networking (MOBICOM'99), pp. 59–68, 1999.
7. Yohei Iwasaki, Nobuo Kawaguchi, and Yasuyoshi Inagaki, "Azim: Direction Based Service using Azimuth Based Position Estimation," The 24th International Conference on Distributed Computing Systems (ICDCS 2004), pp.700–709, Tokyo, Mar. 2004.
8. MicroStrain, Inc, "3DM: solid state 3-axis pitch, roll, & yaw sensor," http://www.microstrain.com/3DM.html
9. NEC TOKIN Corporation, "3D Motion Sensor," http://www.nec-tokin.com/
10. Seon-Woo Lee, Kenji Mase, "Activity and Location Recognition Using Wearable Sensors, " IEEE Pervasive Computing, Vol. 1, No. 3, pp. 24–32, 2002.

11. Nobuo Kawaguchi, "Cogma: A Middleware for Cooperative Smart Appliances for Ad hoc Environment," Proc. of International Conference on Mobile Computing and Ubiquitous Networking (ICMU2004), Jan. 2004.
12. Yohei Iwasaki, Nobuo Kawaguchi, and Yasuyoshi Inagaki, "Touch-and-Connect: A connection request framework for ad-hoc networks and the pervasive computing environment," First IEEE Annual Conference on Pervasive Computing and Communications (PerCom 2003), pp. 20–29, 2003.
13. Goran Djuknic, and Stephen Wilkus, "Geolocation and wireless multimedia," 2001 IEEE International Conference on Multimedia and Expo (ICME 2001), pp.581-584, 2001.
14. Paramvir Bahl and Venkata N. Padmanabhan, "RADAR: An In-Building RF-based User Location and Tracking System," IEEE Infocom 2000, pp.775-784, 2000.
15. Andrew M. Ladd, Kostas E. Bekris, Algis Rudys, Lydia E. Kavraki, Dan S. Wallach, and Guillaume Marceau, "Robotics-based location sensing using wireless ethernet," Proceedings of the eighth annual international conference on Mobile computing and networking (MOBICOM 2002), pp.227–238, 2002.

Designing Transparent Location-Dependent Web-Based Applications on Mobile Environments

Simón Neira and Víctor M. Gulías

MADS Group - LFCIA,
Department of Computer Science, University of Corunna, Spain
sneira@faortega.org, gulias@lfcia.org

Abstract. This paper describes an architecture model designed to allow the development of web-based client-server applications where results should be dependent of the location of the client on a mobile (normally wireless) environment. It has been designed to work with the most popular technologies used nowadays which are available in every modern personal computer such as *HTTP* protocol client-server internetworking, *802.11* wireless networks, *Bluetooth*, *IR*[1] or *RFID* devices. This system is divided into three user transparent subsystems: the first one obtains the location of the client computer from the hardware installed on it, the second one works as a proxy and embeds this obtained location into the *HTTP* request generated by the user's web browser, and the last one, installed in the *HTTP* application server controller, extracts the location from the request and offers the programmer a complete object oriented API that allows to code a web program that will generate a client-location dependent *HTTP* response. Thus the *HTTP* response to a client request is dependent of the location of the client at the moment the request was generated.

1 Introduction

The *HTTP* protocol in combination with the *HTML* language is becoming the most popular and standard user interface used in present software. This allows people to use any running application available from anywhere in the world with independence of the client platform. Another new revolution is the mobility offered by wireless technologies and mobile devices such as laptops or handheld *PDAs*. Furthermore, internetworking is available everywhere now even when the client is moving, so access to all kind of web applications is possible from the most amazing places world-wide.

Mobility and web applications are becoming increasingly popular and standard in all areas of knowledge. In the platform proposed in this paper both concepts are combined so the possibilities of web applications can be improved

---

[1] Infrared lights.

H. Murakami et al. (Eds.): UCS 2004, LNCS 3598, pp. 37–48, 2005.

thanks to user mobility: data processing in those applications are dependent of the physical location of the user. There are multiple possibilities for this architecture, from yellow pages services to location-based museum information systems, on route driver information services or train station on demand timetables. For instance, we can be waiting for a train on a platform of a huge train station browsing the Internet wireless using our laptop computer. Just accessing the train company's Internet homepage with our favourite web browser will show us the scheduled times of all trains expected as well as other information such as delays, etc. Another example could be the case of an art museum where visitors can walk along the rooms with mobile devices accessing to the museum Internet homepage. Depending on the room the user is located, the museum homepage will show general information about that room including a list of art items available in it. If the user gets closer to an item, the homepage will show detailed information about it. Naturally, the museum and train company homepage are accessible from every computer in the world outside the museum or train station thanks to the Internet, but in this case no location dependent information will be shown.

The system proposed in this paper is a complete development platform allowing web application programmers to add location dependence to their software products. The different kinds of locations described in the next section of this paper can be obtained from popular hardware devices available in all present mobile computers. Some of those will be described in the next section. After an objective enumeration and overview, further sections will describe the different subsystems of our approach.

2   Background

Much research has been carried out on location dependence in mobile computing, especially in *GSM* telephone related fields using *WAP*[2] protocol. Such technologies, which have inspired this project, are quite different to this one. The *Cooltown* project described in [1] and [2], from *HP Labs* is probably the most popular project regarding location dependence using the *HTTP* protocol. Mobile computers using this system have an engine installed that reads location from a hardware device. This location is sent by the engine to a *Cooltown* server that will return metadata about the place where the mobile user is located. This metadata conveys a list of hyperlinks to web pages related to that place. The *Cooltown* engine will pop-up a web browser with a list of these links or only one hyperlink. Other projects like *MOGID*[3] and *Mobile Info Search*[4] follow a similar approach. The differences between these projects and the approach presented in this paper are substantial. While in those projects users receive metadata (links to others *URLs* on other servers) in their web browsers related to their location from a single server, in our system users demand information from any web server and will receive it automatically processed in function of the

---

[2] Wireless Application Protocol.

user's location. Aside from this important difference, the process of obtaining location and *ID* translation were inspired by these projects.

2.1 Location

There are many ways to represent location[7] and all of them are supported by this system. The two main models are the symbolic and geometric models.

In the geometric model locations are represented by N-dimension numeric coordinates which represent the exact location of the place itself. The coordinates generated by a GPS^3 device are an example of a location that follows this model. We can also divide this model into other two submodels: Cartesian coordinates (using the *(X, Y, Z)* axis model over a cartesian base) and geographic coordinates (using the classic latitude, longitude model). The cartesian coordinates submodel should be used for the placement of locations over small spaces like a building. In case we need to place locations over a big area such as a city or a country, the geographic coordinates submodel should be used since the Cartesian coordinates submodel becomes invalid due to Earth curvature.

In the symbolic main model, locations are represented by a symbol. A symbol gives the name of the place itself and can be represented by a string, number or others. Like in the geometric main model, we can classify the symbolic model into two submodels: A simple identifier *(ID)* like a string or a number, and a hierarchy *ID* where the location ID is subdivided in hierarchic domains telling us more than one piece of information on location. For instance *mkg.sfc.keio.ac.jp.*

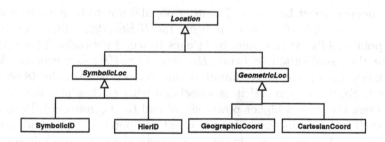

Fig. 1. Location Class hierarchy

This platform will allow us to develop web applications in object oriented programming languages. This will work with `Location` class objects (for instance, the location of the client at the time of the request) from every model described before so, as we can see in the previous figure, an object class hierarchy has been designed for this purpose. Multiple location models can be used by this system at the same time to represent the same location.

---

[3] Global Positioning System.

2.2   Obtaining Location

In our platform, client mobile terminals like laptops or handheld computers obtain their location and send it to the application server. There are many methods a mobile computer can use to get this information, some of them using already integrated and affordable devices like *IR* ports, Bluetooth devices and *802.11* wireless network interfaces, and others requiring more expensive and sophisticated devices like *GPS* satellite receivers. We describe some of them here.

GPS receiver. This device receives signals from several satellites and after comparing the delays between all of them calculates its geographic coordinates. It offers a definition location from 5 to 100 meters, it is available everywhere outside buildings and generates geometric-geographic location.

IR and Bluetooth beacons. Present mobile computers usually integrate them. These can be configured to receive raw data from simple and inexpensive external *IR* or *Bluetooth* transmitters. An external transmitter can be placed anywhere and programmed to transmit *XML* encoded messages including their location in both geometric and/or symbolic models. Granularity and coverage are around 15-20 cm for *IR* and several meters (limited by walls) for *Bluetooth*. A good example of the use of this method could be a museum where each item exposed has an *IR* beacon transmitter streaming its *ID* encoded in *XML* format. If a visitor places his computer near a transmitter, the system will know which item of the museum the visitor is seeing.

802.11 access point beacons. The most popular way to keep online a wireless computer on a *TCP/IP* network is using the *IEEE 802.11* link protocol with access points (*APs*) as repeaters or bridges to wired networks. These APs can transmit their configurable network *ID* string (*ESSID*[4]) as a beacon. Wireless network interfaces from client computers can obtain this *ID* or the 48 bit *MAC*[5] address (*BSSID*[6]) of the *AP* it is associated with at that moment (normally the one received with a higher power signal and the nearest one). Both *ESSID* and *BSSID* can be considered by the client computer as a symbolic location. Granularity and coverage are big (up to 300 meters) but can be limited reducing the transmission power, using building walls or directional 2.4 Ghz antennas. In the example of the museum, each room could be equipped with an *AP* configured with an *ESSID* that includes the name or number of the room where it is placed. Visitors with their wireless mobile computers move from one room to another and their *802.11* network interfaces will associate from one *AP ESSID* to another *AP ESSID*. The system knows where the user is located by obtaining this *ESSID* from the interface driver.

---

[4] Extended Service Set Identification.
[5] Media Access Control.
[6] Basic Service Set Identification.

RFIDs tags.[7][9]. These can be considered as small inexpensive and passive beacons that can be located anywhere without requiring any hardware or power supply to inform about their location. When a magnetic field is induced over these *RFIDs*, they can transmit stored data. As in *IR* and *Bluetooth* beacons this data can contain an *XML* document encoding all kind of location models. Mobile computers can be equipped with Compact Flash or *USB RFID* receivers in order to read information about location. Granularity of this method is small and variable: From 2 centimeters to several meters.

Our approach is designed to use all of these methods and others additional: external modules can be developed and dynamically linked into the system thus support for a new method to obtain location is added. An example of a new method susceptible to be integrated in our platform is the interesting project introduced in [8], that presents a solution to obtain location using the receiving signal strength of many wireless *802.11* access points as a pattern on a trained neural network.

3   System Overview

3.1   Goals

Before designing this architecture some clear objectives were specified in order to propose a solution.

Location dependence of HTTP responses: The contents of an *HTTP* response generated after an *HTTP 1.0/1.1* request using any method (*GET, POST, ...*) will depend on the physical location of the client mobile terminal at the time the request has been sent.

User transparency: Once an initial system installation and setup has been done, mobile users should not notice that a location dependent platform is running in their computers or servers they are accessing to by *HTTP* protocol. This implies compatibility with any *HTTP* request method using any popular web browser, compatibility with other web application servers not supporting our architecture on the Internet (which will just ignore the location dependent request), and of course, efficiency (not causing sensible delays when accessing to any web server that uses or not this system).

Multiple location model support: The system should support working with all the location models described in the past sections, even simultaneously as shown in the deployment example of section 4.

Support for multiple modular methods to obtain location: As exposed before, there are many ways to obtain location using different hardware devices in different ways. This system should support the dynamic inclusion of new

---

[7] Radio Frequency IDs.

methods to obtain location from new hardware devices as external loadable modules.

Mobility: The client side of this platform should be designed to be installed in all kind of mobile devices supporting *TCP/IP* networks. Some of these mobile computers may have low memory and *CPU* resources.

Security: Since we don't want a sniffer in the network to know the place we are, *HTTPS* protocol should be supported. Regarding location beacons, keys on both transmitter and receiver sides could be set up for encryption support.

Support of popular development platforms: A complete *API* for location data processing should be provided to developers for the most popular programming platforms (*J2EE, .NET, Perl, PHP, Erlang, ...*).

3.2   System Interactions

Giving transparency to users is one of the main issues of our approach. The client location should be obtained by web server and the client computer which knows it. The solution used in this platform is an *HTTP* proxy that embeds location information in the client *HTTP* request. It is installed in the mobile client machine as a daemon, so the user should configure his/her web browser to use localhost as a proxy server. This proxy server is called *Client side Location Dependent Information System* (CLDIS). Another subsystem running as a daemon in the same machine will gather information about its physical location from different installed hardware devices and serves it to the *CLDIS* subsystem using a *TCP* socket and *XML* language. This subsystem is called *Location Devices System* (*LDS*).

Figure 2 shows the typical interactions among components in the system. First of all, *CLDIS* receives an *HTTP* request from a user's web browser (1). Then it gets connected to the *LDS* subsystem and finds the client location (2). This location is embedded as a new header of the *HTTP* request and is finally sent to the application web server without any notice of the user (3). The server receives the request, extracts the client location and creates an *HTTP* response which is sent back to the *CLDIS* proxy (4). *CLDIS* just resends this response to the user client browser (5).

Another subsystem called, Server side *Location Dependent Information System* (*SLDIS*) is installed in the application web server for the purpose of extracting the location information from the request and offering several routines to process and translate from one model to other the received client location information before generating the *HTTP* response.

3.3   Location Devices Subsystem

The *LDS* subsystem is responsible for obtaining the location of the computer system where it is installed from the available hardware devices. Several location information from different devices are polled at the same time and then gathered on a single XML buffer. This buffer is served to the *CLDIS* subsystem using a *TCP* socket.

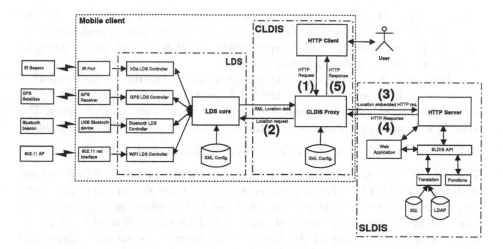

Fig. 2. Interaction among components

The different methods to obtain location from the hardware devices are implemented as external modules that are loaded into the core *LDS* subsystem using a common interface once it has started. These modules access to the operating system hardware drivers to obtain all kind of information about location as exposed in previous sections.

The core *LDS* subsystem is a timer which polls every external module using a *bridge*[10] pattern to transparently access them. When data is already obtained from all different available sources, it is processed in a single *XML* document and served by a socket while the polling process continues.

3.4 Client Side Location Dependent Information Subsystem

As explained before, the *CLDIS* subsystem acts as an *HTTP* proxy. It waits on a socket for an *HTTP* request from the user's web browser. When a connection is received, *CLDIS* is cloned so another process will be waiting for another connection while the initial one is processing the request.

Before processing the request, *CLDIS* will ask its cache system whether it contains non expired information about the client's location. If not, *CLDIS* will open a connection with the *LDS* subsystem and obtain updated *XML* information about the client's location. After updating the cache system, this location data will be parsed and included as a new header in the *HTTP* request.

HTTP/1.0 and *HTTP/1.1* protocols as specified in *RFC 1945* and *RFC 2068* can handle non-standard headers in their request and responses. Such headers are called extension headers and can be used to include encoded location data following the RFC specifications.

A smarter way to include data in the *HTTP* request is the method used in projects like [5] where location information is embedded in the request body as a *SOAP*[6] object encoded in the *XML* language. The problem is that sending *HTTP* requests with *SOAP* embedded information is only limited to POST requests. This circumstance does not make system totally transparent for the user since location dependent *HTTP* queries are limited just to post forms and will interfere with other *POST* requests sent to other servers not prepared to handle location dependent information.

The request, with included location information, is sent directly or by another proxy to the final web server destination. Once the request is processed by the server, an *HTTP* response is generated and sent back to the *CLDIS* proxy. The *CLDIS* will immediately forward it to the web browser that originated the request.

3.5   Server Side Location Dependent Information Subsystem

The *CLDIS* subsystem sends to the web application server an *HTTP* request with the location of the client computer embedded. Once received, a program will be executed by the server to process this request. This program is able to obtain the contents of the *HTTP* request, and so it is also able to read the location of the client at the time of the request. The *Server side Location Dependent Information Subsystem* (*SLDIS*) offers some functions designed for several web application development platforms to extract and parse this location information from the request. These functions will return a vector of Location class objects (see previous sections) corresponding to each location information gathered by the *LDS* subsystem from the client computer.

The *SLDIS* also offers a complete *API* to create, transform, and operate with Location class objects, so all kind of simple and complex queries from the client can be answered. Functions for calculating distances, ranges, bearings, tracking routes or obtaining future client locations from these are examples of implemented methods.

The server can receive the location of the client represented in multiple location models at the same time. One or more of them can be used by the application for its purposes. A mechanism to translate from one model of Location class objects to others is also provided as described in the following section.

3.6   Location Model Translation

Sometimes hardware devices that obtain the geometric geographic location of the client computer (like *GPS*, or beacons broadcasting coordinates) are not available. Only the client can gather symbolic location information, so only Symbolic Location class objects can be processed by the web server program. To solve this problem *SLDIS* offers functions to transform a symbolic location object to a geometric one. The *SLDIS API* uses an external relational database indexed by symbolic *ID* to obtain coordinates from this *ID* so a new Geometric Location class object is created. Not only coordinates are obtained. Action ranges data or *GIS*[8] polygon shapes (area where an *ID* is valid) are also included in the newly created Geometric Location objects.

If the symbolic location data is hierarchic, translation can be done using an *LDAP* directory due to the tree structure and therefore, more efficiency can be obtained.

---

[8] Geographic Information System.

SLDIS also provides functions to make a reverse translation: Let's consider we have a `Geometric Location` class object, and we want to obtain the symbolic name of the place where the coordinates are located. The *SLDIS* will query a relational database where spatial *R-Tree*[11] indexes are used to index regions represented by polygons. *R-Tree* indexing will just give us a reduced list of possible regions where the asked location can be placed since these trees just index the minimum bounding rectangle of these regions. Now, an algorithm to know if the coordinate is inside a polygonal region should be applied to each polygon obtained from the *R-Tree* index.

4   A Deployment Example

A great part of this system has already been implemented for Linux mobile devices (*x86* Laptop and *ARM* handhelds) using the *C++* language in the client side subsystems and a *SLDIS API* for the PHP4/Apache language in the server. Translation `Location` class queries were done against *MySQL 4.1* server (supports spatial indexing) and the *OpenLDAP* directory. Implemented *LDS* controllers to obtain location are the *IR* beacon receiver (using *Linux Kernel IrDa* support), and the *BSSID/ESSID* symbolic location obtained from *802.11* wireless access points.

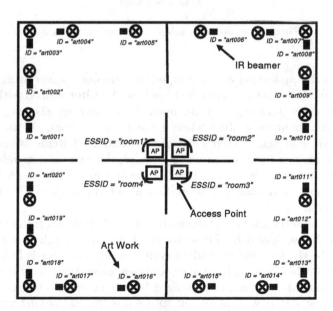

Fig. 3. A deployment example

To validate the system, a real situation in a museum (explained in previous sections) has been simulated: A building with several rooms was equipped with wireless *802.11b* access point, each configured with a name of a museum room as *ESSID* (*room1: Pictures, room2: Sculpture, ...*). Each room was provided with some *IR* beacons (using laptop computers with IR ports), each one streaming an *ID* of an art item of this museum.

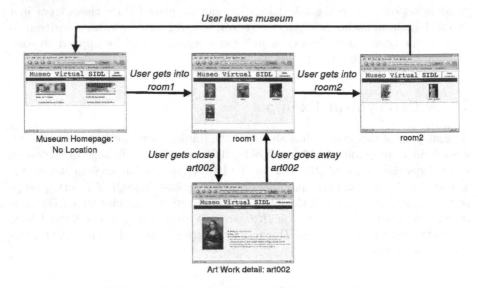

Fig. 4. Location dependent web application states

A *PHP* web application was developed on a network server using the *SLDIS API* to handle the location dependent queries. A visitor walked with a wireless laptop around the building with an opened web browser showing the virtual museum server homepage. Just when getting into a room, the browser automatically refreshed and showed a list of the virtual art items available in that room. When moving from one room to another, the web browser refreshed with information about the new room. Placing the laptop next to an *IR* beacon, the browser automatically showed information about the art item this beacon was associated with.

Results were satisfactory and the system was efficient and totally transparent for the user. Network and *HTTP* server overheads take much longer than those ones caused by the location-dependent system so no difference is found. Refreshing the system when moving from one room to another takes a couple of seconds. This delay depends on the time required by our network interface card to associate the new *AP*. It was important to use directional 2.4 Ghz antennas with low power transmission in order to avoid signals from a *802.11* beacon getting inside a wrong room. Regarding *IR* beacons, refreshing was almost immediate. Significant time delay depends on positioning hardware or the configurable timings of the *LDIS* system. Timings can be set up fast enough so user will not notice delay without a considerable *CPU* usage.

Developing the location dependent web application was very simple. A few conditional instructions with calls to *SLDIS API* were added to the non client location dependent version of the software.

The use of a web browser (*HTTP* protocol) is an advantage in this example as well as in other scenarios since users can take their own standard laptops or handheld computers with their standard web browsers installed to the museum and just use the location dependent system.

5 Conclusions

The system proposed is a very simple and light-weight solution for multiple applications in every area of knowledge where mobility is involved. The simple approach of inserting a client's location in the HTTP request using a proxy architecture allowed this simplicity and transparency for users, one of the main goals of this project:

This simple combination of proxy architecture, compatibility with the Internet and efficiency were the main aspects that helped to achieve it, but the technologies used helped as well. Modern and popular technologies found in every present personal computer, network and software applications are used in this architecture, so no extra effort from the user, system administrator or programmer is necessary to implement our system. In the same way, no special hardware, client web browser or special web application server is needed to run it. That makes it simple and inexpensive to install and use the system for concrete applications: just a simple daemon in client computers, and an *API* library in web application servers should be installed. Similarly, adapting an old web application in order to support this system is also easy.

An important problem of this architecture discussed at UCS 2004 Symposium talks about interruptions. What happen if location changes while client is receiving data streaming from a past location yet? LDIS system is able to know if location changes but, due the compatibility with standard HTTP clients and protocol, it can't communicate with the web browser (and its plug-ins) to interrupt the transfer and start a new updated one. That is the price to pay for the use of all these standard and popular technologies available everywhere.

The main issue of this project is data processing in function of the client's location done by server. This will allow us to be more flexible when developing applications which depend on a user's location, since information returned to the client can be adapted to its location in *real time* with high accuracy instead of being a solid stream of information related to the place where the client is. This will also allow us to integrate this system into any other existing web application software where the user's location will just be another parameter of data processing. Flexibility is increased thanks to the independent-module based design: Different methods and devices for obtaining location and different location models easily help application developers to adapt this architecture to their specific needs allowing a wider range of possibilities.

Future work includes the development of a real-case scenario on a real museum. *RFID* tags will be used for the art works and Video on Demand will stream over the location dependent web pages using the VoDKA[12] video stream server. Client handheld computers with a Compact Flash RFID reader will be available for museum users. A CLDIS subsystem developed in embedded Visual C++ language will be installed in each terminal. Video stream from VoDKA server will be played using a media player after obtaining a location dependent HTTP response that includes a redirection to the stream source.

Acknowledgements

Partially supported by Spanish MCyT (2002-02859 TIC), the private company Alfa21 Outsourcing (FUAC 2/79) and the Amancio Ortega Foundation.

References

1. Kindberg, T., Barton, J.: *A Web-Based Nomadic Computing System.* Internet and Mobile Systems Labs. Hewlett-Packard.
2. Kindberg, T., Barton, J., Morgan, J., Becker, G., Caswell, D., Debaty, P., Gopal, G., Frid, M., Krishnan, V., Morris, H., Schettino, J., Serra ,B.: *People, Places, Things: Web Presence for the Real World. Internet and Mobile Systems Labs.* Hewlett-Packard. http://cooltown.hp.com
3. Belsinger, P., Sun, D., Gómez, M., Pellandini, G. Q., Aeschlimann, M., Dworzak, D., Hubmann, M., Sollberger, A.: *MOGID: Mobile Geo-depended Information on Demand. Workshop on Position Dependent Information Services*, Feb 2000. IN-RIA, France.
4. Takahashi, K.: *A Mobile Portal Service to Provide Location Dependent Information.* Workshop on Position Dependent Information Services. Feb 2000. INRIA, France.
5. Escudero-Pascual, A., Maguire, G. Q.: *Role(s) of a Proxy in Location Based Service.* Royal Institute of Technology, Stockholm, Sweden.
6. W3C: *Simple Object Access Protocol (SOAP) 1.1*, Technical Report. May 2000.
7. Lee, D.L., Xu, J., Zheng, B., Lee, W.C.: *Data Management in Location-Dependent Information Services.* Pervasive Computing, IEEE. July-September 2002.
8. Battiti, R., Villani, A., Le Nhat, T.: *Neural Network models for intelligent networks: deriving the location from signal patterns.* Autonomous Intelligent Networks and Systems, Univerity of California Los Angeles, May 2002.
9. Want, R., Fishkin, K. P., Gujar, A., Harrison, B. L.: *Bridging Physical and Virtual Worlds with Electronic Tags.* Xerox PARC. Palo Alto, California. At CHI'99. April 1999.
10. Gamma, E., Helm, R., Johnson, R., Vlissides, J.: *Design Patterns: Elements of Reusable Object-Oriented Software.* Addison Wesley. 1994.
11. Guttman, A.: *R Tree, A dynamic index structure for spatial searching.* University of California Berkeley. 1984.
12. Gulías, V., Barreiro, M., Freire, J.: *VoDKA: Developing a Video-on-Demand Server using Distributed Functional Programming.* Journal of Functional Programming, special issue on Functional Approaches to High-Performance Parallel Programming. Cambridge University Press, 2005.

Position Tracking Using Infra-Red Signals for Museum Guiding System

Atsushi Hiyama[1], Jun Yamashita[1], Hideaki Kuzuoka[2],
Koichi Hirota[1], and Michitaka Hirose[1]

[1] Research Center for Advanced Science and Technology, the University of Tokyo,
4-6-1, Komaba, Meguro-ku, Tokyo, Japan
{atsushi, jun, hirota, hirose}@cyber.rcast.u-tokyo.ac.jp
[2] Engineering Systems and Mechanics, University of Tsukuba,
1-1-1, Tennoudai, Tsukuba City, Iabaraki, Japan
kuzuoka@esys.tsukuba.ac.jp

Abstract. In this paper, an indoor positioning system has been presented. The proposed system is set up by using infra-red transmitters. The developed system will be utilized as the museum guiding system for the next-generation at the National Science Museum of Japan in this summer. Plenty of research works have been performed for the development of positioning systems or mobile devices of the museum guiding systems. However, user-friendly and more flexible guiding systems are still required for both exhibitors and visitors to the museums. The developed positioning system is a simple system with inexpensive components. In addition, the museum guiding devices should be simple and portable especially for the visitors. Each infra-red(IR) transmitter, which is set on the ceiling of the exhibition hall, transmits its own signal for the identification of the coordinate value of the hall area. Unlike the common IR beacon usage as a part of the museum guiding system, all the IR transmitters are set to have overlap areas for the precise positioning of the visitors with limited number of transmitters.

1 Introduction

As Based on the ubiquitous or mobile computing currently becoming reality, many research works have been promoted for the linking of the real environment and information to the virtual ones stored in the computers. Particularly, such facilities have been received significant interests to increase the motivation of visitors to various types of museums. In most research works, the facilities have been designed especially for specific exhibits or contents. Therefore, reconfigurations of such facilities are always required in the hardware level following the changes of the layout of exhibits. The purpose of this study is to develop a flexible guiding system that can adapt the changes in the circulation planning or the layout of the exhibits in the software level. This paper presents an innovative scheme for the position tracking by using the infra-red signals. To demonstrate the efficiency of the proposed scheme, experimental studies have been performed. The results indicate the highly accurate position tracking by using the proposed scheme.

H. Murakami et al. (Eds.): UCS 2004, LNCS 3598, pp. 49–61, 2005.

2 Requirements

Taking an absolute coordinate of visitors inside an exhibition hall, make exhibition guide contents variable. In the previous studies, an infra-red or a bluetooth beacon is placed nearby each exhibit, or an RFID tag is set toward each exhibit for guiding the exhibits. Such guiding systems are very straightforward and easy to develop, but it is somewhat inefficient to look into the display of PDA in front of each exhibit. In contrast, the proposed system will provide preliminary knowledge and/or additional clues about the exhibit to the visitors heading to it. The way of designing such a system might be easy when the museum guide contents and position are linked together rather than using the contents and the exhibit ID as shown in Fig. 1.

Furthermore, the system should be available to identify precisely the positions of a certain number of visitors at the same time. It is also necessary to make the guiding devises portable for carrying around in the exhibition halls. The proposed system has been designed for the solution of the above requirements.

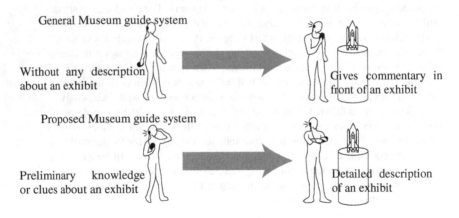

Fig. 1. Content Diagram

3 Positioning System

3.1 Practical Application

The developed system will be utilized at the National Science Museum in Tokyo, Japan. Fig. 2 shows the front gate of the National Science Museum where the exhibition "Video Game" will be held from this July to November. In addition to the function of museum guide on the developed system, it has the feature of a form of future computer games. By taking the real environment as a roll playing game field, the visitor with the museum guiding device becomes a hero following the roll playing game scenarios. Namely, the visitors are navigated through the voices of the popular game characters and they can enjoy to figure out some clues hidden around the exhibition hall.

Fig. 2. The National Science Museum

3.2 Previous Works

Although In our previous studies the handheld GPS receivers have been utilized to monitor the positioning of the visitors in the outdoor filed [1][2]. When using the handheld GPS receivers, the exhibition contents were required to be set quite sparsely in the wider area. Therefore, there was a large "amount of information gap" between the real environment and the virtual one, no information was provided through the wearable computers carried by the visitors when they were moving from one event to another one. To overcome this situation, the development of a high-time-frequency-resolution positioning systems is required by using the other types of devices instead of the handheld GPSs.

In contrast to the outdoor positioning system, the indoor positioning systems are typically based on ultrasonic sensors or infra-red sensors [3][4]. Ultrasonic or infra-red sensors have high accuracy for the positioning. However, the usage of these sensors still have problems to handle massive visitors in the museum and the identification of the visitor position is still difficult by the local mobile device carried by the visitor. Some other positioning systems have been evaluated in [5].

There are several examples adopting the RFID as an interaction trigger for stating to present exhibition contents to museum visitors, such as the digital museum at the University of Tokyo [6] or the Exploratorium in San Francisco [7]. Exhibition systems in the above applications are summarized as follows. When the museum visitor with an RFID tag holds up his/her RFID tag to the RFID readers placed in the exhibition halls, the exhibition system is activated to displays the personalized information to the visitor according to the data retrieved from the RFID tag. These systems have been designed for specific exhibitions. Therefore, the reconfiguration of the systems might be more complex when the number of exhibits increases. On the other hand, the visitor is equipped with an RFID reader and the experimental field is covered with the RFID tags. Visitors can retrieve their position continuously from the fixed tags embedded on the floor. Digital exhibition contents are governed by the positional data of the visitor. Therefore, it is possible to overlap the multiple exhibition topics in a single area. Moreover, the reconfiguration of the system is not required even if the number of exhibits change [8]. However, the RFID reader is still not small enough to carry and also it is not reasonable to embed the RFID tags on the floor. Therefore, an innovative positioning system has been proposed in this study. The proposed system is portable enough to keep the same advantage of our former RFID positioning system, where the infra-red beacons have been utilized just like the RFIDs.

4 Configuration of Proposed System

4.1 Infra-Red Transmitter

Toshiba TLN110 infra-red LED has been introduced as the infra-red transmitter in this study. The half-value angle of the TLN110 is 8 degrees apart from the target direction of infra-red signal. The transmitters will be installed on the ceiling of the exhibition hall in the National Science Museum. The height of ceiling is about 7m. The estimated radius of the infra-red spot is about 0.84m at the height of 1m which is almost equivalent to the ear level of elementary school. For the transmission of the infra-red light further than 7m, the modulation of 38kHz is added to the original infra-red transmitter as shown in Fig. 3.

Fig. 3. Infra-red transmitter

For the receiving unit of the infra-red signal, SHARP GP1UD281XK infra-red receiver is utilized. The GP1UD281XK is embedded onto the monaural headphone connected to the museum guiding device. Fig. 4 is the configuration of the developed museum guiding device designated as iGuide (Impulse Soft). The iGuide has been developed for the coming exhibition "Video Game". Besides the iGuide has a 16x16 tri-colored LED matrix, five RGB LEDs, pager motors and mp3 decoder for the output interface. For the input interface, iGuide has a biaxial accelerometer, a digital compass, a jog shuttle switch and button switches. The iGuide is also equipped with the bluetooth SPP in service.

Fig. 4. Museum guide device (iGuide)

4.2 Overview of Proposed System

The size of the exhibition hall is around 400m². For the installation of infra-red transmitters at every 1m interval, about 400 LEDs are required. In order to achieve the high time resolution of positioning with the limited number of transmitters, the position data length is specified to 12 bits: 6 bit for each x and y coordinate. A position data is transmitted in between the start and the stop bit.

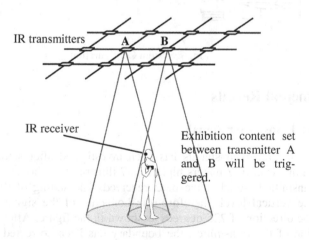

Fig. 5. Usage of Overlapped Area

In our positioning system, there exist the intentional overlapping areas of the infra-red spotlights. When a user is receiving two position data from both the transmitter A and the transmitter B, the iGuide recognizes that the user is standing between the transmitter A and the transmitter B or in the overlapped area created by the both transmitters as shown in Fig. 5.. In this way, the user's position can be calculated resulting in a higher resolution than the transmitter's layout density. However, the operation of a number of infra-red transmitters without a control causes the interference among infra-red signals transmitted from different transmitters in the overlapping areas of infra-red spots. Therefore, sequential transmission of the infra-red signals from a group of transmitters. Namely, during a transmission of position data from one transmitter, its adjacent transmitters should wait for their turn. For the efficient operation of the time-sharing transmission scheme, further investigations are necessary for the specification of the number of transmitters to be set up in the time-sharing relay loop. Overall system configuration is illustrated in Fig. 6.

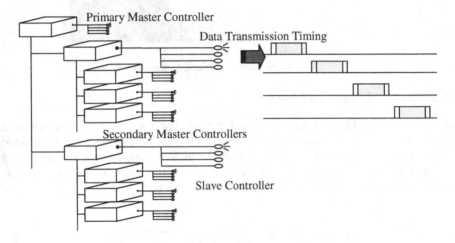

Fig. 6. System Configuration

5   Experimental Results

5.1   Range of Transmitter Signals

The profile of the received signals has been investigated after setting an infra-red transmitter on the level of 7 meters high. Fig. 7 illustrates the boundary of the region where the transmitted signals have been received. The setting of the transmitter is apart from the vertical level, therefore, the boundary of the signal transmission is distorted to the direction of 225 degrees as shown in the figure. After considering the setting position of the transmitter, the boundary has been corrected as shown by a circle in the same figure. The transmission range is almost equal to the range in the specification of the transmitter.

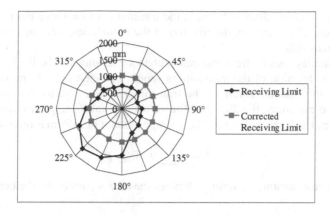

Fig. 7. Boundary of IR Signal Transmission

5.2 Transmitter Layout

Fig. 8 shows an example of the overlapped region of the boundary areas when utilizing three transmitters. The minimum number of the transmitters is three for the positioning through the signals received separately in time. To prevent the interference by receiving more than two signals at the same time, sets of four transmitters have been selected sequentially for the identification of the location of a visitor. Therefore, the locations of the transmitters are essential in order to improve the efficiency of the positioning of the visitors through the proposed scheme. In this study, five different types of the transmitter locations have been investigated as follows: three grid shaped locations, an isosceles triangular shape, and an equilateral triangular shape.

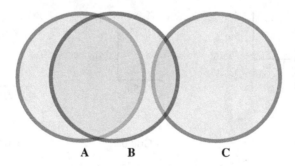

Fig. 8. Example of covered areas by three transmitters

A moving average based method has been proposed for the identification of the current position of a visitor. Namely, the visitor can easily recognize where he/she is following the received signals sent from the transmitters separately in time. The target area should be divided into a certain number of areas with the same size for the efficient usage of the transmitted signals to identify the locations of a visitor or visitors. In the case of Fig. 8, the covered area has three portions of divided areas, however, the transmitted signals does not enable the transmitters to achieve the maximum efficiency because of the uneven distribution of the boundaries, i.e., the uneven distribution of the transmitters.

The positioning signals from the transmitters are assumed to be the Markov source. Therefore, the location of the transmitters should be determined to maximize the entropy of the information given by the transmitters. Namely, the location should be determined to maximize the amount of information sent from the transmitters in each separated area by the boundaries. The average amount of information $\overline{I}$ is given by

$$\overline{I} = -\sum p_i \log_2 p_i$$

In the above equation, the term pi denotes the area separated by the boundaries.

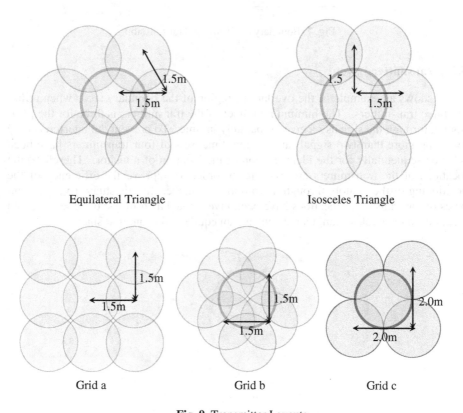

Equilateral Triangle   Isosceles Triangle

Grid a   Grid b   Grid c

Fig. 9. Transmitter Layouts

Fig. 9 illustrates five different shapes of the transmitter locations investigated in the experimental studies.

In the experiments, the interval of neighboring transmitters is basically set to 1.5 meter except the grid shape of case c. Monte Carlo simulations have been performed for the five different shapes of transmitter locations. Table 1 indicates the averaged amount of information $\overline{I}$ for the five different shapes shown in Fig. 9. When considering the averaged amount of information in each spot, the grid shaped location of type b is the best shape among the five shapes. However, the maximum amount of information is achieved for the averaged information per transmitter when applying the equilateral triangular shape. Therefore, the equilateral triangular shape is the most efficient one among the five candidates of the shapes of transmitter locations. Further studies are ongoing for the equilateral triangular shape of the transmitter locations.

Table 1. Average Amount of Information Depending on Shapes of Locations

Shape of Location	Average Information per Spot (bit)	Average Information per Transmitter (bit)
Equilateral Triangle	**3.24**	**2.81**
Isosceles Triangle	**2.62**	**2.62**
Grid a	**2.14**	**2.14**
Grid b	**4.25**	**2.13**
Grid c	**2.3**	**2.04**

6 Accuracy of Positioning

For the calculation of position, the moving average method has been applied. Calculating the moving average from the recent n position data, variation of the estimated position becomes smaller for the larger number of n. When the number n becomes larger, the estimated position is affected by the position data in the past and it causes the degradation of the motion tracking performance. Experiments have been performed for the positioning both of the standing user and the walking one for the different settings of the number n. Four infra-red transmitters are emitting its position data sequentially by the time-sharing, the multiples of four for the number n is considered for the calculation.

6.1 Static Positioning

Experimental studies have been performed for the visitor standing still on the temporary system installed at the National Science Museum. Fig. 10 illustrates the installed transmitters for the static positioning. The infra-red transmitters are fixed at each angle of equilateral triangle frame.

Fig. 11 shows the positioning error for the visitor standing still. From Fig. 11 the root mean square (RMS) of the position error is converging to 10cm when n is set to around 40. When the number n is 20 or 24, the RMS is about 15cm. The difference of 5cm is easily given by shaking head, the proposed system achieves quite accurate positioning even if the number n is set to 20.

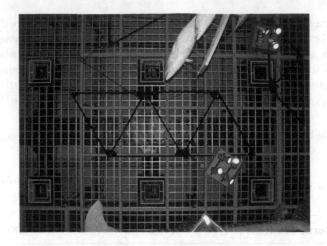

Fig. 10. Installed Transmitters for Static Positioning

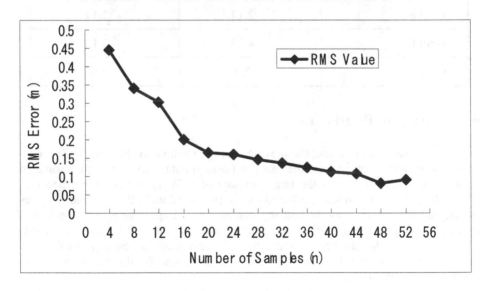

Fig. 11. Static Positioning Error

6.2 Dynamic Positioning

Here, the experimental results of the positioning are summarized for the walking user. In the experimental field, infra-red transmitters are set in a line to a wire stretched under the ceiling as shown in Fig. 12.

Fig. 13 shows the accumulated error depending on the walking speed. The total displacement of position has been measured for the user after walking straight about 11m. For the walking speed of 0.6m/s, the displacement is 50cm even if the number n is 24. For the walking speed of 1.2m/s, about 120cm of displacement is measured if the number n is 20 or 24. When the walking speed reaches to the running speed of

Fig. 12. Installed Transmitters for Dynamic Positioning

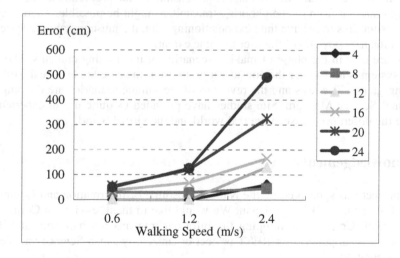

Fig. 13. Accumulated Error Depending on Walking Speed

2.4m/s, the displacement of more than one meter is measured when the number n is no less than 12. As shown in the figure, the stable positioning is still accomplished for the number n of four or eight. Significant difference between the number n of four and eight does not exists.

6.3 Experimental Result

As clearly shown in the experimental results, the proposed positioning system has a highly accurate positioning ability for the number n of larger than 20. In addition, a reliable positioning is still available for a walking user with the number n of less than 8. The following algorithm is utilized to estimate the user's position $\mathbf{P}$.

$$\mathbf{P}n_1 = \frac{\sum_{t=k-n_1+1}^{k}(x_t, y_t)}{n_1} \ , \ \mathbf{P}n_2 = \frac{\sum_{t=k-n_2+1}^{k}(x_t, y_t)}{n_2} \quad (k > n_1 : 20 > n_2 : 8)$$

$$\text{if} \quad |\mathbf{P}n_1 - \mathbf{P}n_2| < 1200[\text{mm}]$$

$$\text{then} \quad \mathbf{P} = \mathbf{P}n_1$$

$$\text{else} \quad \mathbf{P} = \mathbf{P}n_2$$

7 Conclusion and Future Studies

In this study, an infra-red positioning system has been developed for the museum guiding system. Further studies are ongoing to upgrade the positioning algorithm. For example, whenever one infra-red signal is transmitted, the prediction of the next positioning data sent from the neighboring transmitter might be possible. Therefore, even if the visitor fails to receive the next positioning data, the museum guiding system can predict the next position of the user to some extent.

We are now in the phase of making scenarios of the guiding contents. The developed system is now under the consideration to use it in some kinds of real world role-playing games. The tests and the revisions of the sample scenarios are ongoing at the National Science Museum. Site studies have provided us quite useful experiences to notice the difference between the real world and the virtual world.

Acknowledgements

This project was sponsored by the National Institute of Information and Communications Technology (NICT) of Japan. We would like to thank e-withyou Corp. and the Inpulse Soft Corp. for developing the infra-red transmission hardware and iGuide. This study is supported by CREST project organized by Japan Science and Technology Corporation.

We also would like to offer special thanks to the National Science Museum for giving us such a great opportunity.

References

1. Ryoko Ueoka, Michitaka Hirose, et al.:"Wearable Computer Application in EXPO 2005", Proc. of the Second IEEE Pacific-Rim Conference on Multimedia(PCM2001), pp.8-15,2001

2. A. Hiyama, R. Ueoka, K. Hirota, M. Hirose, M. Sone, T. Kawamura:"Development and Demonstration of Wearable Computer Based Interactive Nomadic Gallery",Proc. of the 6th International Symposium on Wearable Computers (ISWC2002),pp.129-130,2002
3. Y. Fukuju, M. Minami, H. Morikawa, and T. Aoyama:"DOLPHIN: An Autonomous Indoor Positioning System in Ubiquitous Computing Environment", In Proceedings of IEEE Workshop on Software Technologies for Future Embedded Systems(WSTFES2003), pp.53-56, Hakodate, Japan, May 2003.
4. Welch, Greg, Gary Bishop, Leandra Vicci, Stephen Brumback, Kurtis Keller, D'nardo Colucci:"The HiBall Tracker: High-Performance Wide-Area Tracking for Virtual and Augmented Environments", Proceedngs of the ACM Symposium on Virtual Reality Software and Technology 1999 (VRST 99)
5. Jeffrey Hightower, Gaetano Borriello:"Location System for Ubiquitus Computing",IEEE Computer,vol.34,no.8,pp. 57-66,2001
6. Ken Sakamura, Noboru Koshizuka:"The ETRON Wide-Area Distributed-System Architecture for E-Commerce", IEEE Micro, vol21, no.6, pp.7-12,2001
7. M.Fleck, M. Frid, T.Kindberg, E. O'Brien-Strain, R.Rajani, M.Spasojevic:"Ubiquitus Systems in Interactive Museums",IEEE pervasive Computing,vol.1,no.1,pp.13-21 ,2002
8. Atsushi Hiyama and Michitaka Hirose: "Wearable Computers and Field Museum",10th International Conference on Human - Computer Interaction, Volume 3, pp.1406-1410, Crete Greece, 2003.6

Navigation with an Adaptive Mobile Map-Application: User Experiences of Gesture- and Context-Sensitiveness

Leena Arhippainen[1], Tapani Rantakokko[2], and Marika Tähti[1]

[1] University of Oulu, P.O. Box 3000,
FIN-90014 University of Oulu, Finland
{leena.arhippainen, marika.tahti}@oulu.fi
[2] VTT Technical Research Centre of Finland, P.O. Box 1100,
FIN-90571 Oulu, Finland
tapani.rantakokko@vtt.fi

Abstract. In this paper, we identify navigation sub-tasks in a mobile map-application, and apply adaptive and gesture-based control methods having improved user experience as our goal. We investigate how automated positioning and rotating of maps and intuitive gesture control for zooming and scrolling facilitates navigation. Several smart features were implemented into a handheld prototype: Map is positioned and rotated according to current location and orientation. Zooming is performed with hand gestures in front of a proximity sensor. Scrolling is operated with tilting movements that are recognized with accelerometers. Graphical icons and effects visualize interesting objects, their directions and distances. We evaluate the prototype by analyzing the effort needed for performing navigation sub-tasks with and without smart control features. Moreover, a user experience study was conducted. The results show that navigation tasks can be facilitated with context-sensitiveness and gesture control, though users may need some practice.

1 Introduction

During the past decade, the use of handheld devices increased exponentially. This phenomenon forced researchers and developers to redirect their design effort from desktop perspective towards small form factor display approach [1].

Small screen size and limited or absent keyboard raised a need to design novel methods for viewing information and controlling the device, such as the Chameleon system that used positions and orientations of palmtop computers as input method [2]. When suitable sensors became technically feasible and commercially available, many researches began to explore with various sensor-based control methods and apply them to handheld devices, in particular to Personal Digital Assistants (PDA). For example, Rekimoto introduced a method for controlling the device based on tilting movements (menu selection, map browsing) [3]. Also Small & Ishii [4], Harrison et al. [5], and Bartlett [6] have used tilting for scrolling and selecting. Applications that integrate several sensor-based techniques have been presented as well, for example Hinckley et al use tilt, proximity and touch sensors together [7].

H. Murakami et al. (Eds.): UCS 2004, LNCS 3598, pp. 62–73, 2005.
© Springer-Verlag Berlin Heidelberg 2005

Intuitive scrolling methods described above facilitate viewing large documents, such as maps, with small and limited displays to some extent. However, also several visualization techniques have been proposed to overcome this particular problem. For instance, Halo technique [8] supports spatial cognition by visualizing the directions and distances of off-screen objects with arcs of circles. Also graphical icons have been used in visualizing off-screen objects by placing them on a border surrounding the drawing area, thus revealing the type of the objects as well as the directions where they can be found [9].

Map-based applications have been developed usually for the purpose of providing detailed information about the surroundings of use. Generally, map-applications have been utilized for guidance purposes. For example, Bellotti et al. [10] and Sumi et al. [11] constructed a handheld tour guide. Aittola et al. [12] introduced map-based interface for a smart library. Davies et al. [13], Simcock et al. [14] and Ojala et al. [15] presented map-based outdoor tourist guidance.

The previous indicates that there is a large body of research on sensor- and map-based applications for mobile terminals. These studies have included user researches (e.g. usability, user experience) to some extent, but they have not been concerned about user behavior as a whole – usually, only one or two mechanisms have been examined at a time. Our goal was to investigate mobile map-application use when several novel techniques are integrated into one versatile prototype.

In this paper, we explore the effects of context-aware adaptation and gesture-based control on the user experience of a mobile map-application. We identify the sub-tasks of navigation with a handheld device, present a simple prototype of a mobile map-application, apply sensor-based methods for viewing and controlling maps with ease, and evaluate the effects of the enhancements from user experience point of view. The prototype is evaluated by analyzing the effort needed for performing navigation tasks with and without the enhancements. Moreover, user experience evaluation was carried out with ten participants in a controlled laboratory environment. We discuss our findings in the conclusion.

2 Prototype Development

We identified the fundamental navigation sub-tasks when using a map as follows: When navigating from, say, location A to location B, the first steps are to (1) recognize one's own position and (2) orientation on the map. This is usually performed based on some visible landmarks and perhaps with the aid of a positioning system and a compass, if available. When the location is solved and the map is adjusted right, one can read it with ease. Next steps are (3) to find the destination on the map and (4) to choose a reasonable route to it. At this point, it is also wise (5) to evaluate the distance to the destination. Finally, before beginning the journey one must (6) solve the direction where to go from the current location. In addition, it is important to check once in a while that one is still following the route. Usually this is accomplished by dividing the journey to several legs, where steps 1-6 are repeated.

In order to carry out the navigation sub-tasks with an electronic map, one should be able to scroll (pan), zoom, and rotate the map similar to what can be reasonably done with a paper map. These features are usually available in commercial hand-held navigation products, such as GPS terminals. However, we concentrate in our study to more versatile and prevalent general purpose terminals, such as smartphones and PDAs. These devices are often equipped with software designed for viewing photographs. Image viewers may include the required functionality for handling map images, but do not perform well enough in navigation where image manipulation occurs frequently and is an essential part of use. Thus, a special map-application is needed.

2.1 Simple Map-Application

At first, we developed a simple map-application that exploits only solutions typical to current graphical user interfaces (Figure 1). It was designed as an independent software application for viewing and navigating with electronic maps, to be utilized as a basis and a reference for the forthcoming enhanced prototype. This way other than designed differences between the two versions could be eliminated. We decided to use a PDA as a terminal device, since planned gesture- and context-sensitivity requires additional sensors that are currently rather difficult to add into a commercial mobile phone. Compared to smartphones, PDAs have larger displays and are designed to be controlled mainly with a small stick called a stylus, using both hands.

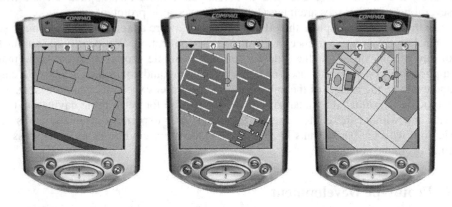

Fig. 1. Example screenshots of the simple map-application with different maps. The toolbar on top allows easy access to scrolling mode, as well as zooming and rotating the map

Since performing navigation sub-tasks often requires manipulating the map, the user should have easy access to these functions. As a compromise to having maximum amount of screen space for the actual information content, we decided to use a small toolbar with four buttons: menu, scrolling, zooming and rotating. In our implementation, scrolling (panning the map) can be performed by dragging the map with a stylus, whereas zooming and rotating exploit pop-up sliders (visualized in Figure 1).

Because of the need to support zooming and rotating of maps, 2-dimensional vector graphics was a natural choice for drawing the map. Constant size bitmap icons are drawn on top of the map to indicate services or other people. The user can select an object on screen simply by pointing it with the stylus (touch screen). Information on pointed object is shown as a default action. Compatibility with different map description formats was taken into account by utilizing XML in map parsing. We developed a simple map description language of our own to allow free experimentation.

The Java programming language was chosen for software implementation, because it supports rapid prototyping and various operating systems. We used CrEme 3.2 Java Virtual Machine from NSICOM on top of Microsoft Windows CE 3.0 OS. CrEme is Personal Java 3.1 compatible and supports various optional Java packages that were needed in the implementation of the enhanced prototype.

The developed user interface was evaluated as follows. Due to time limitations, real usage data could not be collected from actual use of this simple prototype. Thus, we had to estimate based on our own experience which of the control functions (scrolling, zooming, and rotating) users need while performing each of the navigation sub-tasks. The result of our analysis is presented in Table 1.

Table 1. Estimated need for manual map control in navigation with simple map-application. S = scroll, Z = zoom, R = rotate

Navigation sub-task	Operation with simple prototype	S	Z	R
1. Recognize own location	Explore the area, find landmarks	X	X	X
2. Adjust map orientation	Align the map with environment			X
3. Find the destination	Search through the map	X	X	
4. Choose a route to destination	Examine specific areas of the map	X	X	
5. Evaluate distance	Estimate space between locations	X	X	
6. Determine the direction to go	Align the map with right course			X

Clearly, the actions depend on the situation and user preferences, thus one can argue against our classification. However, the analysis revealed that no matter what kind of widgets is used in the user interface, the user experience suffers from frequent need to manipulate the map manually.

2.2 Enhanced Map-Application

We began enhancing the prototype from hardware. Applying sensing capabilities required several additional components: A sleeve and a WLAN card provided means for communicating with other devices (such as network servers) as well as rough positioning based on RF signal strengths [16]. To acquire orientation information and allow gesture-based control, we enhanced the PDA with a SoapBox device [17] via serial connection. SoapBox stands for Sensing, Operating and Activating Peripheral Box. It includes accelerometers (3 axes), an infrared-based proximity sensor, a compass and a light sensor and can be easily enhanced with other sensors. The final hardware setup of the enhanced prototype is illustrated in Figure 2.

To make use of the additional hardware efficiently, an event-based context platform was built between device drivers and the map-application. Raw sensor data is filtered and packaged into a form of context events, which can be passed to all applications that have registered a corresponding event listener to a particular event type (blackboard design pattern). The map-application utilizes following event types: location from WLAN network as coordinates in meters, orientation from SoapBox's

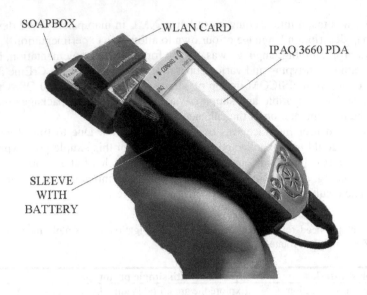

Fig. 2. The PDA hardware enhancements include a sleeve, a WLAN card and a SoapBox

compass as a deviation angle from North in degrees, tilt angles from SoapBox's 3-D accelerometers as three integer values ranging from 0 to 100, and proximity as an integer value ranging from 1 to 10.

Based on received context events, the user interface is modified automatically as follows: The map is scrolled to user's current position utilizing location events. Position is also marked on the map with a cross. The map is rotated automatically based on compass angle to keep it aligned with the environment regardless of user's movements. Since the SoapBox's compass consists of only two magnetometers, it works properly only in the horizontal plane. To prevent incorrect map rotation, tilt angles are utilized for disabling the compass feature whenever the terminal is inclined.

The map can be manually zoomed and scrolled, which allows users to browse the map as they wish. Zooming is performed by altering the distance measured by Soap-Box's proximity sensor, typically by moving one's hand in front of the sensor. Proximity is measured with an infrared transmitter/receiver pair located in the bottom of the device, thus the distance is measured towards floor when the terminal is held in hand horizontally. Manual scrolling is performed in a special scrolling mode, where automatic scrolling to current location is disabled. By tilting the terminal, the map can be scrolled (panned) to the desired direction.

The performance of our prototype has been measured and documented in [18].

In addition to sensor-based control, we enhanced the prototype by combining two visualization techniques for off-screen objects: Halo from Baudisch and Rosenholtz [8] is capable for giving cues of directions and distances of objects out of the screen, but unfortunately their arcs of circles do not reveal the type of the object at all (the arcs look same for all objects). Rantakokko and Plomp [9] visualized off-screen objects with graphical icons placed on a so-called Information Border surrounding the map area. The method helps in perceiving the types and the directions of the objects, but does not reveal distances to them. When the two techniques are combined, objects

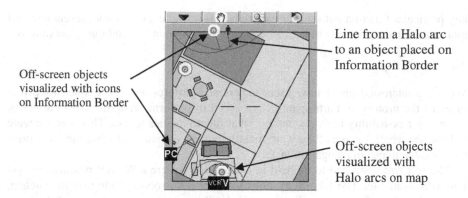

Off-screen objects
visualized with icons
on Information Border

Line from a Halo arc
to an object placed on
Information Border

Off-screen objects
visualized with
Halo arcs on map

Fig. 3. Example screenshot of the enhanced map-application. A straight line combines Halo arc
visualization on map area to icon visualization on Information Border area

can be distinguished and both direction and distance can be perceived. In Figure 3, the
combined implementation is presented.

We evaluated the effects of the enhancements on navigation sub-tasks as follows:
Table 2 explains our own estimation of which of the control functions (scrolling,
zooming, and rotating) users probably need in performing each navigation sub-task
with the enhanced prototype. Because of automation and visualization aids, the total
number of crosses has reduced from eleven in Table 1 to only five in Table 2.

Table 2. Estimated need for manual map control in navigation with enhanced map-application.
S = scroll, Z = zoom, R = rotate

Navigation sub-task	Operation with terminal device	S	Z	R
1. Recognize own location	None, location marked on the map			
2. Adjust map orientation	None, automatically aligned			
3. Find the destination	Check objects on map and border	X	X	
4. Choose a route to destination	Examine specific areas of the map	X	X	
5. Evaluate distance	Estimate with Halo circles			X
6. Determine the direction to go	None, target direction visualized			

In principal, by adding an automatic route guide to the prototype and utilizing the
available visualizations efficiently, also the last 5 marks in Table 2 could be eliminated and navigation performed completely without manual scrolling, zooming and
rotating of maps.

3 User Experience Evaluation

Our goal was to evaluate the effects of the applied gesture- and context-sensitive
enhancements on navigation from user experience point of view. Functions like tilt
scrolling and Halo visualization have been studied individually by others and well-
documented usability tests exist in the literature. We do not focus on the usability of

any particular function but on user experience as a whole, and do not present detailed quantitative measurements but concentrate on users' comments and our observations.

3.1 Test Setup

We were interested about how users experience gesture- and context-sensitive features of the prototype. Participants were asked to perform predefined test cases (3), but given a possibility to freely choose what functionalities to use. This way we were able to see which features they were mostly interested about and what functionalities they wanted to use in navigation tasks.

The test was restricted to be held in a laboratory where a WLAN positioning system was available. The laboratory consists of several rooms (living room, kitchen, etc.) and various domestic appliances (TV, VCR, computer, etc.). A map of the laboratory environment was created for the test (recall Figure 3).

The evaluation included interviews before and after use of the enhanced prototype. The tests and the interviews were recorded on video for later analysis. Each test took about one hour, including the interviews. We had 10 test users. Half of them had used a PDA before (rarely or often), the other half did not know the device at all or had never used it. We call them later as experienced (E) and inexperienced (IE) users.

Case 1

The user is in a health center and is given the enhanced prototype for finding necessary places and objects inside the building. The user familiarizes oneself with the features of the prototype with the aid of the test moderator:
- Positioning: The user observes her measured position by moving around
- Compass: The user observes automatic map alignment by turning around
- Scrolling: The user scrolls the map manually by tilting the device
- Zooming: The user zooms the map manually gesturing near proximity sensor
- Information Border visualization: The user points icons drawn on the screen
- Halo visualization: The user estimates distance to an object using Halo arcs.

Case 2

The user is sitting in a lounge, waiting for to see a doctor. She needs to go to the toilet, and she uses the prototype to find the location of the toilet.

Case 3

The user is still waiting. There is a TV in the lounge and she wants to change the channel, thus she needs to find the remote control unit by using the prototype.

3.2 Required Effort in Terms of Time Usage

All test users were able to carry out all test cases, though some needed a little bit of help. In order to find out how quickly users learned to handle the prototype and what their performance levels at the end of the test were, we measured their time usage in the test. Table 3 depicts the approximate times in minutes used to perform test cases (TC) 1-3, as well as the time differences between consecutive test cases. TC 1 included only familiarization to the functions of the prototype, so it is not comparable with test cases 2 and 3 from navigation point of view. However, TC 1 reveals the amount of time taken to familiarize oneself with the prototype. Table 4 presents average time usage in each test case by user groups (experienced / inexperienced).

The durations in TC 1 (Table 3) seem to be quite similar within experienced and inexperienced user groups, though in average experienced users spent slightly more time to explore with the novel features of the prototype (+1.8 minutes in TC 1, Table 4). In TC 2, experienced users needed in general less time than inexperienced users (TC 2, Table 4). However, in TC 3 inexperienced users improved their performance more than experienced users and eventually were almost as fast as experienced users (TC3, Table 4).

An explanation for the results could be that experienced users are familiar with technical equipment and more interested in new devices and their novel functions, so they were both capable and willing to explore the features of the prototype. Thus, they spent a little more time in familiarization phase, but benefited of that and then quickly learned to handle the prototype during the actual test cases. On the other hand, inexperienced users may have feel stressed and insecure when a new device and many new features were introduced to them at once, and continued to the next case even if they did not yet completely understood how to operate the device. Thus, they needed little more practice during the actual test cases, but then reached to the same level than experienced users.

Table 3. The amount of time used to carry out test cases (TC) 1-3 in minutes

User	TC 1	TC 2	TC 3	TC 2 – TC 1	TC 3 – TC 2
E 1	7	2	2	-5	0
E 2	11	4	3	-7	-1
E 3	13	5	2	-8	-3
E 4	12	2	2	-10	0
E 5	10	4	1	-6	-3
IE 6	4	3	2	-1	-1
IE 7	12	6	1	-6	-5
IE 8	13	6	5	-7	-1
IE 9	7	4	2	-3	-2
IE 10	8	12	4	+4	-8

Table 4. The average amount of time used to carry out test cases (TC) 1-3 in minutes

Users	TC 1	TC 2	TC 3
E users	10,6	3,4	2
IE users	8,8	6,2	2,8
Difference (E-IE)	+1,8	-2,8	-0,8

3.3 Evaluation of Navigation Sub-tasks

The main focus in the evaluation was placed on navigation sub-tasks (ST) and user actions while using the enhanced prototype in order to clarify the need for manual map control in practice. Table 5 presents the number of users who scrolled, zoomed and rotated the map. The need for manipulating the map when using the enhanced prototype turned out to be somewhat similar to what we assumed (recall Table 2), though there were some unexpected exceptions in the usage. For example, the map was rotated automatically by the compass in the test, but some users tried to rotate the map manually by turning the terminal device in hand (Table 5). Also, many users needed manual control in ST 6 – obviously they were a little unsure to which direction to go. Automatic route guide should eliminate this need.

Table 5. The estimated and tested use of manual map control in navigation with enhanced map-application. S = scroll, Z = zoom, R = rotate. On the left, estimated usage is marked with crosses (from Table 2). On the right are measured instances of use. The occasions where more than half of the users used a particular feature are marked with grey background

	Enhanced version, estimate			Enhanced version, user test		
Navigation sub-task	**S**	**Z**	**R**	**S**	**Z**	**R**
1. Recognize own location				1		1
2. Adjust map orientation						2
3. Find the destination	X	X		6	8	
4. Choose a route to destination	X	X		3	6	3
5. Evaluate distance		X		1	7	1
6. Determine the direction to go				3	5	1

ST1: Recognize Own Location

The enhanced prototype includes several features that help users to find their own position. The location is marked with a cross on the map, and the map is automatically scrolled to reveal this location. Also, speech synthesizer gives a voice announcement of the room's name when it changes. Half of the test users noticed the position mark and regarded it as a familiar and clear symbol. The others listened to voice announcements or compared the map to the environment. Despite of these aids, one user utilized scrolling for finding own location, and another turned the map (Table 5). A positioning system is probably more beneficial in a larger environment.

ST2: Adjust Map Orientation

In the prototype the map is rotated automatically based on device orientation (deviation angle from North). The test elicited that 8 of 10 users were able to utilize automatic rotation properly. They considered it useful because they did not have to clarify the direction by themselves. However, the other two users did not really understand how to utilize automatic map alignment; they tried to rotate the map themselves by turning the terminal device in hand (Table 5). Consequently, automatic rotation cancelled their effort and they lost the control of the device.

ST3: Find the Destination

The Information Border was included to help users to find the destination on the map with ease. In the beginning of the test, users typically did not pay attention to this feature much or not at all. Instead, they concentrated on performing the navigation sub-task using other features, such as scrolling (6 users) or zooming (8 users) (Table 5). After the moderator mentioned about this feature, users started to think about it. They understood the benefits of drawing objects on top of the map and regarded it as an important feature, but did not utilize it much or not at all in the test situation. It seemed that using this feature requires more practicing and an environment larger than our test laboratory to become useful.

ST4: Choose a Route to Destination

Earlier, we assumed that route planning would require using scrolling and zooming. In the test, three users utilized scrolling to find a route to destination. Many users experienced tilting movements natural and easy to perform, whereas others felt that they need more practicing with it. Six users utilized zooming, though many of them had troubles controlling it. In addition, three users tried to find the route by turning the map (by turning the terminal). (Table 5)

ST5: Evaluate Distance

In order to evaluate distance to destination, five users needed only the arcs of Halo circles or estimated it without the prototype. Nevertheless, the test illustrated that Halo arcs alone did not give sufficient information for the users – three users mentioned that they wanted to see the distance in meters or steps. In fact, only one user actually followed how the size of the arc changed when she approached the object. Eventually, seven users checked the distance to the destination via zooming and estimating based on the map. (Table 5)

ST6: Determine the Direction to Go

According to our initial assumption, users should be able to perceive the direction of the destination by checking the position of the object on the Information Border. Some users did notice the object's direction from the border, but in practice needed to check it another way as well. Mostly users zoomed (5) and scrolled (3) to find the direction. Once again, one test user tried to rotate the map by turning the device in hand. (Table 5)

3.4 Summary of the Evaluation

Positioning and map rotation were automated and visualizations in use, thus users should have been able to perform sub-tasks 1, 2 and 6 without manipulating the map (Table 5). In sub-tasks 1 and 2, this seems to be accomplished rather well despite of a couple of stray values on lines one and two. In sub-task 6, the direction of the destination was visualized on the Information Border, but users did not utilize the border much and thus needed to access scrolling and zooming features. Also, since rotation was automated its column should be empty. A few users had constant difficulties in understanding automatic rotation, which explains stray values in that column.

Performing sub-task 3 required finding a suitable icon on the map or on the border, and clicking it to see its details and to make sure it really represents the target. Instead of utilizing the border, scrolling and zooming were often accessed. In sub-task 4, most of the users preferred zooming to examine areas of the map. When users needed to evaluate distance to the destination (ST5), they wanted to check it via zooming instead of utilizing Halo visualization, which turned out to be difficult to understand.

In Table 5, the cases where more than half of the users utilized a particular control method are marked with a gray background. The pattern seems close to our estimation (pattern formed by crosses). Differences suggest that we were too optimistic about the benefits of visualizations. One reason for little use of visualizations is very likely the small size of the laboratory; it was often too easy see the requested information directly. Also, users were clearly more excited about the sensor-based features.

4 Conclusion

We identified the fundamental navigation sub-tasks in mobile map-applications, developed a simple prototype, and after evaluating it enhanced it with automatic positioning and rotation of maps as well as gesture-based scrolling and zooming, and combined two visualization techniques to provide information of off-screen objects and thus reduced the need for browsing the map. We estimated the benefits of our enhancements by comparing the need for map manipulation with and without the enhancements in each navigation sub-task. In order to validate our estimation, we tested the enhanced prototype with ten users in a laboratory environment, measured how much time they needed to learn to handle the prototype, how they utilized the features of the prototype in navigation tasks, and collected their experiences.

The results revealed that our initial assumptions were mostly correct. When automatic positioning and rotating of maps based on user location and orientation were applied, the users could perceive their location and orientation mainly without manipulating the map. However, a few users had troubles in understanding automatic rotation of maps. Intuitive gesture control performed well enough and users were able to browse the map, though it became obvious that some practice is needed. Most of the users liked scrolling by tilting the device. Zooming by altering the device's proximity to other objects was not that popular in comments, but was utilized very often.

The major difference between our assumptions and user experience tests was in the utilization of visualizations. Users did not pay much attention to them and preferred scrolling and zooming in solving navigation sub-tasks. One of the probable reasons was the small size of the test environment. Another explanation to low utilization of visualization is that users were more excited about sensor-based control.

Our research validated that navigation using a mobile map-application can be facilitated with sensor-based context-aware adaptations, such as automatic map positioning and alignment, as well as with intuitive gesture-based control. In the future, we would like to study the benefits of visualization techniques more carefully and test the prototype in outdoor environment for a longer test period.

References

1. Marcus, A., Ferrante, J.V., Kinnunen, T., Kuutti, K., Sparre, E.: Baby Faces: User-Interface Design for Small Displays. CHI (1998) Panel, 96-97
2. Fitzmaurice, G.W., Zhai, S., Chignell, M.H.: Virtual Reality for palmtop computers. ACM Transactions on Information Systems, 11 (3) (1993) 197-218
3. Rekimoto, J.: Tilting Operations for Small Screen Interfaces, UIST (1996)
4. Small, D., Ishii H.: Design of Spatially Aware Graspable Displays, CHI (1997) Companion, 367-368
5. Harrison, B., Fishkin, K., Gujar, A., Mochon, C., Want, R.: Squeeze Me, Hold Me, Tilt Me! An Exploration of Manipulative User Interfaces, CHI (1998)
6. Bartlett, J.F.: Rock 'n' Scroll Is Here To Stay. IEEE Computer Graphics and Applications, May/June (2000)
7. Hinckley, K., Pierce, J., Sinclair, M., Horvitz E.: Sensing Techniques for Mobile Interaction. ACM UIST (2000)
8. Baudisch, P., Rosenholtz, R.: Halo: A Technique for Visualizing Off-screen Objects. CHI (2003) 481-488
9. Rantakokko, T., Plomp, J.: An Adaptive Map-Based Interface for Situated Services. Smart Objects Conference (2003)
10. Bellotti, F., Berta, R., deGloria, A., Margarone, M.: User Testing a Hypermedia Tour Guide. IEEE Pervasive Computing (2002) 33-41
11. Sumi, Y., Etani, T., Fels, S.: C-MAP: Building a Context-Aware Mobile Assistant for Exhibition Tours. AAAI (1998)
12. Aittola M., Ryhänen T., Ojala T.: SmartLibrary - Location-aware mobile library service. MobileHCI (2003) 411-416
13. Davies, N., Cheverst, K., Mitchell, K., Efrat, A.: Using and Determining Location in a Context-Sensitive Tour Guide. IEEE Computer (2001) 35-41
14. Simcock, T., Hillenbrand, S.P., Thomas, B.H.: Developing a location based tourist guide application. ACSW frontiers (2003), Volume 21.
15. Ojala, T., Korhonen, J., Aittola, M., Ollila, M., Koivumäki, T., Tähtinen, J., Karjaluoto, H.: SmartRotuaari - Context-aware mobile multimedia services. MUM, (2003) 9-18
16. Haataja, V.: Indoor Positioning Based on Wireless Networks, University of Oulu, Oulu 2001.
17. Tuulari, E., Ylisaukko-oja, A.: SoapBox: A Platform for Ubiquitous Computing Research and Applications. Pervasive Computing, (2002)
18. Rantakokko, T., Arhippainen L., and Tähti M., Evaluation of Sensor-Based UI Adaptation and Control in a Map-Application for Mobile Terminals, PSIPS, (2004)

Real-World Interaction with Camera Phones

Michael Rohs

Institute for Pervasive Computing,
Department of Computer Science,
Swiss Federal Institute of Technology (ETH) Zurich, Switzerland
rohs@inf.ethz.ch

Abstract. With the integration of cameras, mobile phones have evolved
into networked personal image capture devices. Camera phones can perform image processing tasks on the device itself and use the result as
an additional means of user input and a source of context data. In this
paper we present a system that turns such phones into mobile sensors for
2-dimensional visual codes. The proposed system induces a code coordinate system and visually detects phone movements. It also provides the
rotation angle and the amount of tilting of the camera as additional input parameters. These features enable applications such as item selection
and interaction with large-scale displays. With the code coordinate system, each point in the viewed image – and therefore arbitrarily shaped
areas – can be linked to specific operations. A single image point can
even be associated with multiple information aspects by taking different
rotation and tilting angles into account.

1 Introduction

With the integration of CCD cameras, mobile phones have become networked
personal image capture devices. As image resolution improves and computing
power increases, they can do more interesting things than just taking pictures
and sending them as multi media messages over the mobile phone network. For
example, programmable camera phones can perform image processing tasks on
the device itself and use the result as an additional means of input by the user
and a source of context data.

In this paper, we present a visual code system that turns camera phones
into mobile sensors for 2-dimensional visual codes. For that, we elaborate on
and extend our initial ideas presented in [1]. We assume scenarios where camera
phones are used to sense a scene that contains one or more visual codes. By
recognizing a code tag, the device can determine the code value, the targeted
object or image element (even if the object or image element itself is not equipped
with a code tag), as well as additional parameters, such as the viewing angle of
the camera. The system is integrated with a visual phone movement detection
scheme, which provides three degrees of freedom and turns the mobile phone
into an optical mouse. Code recognition and motion detection are completely
performed on the phone itself. The phone's wireless communication channel is

H. Murakami et al. (Eds.): UCS 2004, LNCS 3598, pp. 74–89, 2005.

used to retrieve online content related to the selected image area or to trigger actions (either in the background infrastructure or on a nearby larger display), based on the sensed code and its parameters.

These features enable local interaction with physical objects, printed documents, as well as virtual objects displayed on electronic screens in the user's vicinity. Mobile phones are in reach of their users most of the time and are thus available in many everyday situations. They are therefore ideal bridging devices between items in the real world and associated entities in the virtual world. Visual codes provide visible "entry points" into the virtual world, starting from the local surroundings. This offers a natural way of local interaction and strengthens the role of mobile phones in a large number of usage scenarios. The visual code system also provides the basis for superimposing textual or graphical information over the camera image in close real-time in the sense of augmented reality. This entails a manifold of application possibilities in situations where information is to be closely linked to physical objects. An example is the maintenance of devices or apparatuses in the field: Individual parts of an apparatus are associated with visual codes. With the help of the visual code system, graphical information which is aligned with the items in the image, is superimposed over the camera image.

The novelty of the proposed system is its code coordinate system, the visual detection of phone movement, and the determination of the rotation angle and amount of tilting. These features enable interesting applications, beyond simple item selection, such as interaction with nearby active displays. The recognition algorithm precisely determines the coordinates of a targeted point in the code coordinate system, which is independent of the orientation of the camera relative to the code tag (distance, rotation, tilting) and also independent of the camera parameters (focal distance, etc.). This enables the association of each point in the viewed image – and therefore arbitrarily shaped areas – with specific operations. A single visual code can be associated with multiple such areas and a single image point can be associated with multiple information aspects using different rotation and tilting angles.

2   Related Work

Sony's *CyberCode* [2] is related to our approach, but does not operate on mobile phone class devices and does not use phone movement and other additional parameters for interaction in the way we propose. CyberCodes store 24 bits of data. In addition to the ID, the 3-D position of the tagged objects is determined. The proposed applications for CyberCodes are augmented reality systems, various direct manipulation techniques involving physical objects, and indoor guidance systems.

TRIP [3] is an indoor location tracking system based on printable circular markers, also called "TRIPtags". It employs CCD cameras plugged into standard PCs for code recognition, 3-D location, and orientation detection. TRIPtags have an address space of just 19683 ($= 3^9$) possible codes, which makes them impracticable to encode universally unique IDs, like Bluetooth MAC addresses. In contrast to our system, TRIP is designed for use with stationary cameras which are distributed in a networked environment. It relies on a CORBA infrastructure and a centralized recognition engine named "TRIPparser". In our system, code recognition is completely done on the mobile phones, which enhances scalability, and code sightings are distributed wirelessly.

The *FieldMouse* [4] is a combination of a barcode reader and a pen-shaped mouse. The mouse detects relative $(\Delta x, \Delta y)$ movement. If the location of a barcode on a flat surface is known to the system, absolute locations can be computed by first scanning the barcode and then moving the FieldMouse. This enables various kinds of paper-based GUIs.

A number of commercial efforts exist to recognize product codes with mobile phones. An example is *AirClic* (www.airclic.com), which provides tiny barcode readers that can be attached to mobile phones. The disadvantage of this approach is the necessity of an additional device, which increases the physical size and weight of the mobile phone and consumes additional energy. Barcode readers also do not provide the orientation and selection features of camera based approaches.

SpotCodes (www.highenergymagic.com) are a commercialized derivative of the TRIP tags mentioned above for use with camera phone devices. They recognize the rotation of the code tag in the image, but do not provide an orientation-independent code coordinate system and do not detect relative camera movement independent of codes in the camera image. A number of interaction possibilities are described on the Web page and in [5], such as rotation controls and sliders.

An increasing number of companies offer mobile phones with the ability to read *QR Codes* [6]. They implement the core functionality of decoding QR Codes. They do not, however, have the code coordinate system, rotation, tilting, and visual movement detection features that are integrated in our system.

The same applies to Semacode (semacode.org), which uses standard *Data Matrix* [7] codes to implement physical hyperlinks and load Web pages in the phone's browser. Example applications are live urban information, such as the position of GPS-equipped buses, information on nearby shops and services, and semacodes on business cards and conference badges.

3   Visual Code, Recognition Algorithm, and Phone Movement Detection

The mobile phone devices we consider have severely limited computing resources and often lack a floating point unit. Hence, the use of floating point operations has to be minimized. The typical phone camera generates low to medium quality color images in VGA (640×480 pixels) or lower resolution. The relatively poor image quality determines the minimal size of code features that can be reliably recognized. The code features therefore have to be more coarsely grained than those of most available visual codes. In our evaluation it became clear that color should not be used as a code feature, because of the large differences in color values, depending on varying lighting conditions. Moreover, color codes are more expensive to print and harder to reproduce than simple black-and-white codes.

Because of the mobility inherent to camera phones, scanned codes might appear at any orientation in the camera image. They can be arbitrarily rotated and tilted, which complicates image recognition. We decided to constructively use these characteristics by measuring the amount of tilting and rotation of a code tag in the image and use them as additional input parameters. Another feature we deemed essential is the ability to map arbitrary points in the image plane to corresponding points in the code plane, i.e. to compute the code coordinates of arbitrary image pixels, and vice versa. In particular, this enables the conversion of the pixel coordinates of the camera focus – which is the point the user aims at – into corresponding code coordinates and the selection of image elements located at these code coordinates. This coordinate mapping can also be used for removing the perspective distortion of image parts.

These characteristics mark out the design space for the visual codes and form the basis for the further discussion. The code layout is pictured in Fig. 1. It consists of the following elements: a larger and a smaller guide bar for determining the location and orientation of the code, three cornerstones for detecting the distortion, and the data area with the actual code bits. The combination of larger and smaller guide bars is beneficial for detecting even strongly tilted codes. In the bottom of Fig. 1 the code coordinate system is shown. Each code defines its own local coordinate system with its origin at the upper left edge of the code and one unit corresponding to a single code bit element. Depending on the code size, the mapping between points in the image plane and points in the code plane is more precise than a single coordinate unit. The x-axis extends in horizontal direction to the left and to the right beyond the code itself. Correspondingly, the y-axis extends in vertical direction beyond the top and bottom edges of the code. For each code found in a particular input image, the code recognition algorithm establishes a bijective mapping between arbitrary points in the code plane and corresponding points in the image plane.

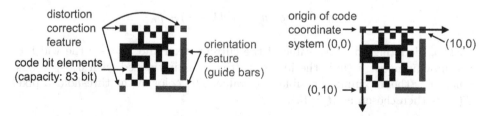

Fig. 1. The layout of the visual code (left) and the code coordinate system (right)

3.1   Recognition Algorithm

The recognition algorithm performs the following main steps on the camera image and produces a code information object for each detected code.

- **Input:** Camera image
- **Output:** Set of code information objects, comprising
  - the code value,
  - the image pixel coordinates of the corner stones and guide bars,
  - the rotation angle of the code in the image,
  - the amount of horizontal and vertical tilting,
  - the distance of the camera to the code,
  - a projective warper object for the code, which implements a planar homography (see below) used to transform image coordinates to code coordinates and vice versa,
  - the width and height of the originating image,
  - a flag indicating the result of error checking.

Gray Scaling and Adaptive Thresholding. To produce a gray scaled version of the colored input image, we use the formula $gray = (red + green)/2$, instead of the ITU-standardized formula for luminance $Y = 0.2126 \times red + 0.7152 \times green + 0.0722 \times blue$. The blue color component is omitted, since it has the lowest quality in terms of sharpness and contrast. Our simple formula is computationally efficient and produces an adequate starting point for thresholding. Efficiency in this step is of utmost importance for the performance of the whole recognition algorithm, because every single image pixel has to be gray scaled.

An adaptive thresholding method is taken to produce a black-and-white version of the gray scaled image, because the brightness of the camera image is not constant and the visual code may be unevenly illuminated. We slightly modified the adaptive thresholding algorithm described in [8], where the basic idea is to use a weighted moving average of the gray values while running through the image in a snake-like fashion (alternating left to right and right to left scanline traversal). Our adaptation takes the previous scanline of each examined scanline into account in order to avoid artifacts in every other line, resulting from the zigzag traversal of the scanlines. The average $g_s(n)$ is updated according to

$$g_s(n) = g_s(n-1) \cdot (1 - \frac{1}{s}) + p_n$$

with p_n denoting the gray value of the current pixel and $s = \frac{1}{8}w$ the width of the moving average (w is the image width). g_s is initialized with $g_s(0) = \frac{1}{2}cs$, where c is the maximum possible gray value. The color of the thresholded pixel $T(n)$ is then chosen as ($t = 15$):

$$T(n) = \begin{cases} 1 \text{ if } p_n < \frac{g_s(n)}{s} \cdot \frac{100-t}{100} \\ 0 \text{ otherwise} \end{cases}$$

Gray scaling and adaptive thresholding turned out to be the most time consuming phase of the recognition process. Therefore, we replaced any floating point operations in this part by shifted integer operations, which resulted in a significant performance improvement.

Region Identification and Labeling. This step consists of finding regions of neighboring black pixels, counting them, and assigning a number to each. The algorithm we use is a well known two-phase method: In the first phase, the image is traversed row by row, assigning preliminary labels to the regions found. During this process, it may happen that two regions with different labels turn out to be in fact the same region. In this case, the equivalence of the two temporary labels is stored in a table. The second phase resolves the equivalencies by merging the corresponding regions and assigns a final label to each region.

In the implementation, gray scaling, adaptive thresholding, and the first phase of region labeling are bundled for performance reasons and are done in a single scan through the image, i.e., pixels that are thresholded as foreground pixels are immediately assigned a label and any label equivalences are recorded.

Calculation of Region Shapes and Orientations. In order to identify candidates for orientation bars among the regions found, the notion of second-order moments is used [9]. From these moments, the major and minor axis of each region is determined. The ratio of the lengths of these axes is a good measure for the "eccentricity" of a region: perfect circles and squares have a ratio equal to one whereas line segments have a ratio close to zero. This is very useful to identify regions with a bar-like shape.

The second-order moments of a region consisting of the set of pixels R and having the center of gravity $(\bar{x}, \bar{y})$ are defined as follows:

$$\mu_{xx} = \frac{1}{|R|} \sum_{(x,y)\in R} (x - \bar{x})^2,$$

$$\mu_{yy} = \frac{1}{|R|} \sum_{(x,y)\in R} (y - \bar{y})^2,$$

$$\mu_{xy} = \frac{1}{|R|} \sum_{(x,y)\in R} (x - \bar{x})(y - \bar{y}),$$

$$\text{where} \quad \bar{x} = \frac{1}{|R|} \sum_{(x,y)\in R} x, \qquad \bar{y} = \frac{1}{|R|} \sum_{(x,y)\in R} y$$

From these moments, an ellipsis $E = \{(x, y)|dx^2 + 2exy + fy^2 \leq 1\}$ that has the same major and minor axis as the region can be defined by setting:

$$\begin{pmatrix} d & e \\ e & f \end{pmatrix} = \frac{1}{4\mu_{xx}\mu_{yy} - \mu_{xy}^2} \begin{pmatrix} \mu_{yy} & -\mu_{xy} \\ -\mu_{xy} & \mu_{xx} \end{pmatrix}$$

Furthermore, the orientation vector of the major axis is calculated as

$$\begin{pmatrix} -\sin\alpha \\ \cos\alpha \end{pmatrix}, \quad \text{where} \quad \alpha = \frac{1}{2}\arctan\frac{2e}{d - f}.$$

Locating and Evaluating the Codes. Locating codes in the image is done by looking for guide bar candidates and by finding corresponding cornerstones. Guide bar candidates are found by simply selecting those regions whose axis ratio lies in a certain range around the expected ideal axis ratio. The range has to be large enough to allow for tilted codes. For each of these candidates, the size and orientation of the region is used to estimate the expected positions of the second guide bar and the three cornerstones. It is then checked whether these features are actually present at the estimated positions. Cornerstone candidates found are only accepted if their axis ratio is above a certain limit.

Computing the Projective Mapping from Code Coordinates to Image Coordinates. Since the code elements are coplanar, there exists a unique homography (projective transformation matrix) between the code plane and the image plane. The projective mapping can be calculated once four corresponding points are known [10]. In our algorithm, the correspondences are the centers of the three cornerstones plus the center of the second guide bar:

Code element	Image coordinates	Code coordinates
upper left cornerstone	(x_0, y_0)	$(0, 0)$
upper right cornerstone	(x_1, y_1)	$(10, 0)$
second guide bar	(x_2, y_2)	$(8, 10)$
lower left cornerstone	(x_3, y_3)	$(0, 10)$

Code coordinates (u, v) are mapped to image coordinates (x, y) with

$$x = \frac{au + bv + 10c}{gu + hv + 10}, \quad y = \frac{du + ev + 10f}{gu + hv + 10}.$$

The parameters a to h are calculated from the four reference points (x_i, y_i), $i \in \{0, \ldots, 3\}$, as follows:

$$\Delta x_1 = x_1 - x_2 \qquad \Delta y_1 = y_1 - y_2 \qquad \Delta x_2 = x_3 - x_2 \qquad \Delta y_2 = y_3 - y_2$$

$$\Sigma x = 0.8x_0 - 0.8x_1 + x_2 - x_3 \qquad \Sigma y = 0.8y_0 - 0.8y_1 + y_2 - y_3$$

$$g = \frac{\Sigma x \Delta y_2 - \Sigma y \Delta x_2}{\Delta x_1 \Delta y_2 - \Delta y_1 \Delta x_2} \qquad a = x_1 - x_0 + gx_1 \qquad d = y_1 - y_0 + gy_1$$

$$h = \frac{\Sigma y \Delta x_1 - \Sigma x \Delta y_1}{\Delta x_1 \Delta y_2 - \Delta y_1 \Delta x_2} \qquad b = x_3 - x_0 + hx_3 \qquad e = y_3 - y_0 + hy_3$$

$$c = x_0 \qquad f = y_0$$

Computing the Projective Mapping from Image Coordinates to Code Coordinates. The inverse mapping to the one described above is important for applications which select items visible in the image. Given the coordinates of a pixel, the corresponding code coordinates can thus be obtained. Image coordinates (x, y) are mapped to code coordinates (u, v) as follows:

$$u = 10 \cdot \frac{Ax + By + C}{Gx + Hy + I}, \quad v = 10 \cdot \frac{Dx + Ey + F}{Gx + Hy + I}, \quad with$$

$$A = e - fh \qquad D = fg - d \qquad G = dh - eg$$
$$B = ch - b \qquad E = a - cg \qquad H = bg - ah$$
$$C = bf - ce \qquad F = cd - af \qquad I = ae - bd$$

Rotation Angle. The rotation angle gives the rotation of the visual code in the image in degrees counterclockwise (0-359°). A code that has the same orientation as the image has rotation angle 0° (like the ones in Fig. 1). The rotation is determined by mapping the points (0,0) and (100,0) from the code coordinate system to the image coordinate system, resulting in the image points (a_x, a_y), and (b_x, b_y). The rotation angle is then determined as the arc tangent of the difference quotient of a and b.

Horizontal and Vertical Tilting. The term *tilting* denotes the amount of inclination of the image plane relative to the code plane. *Horizontal tilting* is the amount of inclination of the image plane relative to the horizontal axis of the code. Analogously, *vertical tilting* denotes the amount of inclination of the image plane relative to the vertical axis of the code. Tilting values of 1 mean no tilting, a value less than 1 means tilting towards the left/top, and a value greater than 1 means tilting towards the right/bottom.

The tilting parameters are computed as follows: Four image points with constant distance h (image height) from the image center point in the axis directions of the code coordinate system are computed. They are mapped to corresponding code coordinates and their distances to the center point are computed. The ratios of these distances determine the tilting parameters t_x and t_y. They are independent of the size of the code in the image. From these ratios the tilting angles t_x^α and t_y^α can be determined, if a constant r is known that depends on the camera parameters. It can be obtained experimentally. For the Nokia 6600, e.g., this parameter has the value $r = 1.64177$.

$$i = \text{image coordinates of the image center point}$$
$$c = \text{CodeCoordinates}(i)$$

$$x = \text{ImageCoordinates}(c + (1, 0)) - i$$
$$y = \text{ImageCoordinates}(c + (0, 1)) - i$$
$$u = x/|x|$$
$$v = y/|y|$$

$$l = |\text{CodeCoordinates}(i - hu) - c|$$
$$r = |\text{CodeCoordinates}(i + hu) - c|$$
$$t = |\text{CodeCoordinates}(i - hv) - c|$$
$$b = |\text{CodeCoordinates}(i + hv) - c|$$

$$t_x = l/r$$
$$t_y = t/b$$

$$t_x^\alpha = \arctan\left(r\frac{t_x - 1}{t_x + 1}\right)$$
$$t_y^\alpha = \arctan\left(r\frac{t_y - 1}{t_y + 1}\right)$$

Code Distance. If the real code size s_{real} (the real distance between the centers of the upper left and the upper right cornerstones) and the camera's focal distance f are known, the metric distance from the camera to the untilted visual code can be computed from s_{image} (the pixel distance between the centers of the upper cornerstones in the camera image) using the pinhole model as (w_{image} is the pixel width of the image)

$$D_{camera,code} = \frac{s_{real} \times f}{s_{image}/w_{image}}.$$

Since s_{real} and f are typically not known and we want to use the code distance for interaction purposes rather than measuring its exact value, we define the distance in terms of the size of the visual code in the image. We set $d_{camera,code} :=$ 100 for the farthest distance at which a code is recognized in view finder mode. For the Nokia 6600 this is the case when $s_{image} = 25$ pixels, which amounts to 15.625% of the image width. Hence the distance is computed as

$$d_{camera,code} = \frac{15.625}{s_{image}/w_{image}}.$$

Should s_{real} and f be known, the metric distance can still be computed from $d_{camera,code}$. For the Nokia 6600, the range of distances at which codes are recognized in view finder mode are: $11 - 46$ cm for $s_{real} = 69$ mm, $3.5 - 14$ cm for $s_{real} = 21$ mm, $2.3 - 9$ cm for $s_{real} = 13.6$ mm.

Reading the Encoded Bits. Once the positions of the guide bars and corner stones have been identified and a suitable projective mapping has been computed, reading the encoded bits is simply a matter of testing the appropriate pixels (x, y) of the black-and-white image, using code coordinates (u, v) with $u, v \in \{0, ..., 10\}$ and $(x, y) = \text{ImageCoordinates}((u, v))$.

Error Detection. In order to detect pixel errors and false orientation features, the code bits are protected by an (83,76,3) linear code that generates an 83-bit code word from a 76-bit value and has a Hamming distance of 3.

3.2 Phone Movement Detection

The code recognition algorithm is combined with a phone movement detection algorithm that solely relies on image data obtained from the camera. It does not require any additional hardware components, such as accelerometers. It is integrated with the visual code recognition algorithm in such a way that the latter only examines images for visual codes when the detected phone movement is below a certain threshold. If the phone is quickly moved, it is very unlikely that the user aims at a specific code. Trying to locate codes in the image in such a case would not be sensible.

The algorithm provides the relative x, y, and *rotational* motion of the phone, representing three degrees of freedom. With the movement detection, the camera phone thus becomes an optical mouse. The algorithm works as follows: Successive images from the camera are dispatched to the view finder to render them on the device display. Every n-th frame (depending on the performance of the phone) is used for phone movement detection. The image is divided in 16×16 pixel blocks. For each block, 16 pixels are sampled (out of the 256 available pixels in each block) and their average gray value is computed. Then, the blocks of the current image are compared to the blocks of the previously sampled frame. The block arrays are displaced against each other in x and y direction using values for Δx and Δy from $\{-3, \ldots, 3\}$. The difference values are computed and normalized with the number of compared blocks (which depends on the amount of displacement) and the minimal difference is chosen as the most likely amount of $(\Delta x, \Delta y)$ movement relative to the image before. Relative rotation θ is computed in a similar fashion, but rotating the block images against each other. The current block image is rotated by $\Delta \alpha$ values between $-24°$ and $24°$, with a step width of $6°$. The rotational coordinate mappings are precomputed and stored in tables for performance reasons. Again, the differences of the resulting block images are compared to the previous block image and the minimal difference is chosen as the most likely amount of relative rotation.

This simple algorithm works quite reliably and detects the relative motion even if the sampled backgrounds only have a limited number of features, like a wall or a floor. Because only a few pixels are sampled, the algorithm performs quickly and leaves enough time for doing the actual code recognition. On a Nokia 6600, it produces about five (x, y, θ) triples per second.

The code recognition and motion detection algorithms were implemented in C++ for Symbian OS (v6.1, v7.0s, and v8.0a). Replacing floating point operations by shifted integer operations reduced the time consumption of the thresholding phase from 2000 ms to less than 400 ms on a Nokia 7650 for a 640×480 pixel camera image. The total execution time of the recognition algorithm on the same device amounts to about 700 ms if less than 5 codes are present, and up to 1500 ms if 30 codes are present – which is rather uncommon in typical applications. The picture-taking process for 640×480 pixel images takes about 850 ms, resulting in an overall average delay of about 2000 ms. Low resolution 160×120 pixel images that are generated during the view finding process are recognized much faster, i.e. in close real-time as the device moves relative to the detected code(s).

4 Item Selection Using Relative Focus Position, Rotation Angle, and Tilting Determination

In this section we show how the additional input parameters that the code recognition algorithm provides can be combined to realize novel interaction patterns.

Fig. 2. Selection from a table: the code coordinates determine the table row, the camera rotation specifies the concrete information aspect to display

When aiming the phone camera at the target item, the image of this target item appears on the display. It is continuously updated as the phone is moved. The center of the display contains a crosshair to facilitate precise selection, as can be seen in the screenshots in Fig. 2. To further facilitate item selection, the display contains a magnified portion of the area around the display center. The level of magnification can be adjusted with the joystick. The mapping from image coordinate system to code coordinate system enables the precise selection of items in the image, requiring just a single code element for multiple items. Image items may be menu entries, arbitrarily shaped regions in a picture, or the cells of a table.

Further input parameters comprise the rotation of the code tag in the image and the amount of tilting of the image plane relative to the code plane. The tilting parameter identifies the viewing position (from left, from right, from top, from bottom). Both parameters can be used to associate multiple information aspects with a single point in the code coordinate system.

For an effective interaction, the user has to be provided with indications about the possible interactions. This can be achieved by superimposing visual cues on the display image that indicate at what rotation angles and viewing positions what kind of information is to be expected. We currently investigate different kinds of symbols that guide the user in his or her interactions with visual codes. An indication of user interaction normally consists of a symbol denoting the kinds of physical interaction – like movement, rotation, or tilting – and a set of symbols for the associated actions that are triggered as a consequence of the interaction. The latter comprise symbols for typical functions of a mobile phone, such as placing a phone call or starting the WAP browser. Another possibility is to print interaction cues next to the code. This was realized with a visual code dialer application. The printed code contains a phone number and is surrounded by words indicating the function that is triggered when the phone is tilted in that direction: Just below the code it says "Call", to the left it says "SMS", and to the right the word "Store" is printed. Scanning from a central position immediately places a call, scanning from the left opens the phone's SMS editor with the number already entered into the appropriate field, and scanning from the right looks up the contact information on a server and stores it on the phone.

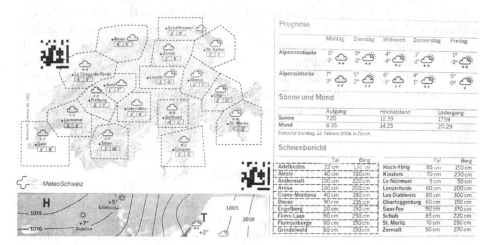

Fig. 3. Example of a weather forecast newspaper page containing visual codes. The 17 regions on the map and all entries in the table are individually mapped to different URLs and thus hyperlinked to specific online content

In newspapers, online background information to articles, advertisements, or information which quickly gets obsolete, like weather forecasts or stock quotes, can be linked via visual codes. Fig. 3 shows a cut-out of a newspaper page containing a geographic map with the current weather data and a table containing the snow conditions for various regions. The dotted lines drawn on the newspaper page indicate sensitive areas that are individually linked to online content. Such a mapping can be easily created with suitable content creation software. As a prototype, we developed a mapping tool for drawing the areas in the image and specifying the associated URL for each region. The tool computes the coordinates of these areas in the coordinate systems of the codes present in the image, and stores this data as an XML file. Multiple URLs can be specified for each region by taking into account rotation, distance, and tilting. As shown in Fig. 3, a single code suffices to select any one of the multiple areas and table entries, respectively. By rotating the mobile device, different aspects of the online information can be chosen: In the example, vertical orientation shows the snow depth for the selected area, while a slight rotation shows the current temperature. Other conceivable operations include showing the currently open skiing trails, calling the local tourist information office, and booking rail and lift tickets. The current weather data is retrieved from a server and the display of the phone is updated in real time as the crosshair is moved across the table entries and geographic regions and as the phone is rotated clockwise and counterclockwise. A video that demonstrates this type of interaction is available at visualcodes.sourceforge.net.

The ability to link multiple items to a single code based on their code coordinates and to associate multiple information aspects to a single point depending on rotation and tilting has a number of usability advantages. In the example above, it would of course be possible to present a table of the current snow conditions of all regions on the map to the user once the code has been recognized. But it is difficult to effectively show a table containing all the attributes on the small amount of available display space. It also requires the user to scroll through the – possibly lengthy – table and locate the data of interest in a second step. The presented approach avoids both of these problems. It gives direct and immediate feedback to the user and presents exactly the scanned item and selected information aspect.

5   Visual Codes and Large-Scale Displays

A compelling class of applications for visual codes, the code coordinate system feature, and the relative movement detection involves the interaction with large-scale wall displays, as they are increasingly found in public or semi-public places. Today's wall displays are mostly limited to the passive reception of information. At public places, keyboards and other input devices are often not installed, because of potential problems with vandalism. If passers-by carry their own interaction devices in the form of a camera phone, this problem is eliminated. Example locations for interactive public wall displays are train stations, airports, bus stops, shopping malls, and museums.

To investigate the interaction possibilities, we set up a projected display that contains a 3-D model of a number of visual codes arranged on an invisible sphere as shown in Fig. 4. The model is implemented using Java 3D [11]. The screen model is controlled by the motion of the camera phone. The phone and the screen are connected via Bluetooth. Motion updates are sent as (x, y, θ) triples to the active display. Phone movement in horizontal direction results in a rotation of the sphere around the y-axis, vertical motion results in a rotation around the x-axis, and rotating the phone results in sphere rotation around the z-axis. Because of the relatively low update rate, the movement of the sphere is interpolated between motion updates from the phone, in order to obtain a smooth visually pleasing movement. The updates are frequent enough to be able to effectively control the display contents.

In addition to rotating the sphere containing the codes, aiming at a visual code shown on the wall display brings up an associated menu. Individual menu

Fig. 4. Phone movement detection and item selection for interaction with a projected wall display

items can now be selected, whereupon the related content is transferred to the phone and shown on the device screen. In the demo application, the visual codes are permanently visible. They could also be superimposed over the large-scale display image just before scanning them. This could be synchronized by the Bluetooth connection between the phone and the display.

The motion detection was informally tested by a number of subjects and worked very well. We provided the test subjects with a number of tasks, such as rotating a certain menu to the foreground and selecting a specific menu item. After a short period of practice, the subjects quickly became familiar with this type of interaction. This application was shown as a demonstration at [12].

We are currently investigating the idea of a "Photo Wall", which uses a large-scale display to organize photos taken with the camera phone, because this is difficult to do on the device itself. The large-scale display is also used as an access point to a photo printing service or one's online photo collection. The interaction mechanisms described above are investigated to perform interaction tasks such as navigating through, selecting, deleting, rotating, and manipulating the photos.

6   Conclusion

In this paper we have presented extended features of a visual code system for camera equipped mobile phones. It performs well on resource constrained phone devices with low to medium resolution cameras. Besides detecting visual codes in the user's vicinity and thus linking physical objects to online content, it has a number of supplementary features. It provides the code coordinates, the code rotation angle, and the tilting of the image plane relative to the code plane as additional input parameters. These parameters can be determined without prior calibration. Phone movement detection is integrated with the visual code system. It provides (x, y, θ) motion parameters and turns the mobile phone into an optical mouse.

We have shown how these input parameters can be used and combined to provide novel interaction patterns with objects in the user's local environment. The user can pick up multiple information items which are located at known code coordinate positions relative to a single code tag, by aiming the camera focus at the appropriate location. By slightly rotating or tilting the phone, the user has the opportunity to select between different information aspects. We have also shown how phone movement detection and visual code recognition can be combined to interact with individual items on a large-scale wall display.

In the future, camera phones might play a prominent role as ubiquitous personal image recognition devices and for local interaction with physical objects that their users encounter in everyday settings. New services can be associated with printed documents, wall displays, TV programs, or general consumer products when they are made interactive by techniques as described in this paper.

References

1. Rohs, M., Gfeller, B.: Using camera-equipped mobile phones for interacting with real-world objects. In Ferscha, A., Hoertner, H., Kotsis, G., eds.: Advances in Pervasive Computing, Vienna, Austria, Austrian Computer Society (OCG) (2004) 265–271
2. Rekimoto, J., Ayatsuka, Y.: CyberCode: Designing augmented reality environments with visual tags. In: DARE '00: Proceedings of DARE 2000 on Designing augmented reality environments, ACM Press (2000) 1–10
3. de Ipiña, D.L., Mendonça, P.R.S., Hopper, A.: TRIP: A low-cost vision-based location system for ubiquitous computing. Personal Ubiquitous Comput. **6** (2002) 206–219
4. Siio, I., Masui, T., Fukuchi, K.: Real-world interaction using the FieldMouse. In: UIST '99: Proceedings of the 12th annual ACM symposium on User interface software and technology, ACM Press (1999) 113–119
5. Madhavapeddy, A., Scott, D., Sharp, R., Upton, E.: Using camera-phones to enhance human-computer interaction. In: Sixth International Conference on Ubiquitous Computing (Adjunct Proceedings: Demos). (2004)
6. International Organization for Standardization: Information Technology – Automatic Identification and Data Capture Techniques – Bar Code Symbology – QR Code. ISO/IEC 18004 (2000)
7. International Organization for Standardization: Information Technology – International Symbology Specification – Data Matrix. ISO/IEC 16022 (2000)
8. Wellner, P.D.: Adaptive thresholding for the DigitalDesk. Technical Report EPC-93-110, Rank Xerox Research Centre, Cambridge, UK (1993)
9. Veltkamp, R.C., Hagedoorn, M.: State of the art in shape matching – principles of visual information retrieval. In Lew, M.S., ed.: Series in Advances in Pattern Recognition, Springer (2001)
10. Heckbert, P.S.: Fundamentals of texture mapping and image warping. Master's Thesis, Department of Electrical Engineering and Computer Science, University of California, Berkeley (1989)

11. Sun Microsystems: Java 3D API Specification, version 1.3. Available at: java.sun.com/products/java-media/3D (2002)
12. Rohs, M., Gfeller, B.: Visual code recognition for camera-equipped mobile phones. Pervasive 2004 Demonstrations D06. Demonstration description available at: www.pervasive2004.org/program_demonstrations.php (2004)

Appendix

We have explored the integrated phone movement detection features in a number of ways. As the camera detects phone movement relative to the background, the content of the phone display is continuously updated. No visual code needs to be present in the view of the camera. With this technique we have built a camera controlled wireframe model of a house, a pong game whose slider can be controlled by tilting the wrist left and right, and an application showing a large subway map that is scrolled in response to phone movement. These applications are shown in Fig. 5 and are available for download at `visualcodes.sourceforge.net`.

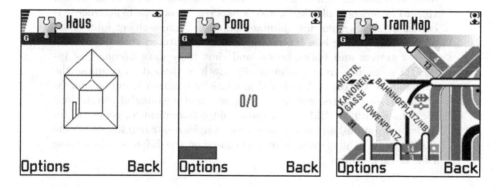

Fig. 5. Wireframe model (left), pong game (middle), and subway map (right), all controlled by the visual detection of phone movement

Experience-Sharing System Using Ubiquitous Sensing Environments

Megumu Tsuchikawa[1,2], Shoichiro Iwasawa[1,2], Sadanori Ito[1,2],
Atsushi Nakahara[1], Yasuyuki Sumi[1,3], Kenji Mase[1,2,4], Kiyoshi Kogure[2],
and Norihiro Hagita[1,2]

[1] ATR Media Information Science Laboratories
[2] ATR Intelligent Robotics and Communications Laboratories
[3] Graduate School of Informatics, Kyoto University
[4] Information Technology Center, Nagoya University
megumu@atr.jp

Abstract. This paper proposes an experience-sharing system that captures experience by using ubiquitous sensing environments and a humanoid communication robot. For experience sharing, a summarizing method is absolutely necessary because it is impossible to spend enough time to experience all other person's experiences or past experiences vicariously. This system uses human-human or human-object interaction as the summarizing key. Interaction data are captured with an infrared ID tag system and microphones, and thus these data become the index for streaming data automatically. Both of these data compose the hInteraction Corpus.h Another characteristic function is interaction facilitation, that is, the system creates new and meaningful interactions for a user with an HMD or a humanoid communication robot. In an actual exhibition hall environment, we examined our hypothesis on the differences in exhibit visitors'interests based on the differences in staying time at each exhibit.

1 Introduction

It is possible to apply available technology to automatically record various experiences in daily life and then to share the experiences of other people or past experiences. This is very useful for both vivid and common understanding of experiences and for sharing impressions of those experiences. Moreover, when the interests and intentions of a person are classified automatically in a place where many people gather, such as an exhibition hall or a stadium, much information can be offered to match the individual's interests and intentions. Furthermore, through integrating such knowledge among users, each user can be provided the chance to meet or communicate with other individuals who have similar interests or intentions. On the other hand, the owner or organizer of the system can obtain much information that was previously difficult to acquire or overlooked, such as what the exhibition's visitors are actually interested in.

H. Murakami et al. (Eds.): UCS 2004, LNCS 3598, pp. 90–103, 2005.

In recent years, many research efforts have been devoted to developing experience capturing and human memory assisting systems [1]-[6]. These systems store and use various kinds of information on human experiences, for example, movies, sound, still images, and position data.

Our approach is based on non-cumbersome recording of experiences by using ubiquitous sensing environments and on interpretation of the experiences [7]-[10].

We view gexperienceh as being constructed by human-human or human-object interaction, where the actor is physically facing the target in many cases. To take advantage of this characteristic, we introduce an infrared tag system to capture interactions. These sensors detect the human-human or human-object interaction easily, and the data becomes an important indexing key for experience. These data and the captured streaming data compose corpora for experience, which we call in its entirety the gInteraction Corpus.h The interaction corpus has a layered structure categorized by data type - physical data or symbolized data - and data structure - elementary data or compositive data.

Furthermore, our experience-sharing system can facilitate new interactions with its head mounted display (HMD) and a humanoid communication robot. Accordingly, the system offers the user information specialized for the individual.

This paper presents a developed prototype experience system and uses it to confirm the proposed system's mechanism for use in an exhibition environment.

Moreover, we examine the validity of our hypothesis on the differences in visitors' interests. This hypothesis states that the importance of a visitor's experience can be determined by the amount of time that he or she stays at an exhibit in an exhibition situation.

2   Overview of Experience-Sharing System

From among various types of experience-sharing situations, we selected an exhibition hall event because it typically involves a great amount of human-human and human-object interactions. Consequently, we created a prototype system for this situation. The system is built upon stationary sensors and wearable sensors. The system captures data from theses sensors and stores them while indexing the interactions. In addition, a communication robot and HMD applications facilitate new experiences. Visitors may share other (past or current) visitors' experiences by using the HMD or other applications in the exhibition hall during the visit, and they can also share their own experiences with other persons after leaving the room. Our prototype system has been implemented as an exhibit room, and it is thus called the gUbiquitous Sensing Sensor Roomh (Figure 1). This system performs four functions: eCapturing,' eStoring,' eFacilitation' and eSharing.'

2.1   Interaction Capturing

In this prototype system, stationary sensors are located near potential focal points, that is, posters and displays, and wearable sensor units are worn by both presenters and visitors. The sensor units include video cameras, microphones,

Fig. 1. Ubiquitous Sensor Room

and infrared ID tags and trackers and other sensors. These sensors are connected to the database server by a wired or wireless network.

The infrared ID system, consisting of infrared tags and trackers (Figure 2), plays an important role in segmenting interactions. The ID tag sends a unique ID number with a blinking pattern of an infrared LED. The ID tracker finds the two-dimensional locations of ID tags in the sight of its infrared image sensor and recognizes their ID numbers. The specifications of the infrared ID tags and trackers are as follows.

Infrared ID tags

- Device: infrared LED
- Peak wavelength: 850 nm
- Reduction-by-half angle: 60 degrees
- Blinking speed: 200 Hz

Infrared ID trackers

- Sensor Device: Mitsubishi M64283FP
(infrared CMOS Active Pixel Image Sensor)
- Image size: 128 x 128 pixels
- View angle: 90 degrees
- Capture speed: 400 Hz

ID signal

- Bit length: 10 bits
(including 1 start bit, 1 parity, 2 stop bits)

We can obtain the ID every second at a 0.38even while users are walking.

When two persons wear the infrared ID tags and trackers and these devices detect each other, we can determine whether the users are facing each other because the infrared ID tags and trackers have strong directivity. We placed infrared ID tags and trackers (sometimes tags only) to the side of exhibition objects (e.g. posters) in the Ubiquitous Sensor Room. This allowed us to record the time spent and participants in face-to-face communication (in the case of human-human interaction) or who looked at what (in the case of human-objects interaction). The directions of the image sensors of the ID tracker and video

Infrared ID tag & tracker@@@Infrared ID tag@@

Fig. 2. Infrared ID tags & trackers

cameras are set to stationary, and the wearable units are aligned to operate in parallel, with their view angles set to be almost the same.

There are two kinds of stationary sensors: environmental data-capturing clients and infrared ID tags. The environmental data-capturing client has a video camera, microphone, infrared ID tag and tracker, and a personal computer (PC). The PC collects the sensors' data and transmits them to the server, which has a wired connection to the network. Two environmental data-capturing clients are set in each exhibition booth. One is placed above the poster in a booth to take images from the front-upper side of the visitors who face the poster, and the other is in front of the poster to capture the same visitors from the behind-upper viewpoint. The infrared ID tags are installed around the posters, five tags for each poster.

Complementing the stationary sensors, visitors and the exhibitor have wearable data-capturing clients. This client has a video camera, two microphones, infrared ID tag and tracker, other sensors, head mounted display (HMD), and a lightweight notebook type PC. The video camera and infrared ID tag and tracker can be adjusted for face direction. One sensor is a conventional microphone that records the person's voice along with environmental sound, and another is a throat-mounted microphone for detecting whether the person is making an utterance. The conventional microphone gathers environmental noise, while the throat microphone only obtains the voice of the person wearing it; consequently, we can detect the utterance time by using simple threshold processing. The infrared ID system and throat-mounted microphone are very important devices for capturing interaction because they find gazing and talking, respectively, and they permit automatic indexing for interactions. The data from these sensors can indicate a visitor's interest. These sensor devices are mounted on a cap-type headset, the PC is carried in a bag, and they are connected by a wired data line. Next, the PC sends these data (video, audio, other sensor data) to the data server over a wireless network. The HMD is also mounted on the headset. The headset weighs 500 g and the bag with the PC weighs 2720 g. Figure 3 shows the wearable data-capturing client.

2.2   Storing

All of the captured data are stored in the data server. These data are recorded with time information. We detect human-human or human-object interaction

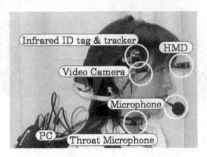

Fig. 3. Wearable Client

from these sensor data automatically, and the interaction information is entered into the database for indexing. We call this the gInteraction Corpus.h The interaction corpus can be used as a well-structured stored experience.

Gazing information can be obtained from infrared ID data. If an infrared ID tracker attached to a person's headset detects an infrared ID tag, this means that the person is gazing at another person or an object to which the infrared ID tag is attached. This gazing information, together with utterance information, is used for automatic interaction segmentation and classification. We employ a four-layered data structure categorized by data type - physical data or symbolized data - and data structure - elementary data or compositive data. This layered structure manages the interaction data systematically and clearly describes the symbolizing role of the interaction.

This structure is designed to be domain-independent (Figure 4).

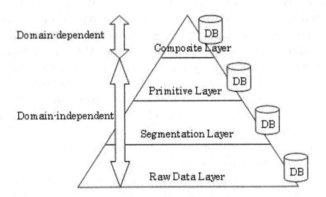

Fig. 4. Layers of Interaction Corpus

The lowest layer, called the gRaw Data Layer,h stores pairs consisting of raw sensor data and their time stamps. These data are the most instantly obtained data because they are stored with a very short time lag. They are elementary physical data.

The second layer is called the gSegmentation Layer.h These data are segmented by routine work from raw data. They are compositive physical data. The previous layer contains raw ID tag data and raw utterance data detected from the throat microphone. Each of the infrared ID data items represents a very short gazing interval. On the other hand, utterance information includes burst noises and short intervals. These are clustered into more meaningful intervals by combining two such intervals within a temporal threshold. Information on these longer intervals is stored in this layer. We store start time, end time, and a flag for each data cluster because we want to store data quickly. If we want to store them after clustering is finished, the timing is stored after finishing each interaction, which sometimes causes a long delay. Consequently, it becomes too late to use these data for real-time applications (c.f. interaction facilitation by communication robot). When an interaction start is found, we store the segmentation data with the start time and a gnot completedh flag, and when it is finished, we add the end time and change the flag to gcompleted.h We can determine that an interaction is continuing when we see that the flag is gnot completed,h and we can use this information for real-time applications.

The third layer, called the gPrimitive Layer,h stores interaction primitives, each of which is defined as a unit of interaction. These are elementary symbolized data. In this layer, an interpretation of the interaction is made into data. We detect the interaction primitives based on gazing information from the segmented tag data and utterance information from the segmented throat microphone data. We believe that gazing and utterance provide very important data for finding human-human or human-object interactions. For example, when an infrared ID tracker captures an infrared ID tag, we detect the interaction primitive for a gLOOK_ATh situation. When a person's tracker captures the tag and utterance, the primitive is gTALK_TO. Figure 5 shows some examples of interaction primitives. The interaction primitive data has the interaction primitive type, time, and target of interaction, and it is stored for every client (person or object). These three layers have low dependence on the domain.

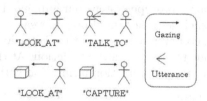

Fig. 5. Interaction Primitives

The upper layer, called the gComposite Layer,h stores the social meaning of interaction, and we call this kind of interaction gComposite.h For example, mutual interaction between two persons or among three or more persons (or objects) is composite interaction, which has a greater dependence on the situation.

These are compositive symbolized data. This information is detected by primitive interaction data or this layer's data. In the exhibition situation, we store correlation interaction data between two or more clients (persons or objects). If two persons talk to each other, the interaction is recorded as gTALK_WITH.h When three or more persons have the gTALK_TOh or gLOOK_ATh primitive (sometimes the target changes in a short time), the Composite is presumed to be gGROUP_DISCUSSION.h Figure 6 shows some examples of Composite. Composite is the most abstracted form of data but has the largest delay.

Fig. 6. Interaction Composites

The interaction corpus is built automatically, which makes it very useful for indexing huge quantities of video and audio data. We can manipulate multimedia data easily with the interaction corpus. In this experience-sharing prototype system, we use the interaction corpus for interaction facilitation and experience-sharing applications.

2.3   Interaction Facilitation

The Ubiquitous Sensor Room not only captures interactions passively but also creates new interactions by using the communication robot or the HMD applications to facilitate the initiation of new interactions by the users.

In an exhibition situation, an assistant often guides a visitor to pay attention to a specific event. In our prototype system, our humanoid communication robot, Robovie-II, serves as such an assistant. Robovie wears an infrared ID tag and tracker and engages in communication with the visitor in front of it by referring to the interaction corpus to create a new interaction. At the ATR exhibition, we demonstrated several types of interaction facilitation with Robovie as follows.

1) Calling visitor's name

Robovie greets the visitors in front of it by calling their names, since it knows each visitor's name by referring to the interaction corpus.

2) Guiding the visitors to other booths

For example, if Robovie finds that the visitor in front of it has not yet visited a booth, Robovie will guide him or her to the booth title and location by using speech and various kinds of body movements (Figure 7).

Fig. 7. Robovie's interaction facilitation

3) Talking about other visitors
For example, Robovie talks about other visitors who have met both Robovie and the visitor in front of it.
4) Announcing exhibition information
For example, Robovie informs the user of the number of this exhibition's visitors.

Robovie uses its gJoint Attentionh behavior, which directs a person's attention by first gazing at a person and then pointing to an object by hand and gazing at it. Furthermore, by using its sensors (video camera, microphone and infrared ID tag and tracker), Robovie can capture interaction actively.

Another interaction facilitation method uses the HMD applications. HMD can sometimes show the recommended person or booth to a user when the user's infrared ID tracker does not detect any tag. The recommended persons are selected based on similarity of interest estimated by the ratio of the length of staying time at each booth. The recommended booths are selected from the length of staying time of other visitors whose interests are similar to those of the user. Figure 8 shows the HMD applications used for interaction facilitation. The visitor's actions are modified by these interaction facilitation methods to make new or better interactions.

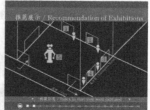

(a) Recommended Person@(b) Recommended Booth

Fig. 8. Directing Interaction with HMD

2.4   Experience Sharing

We have developed two kinds of experience-sharing applications. The first is a real-time application that shows current or previous information on the exhibition room or persons. The other is a recollection-type application that shows visitors' experiences after leaving there.

We have made three kinds of real-time applications for this prototype system.

1) HMD shows the rate of similarity of interest between the user and the person in front of the user (Figure 9(a)). Similarity of interest is estimated by the ratio of the length of staying time at each booth.

2) HMD shows the popularity degree of the booth that the user is visiting (Figure 9(b)).

3) A large-sized monitor, located next to the room's exit, shows the interaction mode of each booth (Figure 10).

The exhibitor's behavior in conversation is categorized as either glecture modeh or ginteraction modeh [11]. This application's display shows glecture mode,h ginteraction modeh or no visitor present. These applications are based on previous visitors' experiences, so they can be considered kinds of experience sharing.

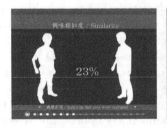

(a) Similarity of Interaction@@(b) Popularity Degree@

Fig. 9. Experience Sharing with HMD

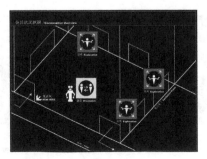

Fig. 10. Experience Sharing with Monitor

The HMD applications display information on what is currently in front of the user, so these applications mainly use gSegmentation Layerh data, which has a small delay. However, the large-sized monitor application displays information over a certain range, so it involves some delay and thus requires analysis of the interactions. Accordingly, it uses gComposite Layerh data. All of the HMD applications, including the interaction facilitation applications, are designed under the following policy for facilitating effective interaction or experience sharing.

1) User needs no operation.

This is important because the user should not feel an impression of complicated use.

2) The entire region is used for one kind of information.

This is necessary because the user cannot get much information from HMD at once while they are walking.

3) Thumbnail images are used and screen color is changed according to the kind of information.

Gazing with HMD is not required, but the displayed information is known instantly.

4) Information blinking is used.

Blinking gets the user's attention when he or she has not paid attention to the HMD.

5) Nothing is drawn when there is no information for display.

Attention is expected only when information is shown.

We made two experience-sharing applications for recollected experiences: gExperience Video Summaryh and gExperience Video Catalogh. Experience Video Summary is a digest of one user's experience, which is composed of a summary page and streaming data of one user's experience (Figure 11). A summary page is created by chronologically listing video scenes that were automatically extracted based on Composite Layer data. We draw thumbnail images of each video scene and coordinate the images with shading for quick visual cues. The shading rate is determined by interaction type or continuation time. The streaming data of each thumbnail image can be seen by clicking the thumbnail on the display.

This streaming data is constructed from not only the data captured by the user's video camera and microphone but also the data from a partner's or stationary video camera or microphone that captured the user. These are selected by using automatic indexing data from the interaction corpus.

The Experience Video Catalog is the message based on a visitor's experience and an exhibition sponsor's intention (Figure 12). It is a kind of summary provided for each visitor, and it is created from the summary of the visitor's experience and the information that the exhibition sponsor provides, for example the aim of each exhibition or the number of visitors. The thumbnail images are arranged as templates that the sponsor prepared, and characters on the screen speak information about each booth or exhibition, such as the concept of the booth and the number of visitors. This information cannot be obtained by vis-

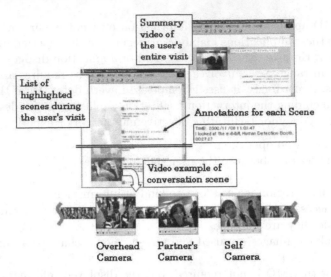

Summary video of the user's entire visit

List of highlighted scenes during the user's visit

Annotations for each Scene

Time: 2002/11 /08 11:02.47
I looked at the exhibit, Human Detection Booth.
00:27.27

Video example of conversation scene

Overhead   Partner's   Self
Camera   Camera   Camera

Fig. 11. Experience Video Summary

Fig. 12. Experience Video Catalog

itors without an explicit announcement by the sponsor. We believe that this Experience Video Catalog can help visitors to understand the exhibition and that it can be effective in imparting the sponsor's intention and in guiding the user's action.

3 Experiment and Results

To confirm the mechanism of the experience-sharing system, that is, capturing, storing, interaction facilitation and experience sharing, in an actual situation involving many people using the system at the same time, we used our proto-type system in a room at the annual ATR Exhibition. The environment of the experiment is as follows.

- There were five booths in the room, and each booth had two stationary clients and ten infrared ID tags around the poster.

- All five presenters wore wearable clients.

- A maximum of nine visitors wore wearable units, and other visitors wore infrared ID tags only.

- There was a humanoid communication robot, called Robovie-II, in the room that facilitated interaction by talking and gesturing.

For the two-day experiments, 105 visitors wore wearable clients, and we checked how our experience-sharing system operated with a maximum of fourteen persons (including presenters) using the wearable sets at any given time. We obtained 290 hours of video and audio data, 6,120,000 items of Raw Data Layer data, 1,190,000 items of Segmentation Layer data, 230,000 items of Primitive Layer data, and 2,000 items of Composite Layer data. We asked some questions using a subjective questionnaire sheet to visitors when they finished looking at the exhibits and obtained 71 valid answers.

About 70booth and the booth at which they stayed for the longest time. This supports our hypothesis that if a visitor is interested in a booth he/she will stay there for the longest time, indicating that duration of staying time is an important key for experience summarization. But in a preliminary experiment before the ATR experiment, we obtained different results, which showed that the most interesting booth and the booth where one stayed for the longest time were not the same; here, the booth receiving the longest stay was the one most difficult to understand. We think the main factor of the different results lies in the task and situation. At the ATR exhibition, visitors had no given task, so they looked at exhibits at their whim; however, in the preliminary experiment, we assigned a task for visitors that required them to understand each presentation. Furthermore, there were many people in the room at the ATR exhibition, while there were only a few people present in the preliminary experiment, which allowed the latter group to stay a long time with no concern about interfering with others' visits. Consequently, we think there is a strong relation between the length of stay at a booth and the degree of the visitor's interest under a no-control situation. This confirms our hypothesis about the differences in visitors' interests, that is, the importance of a visitor's experience can be determined by the time he or she stays at the exhibit in an exhibition situation.

We could obtain no tendency explaining the validity of particular applications; we believe this is because the experiment used only one room and visitors could view all booths at once.

Through construction of this system, it was confirmed that the four-layered data structure of an interaction corpus can manage interaction data systematically and more clearly describe the symbolizing role of the interaction.

4   Conclusions

We proposed an experience-sharing system using ubiquitous sensing environments. We also developed a prototype system and used it to confirm the mechanism. The supporting process consists of four phases; capturing, storing, facilitating and sharing. The capturing accuracy of interaction is a key for later processing. We have created an infrared ID system for interaction capturing, obtaining 0.38A four-layered hierarchical data structure is employed to store the captured data as the interaction corpus. This structure is selected from the analogy of language understanding, and the effectiveness of this structure in managing interaction data was confirmed. The system provides flexibility in manipulating collaborative interactions and events such as joint attention and discussions by multiple participating users. The hierarchical structure makes it possible to implement both the interaction facilitation application, which requires use of short-delay data, and the experience sharing application, which requires long-span interaction data. A humanoid communication robot is introduced to facilitate human interactions and communication adapted for each visitor. The robot interacts with people based on the captured situation of users, which can be obtained via a network. A small HMD system is incorporated in the prototype system, and it displays context information on the event in real-time to enhance he ongoing experience sharing. This experience-sharing prototype system focuses attention on the visitor's interest. The experiment confirmed our hypothesis about the differences in visitors' interests, showing that the importance of a visitor's experience can be determined by the time he or she stays at the exhibit in an exhibition situation.

Acknowledgments

We would like to acknowledge the help of all members of the ATR Media Information Science Laboratories and ATR Intelligent Robotics and Communication Laboratories. This research was supported by the National Institute of Information and Communications Technology.

References

1. DARPA Life Log Program (2003), http://www.darpa.mil/ipto/programs/lifelog/index.htm
2. Gordon Bell's MyLifeBits (2002), http://research.microsoft.com/research/barc/MediaPresence/MyLifeBits.aspx
3. UK CRC Grand Challenge "Memories for Life" (2003), http://www.nesc.ac.uk/esi/events/Grand_Challenges/proposals/Memories.pdf
4. Aizawa, K., Hori, T., Kawasaki, S. and Ishikawa, T.: Capture and Efficient Retrieval of Life Log, Proceedings of Pervasive 2004 Workshop on Memory and Sharing of Experiences, pp. 15-20, Apr. 2004.
5. Kawamura, T., Ueoka, T., Kono, Y. and Kidode, M.: Relational Analysis among Experiences and Real World Objects in the Ubiquitous Memories Environment, Proceedings of Pervasive 2004 Workshop on Memory and Sharing of Experiences, pp. 79-84, Apr. 2004.

6. Ueoka, R., Hirose, M., Kuma, K., Sone, M., Kohiyama, K., Kawamura, T. and Hiroto, K.: Wearable Computer@Application for Open Air Exhibition in EXPO 2005, Advances in Multimedia Information Processing PCM 2001, pp. 8-15, Oct. 2001.
7. Hagita, N., Kogure, K., Mase, K. and Sumi, Y.: Collaborative capturing of experiences with ubiquitous sensors and communication robots, in Proceedings of the 2003 IEEE International Conference on Robotics and Automation, pp. 4166-4171, Sep. 2003.
8. Kogure, K., Hagita, N., Sumi, Y., Kuwahara, N. and Ishiguro, H.: Toward Ubiquitous Intelligent Robotics, in Proceedings of the 2003 IEEE International Conference on Intelligent Robots and Systems, pp. 1826-1831, Oct. 2003.
9. Sumi, Y., Matsuguchi, T., Ito, S. and Mase, K.: Collaborative Capturing of Interactions by Multiple Sensors, Adjunct Proceedings of the Fifth International Conference on Ubiquitous Computing, pp. 193-194, Oct. 2003.
10. Mase, K., Sumi, Y., Tsuchikawa, M. and Kogure, K.: Interaction Corpus and Memory for Experience Sharing, International Symposium on Large-scale Knowledge Resources, Mar. 2004.
11. Bono, M., Suzuki, N. and Katagiri, Y.: An analysis of non-verbal cues for turn-taking through observation of speaker behaviors, in Proceedings of the Joint International Conference on Cognitive Science, (CD-ROM), Jul. 2003.

Augmented Classroom: A Paper-Centric Approach for Collaborative Learning System

Motoki Miura[1], Susumu Kunifuji[1], Buntarou Shizuki[2], and Jiro Tanaka[2]

[1] School of Knowledge Science,
Japan Advanced Institute of Science and Technology,
1-1 Asahidai, Nomi, Ishikawa, 923-1292, Japan
{miuramo, kuni}@jaist.ac.jp
[2] Department of Computer Science,
Graduate School of Systems and Information Engineering,
University of Tsukuba, 1-1-1 Tennodai, Tsukuba, Ibaraki, 305-8573, Japan
{shizuki, jiro}@cs.tsukuba.ac.jp

Abstract. We developed *AirTransNote*, a computer-mediated classroom collaboration system. The system enables real-time note-sharing. Air-TransNote manages notes written by students on paper and enables the teacher to browse through the notes or show them to the students. AirTransNote can analyze students' answers, helping the teacher better understand their problems. The system is not meant to provide an alternative to the conventional way of instruction; rather, it is designed to enhance class interaction. We conducted a preliminary study using questionnaires and found that this system can be feasible to apply for classroom environment.

1 Introduction

In the last decades, many educational institutions have started to introduce computers into the classroom. Most schools in Japan already have PC rooms for computer literacy classes, collaborative activities, and individual study. However, computers have not yet become part of everyday school life because they can seldom be used outside the PC room.

There is an increasing interest among school professionals and administrators in using computers for everyday classes. For example, *The Computers in Education project in Japan* [1] is designed to promote the use of network-connected computers and LCD projectors in the regular classroom. Computers are used to show digitally the main points of lectures through images, short video clips, animation, and other applications. The use of computers for demonstration purposes is justified because it helps students better understand the content of lectures. Yet in this approach, the use of computers in the classroom is limited.

We believe that the main purpose of using computers is to promote interaction among students and teachers and create a collaborative learning environment. To enable student participation in computer-mediated learning, classrooms must be equipped with a sufficient number of computers. However, there

H. Murakami et al. (Eds.): UCS 2004, LNCS 3598, pp. 104–116, 2005.

is usually not enough room in a typical classroom to install computers for all students. Also, devices such as PCs and PDAs which require special skills to operate are not appropriate for students.

2   System "AirTransNote"

We developed a computer-mediated collaborative learning system called Air-TransNote. AirTransNote is designed to augment the traditional way of communication in the classroom. AirTransNote is similar to systems designed for chat-augmented conferences[2]. We believe that the system can be incorporated into conventional classrooms to become part of everyday class interaction and learning.

AirTransNote enables real-time sharing of notes. When a student writes notes on a regular sheet of paper, the handwritten data are immediately sent to the teacher's computer. In our current implementation, the transmitter in Air-TransNote is a PDA with a wireless local area network connection and a digital pen. The digital pen is a device which is used to write notes and scribbles on paper. The pen enables recording the coordinates of notes and the timestamp in digital form. The notes are stored into the local memory of the PDA first, and then the notes are transferred to PC by an explicit operation for synchronization. AirTransNote stores data into the local memory of the PDA for backup purposes, but the data are sent to the server in real time. Successive transfer of data improves the effectiveness of communication. We used this feature for interactive communication among the teacher and students.

2.1   Transmitter (Client)

Figure 1 shows the transmitter of AirTransNote. It combines a digital pen (InkLink[3]) and a PDA with a wireless LAN device. The digital pen consists of a sensor, an IrDA relay, and a regular pen.

The transmitter works as follows. Using a clip, a student attaches a sheet of paper to the sensor and connects the sensor to the IrDA relay. Then the student arranges the IrDA relay and PDA in such a way that an infrared connection is established.

Basically, the transmitter is designed to free the student from the need to operate the PDA during class. The only operation the student needs to perform is pressing a hot-key on PDA at the beginning of the class. The hot-key wakes up the PDA device and activates the AirTransNote transmitter.

When the student puts the pen down, ultrasonic waves are generated from the tip of the pen. The sensor recognizes the waves and calculates the current position of the pen tip. The tip position is transmitted to the PDA via the IrDA relay. Finally, the PDA transfers the data to the server through the wireless LAN device.

2.2 Manager (Server)

Figure 2 shows the note-browsing interface of the AirTransNote manager. Transmitted notes are received by the manager, who immediately updates the browser by adding the notes to the corresponding student panel. The teacher can use the browser not only to check the students' progress, but also to show them the notes with explanations.

Fig. 1. Transmitters in AirTransNote. The rectangle indicates the area on which the student should concentrate

The student panels have the form of a regular paper sheet. When the teacher activates a student panel by clicking on it, the browser zooms in onto the activated student panel. The zoom level and focus can be easily adjusted by using FlowMenu[4] and a mouse with a wheel. So that the class could better understand the notes, they can be displayed in an image of content printed on the answer sheet (see Figure 3). The teacher can choose the image and apply it using a page chooser (bottom left corner in Figure 2).

The upper left corner in Figure 2 shows the connection status of each client (a student number filled by yellow color means connected). The status window is also used for shortcuts to turn on an activated student panel by clicking on the corresponding student number. When the teacher uses this shortcut, the view in the current student panel is preserved in the new activated panel. The

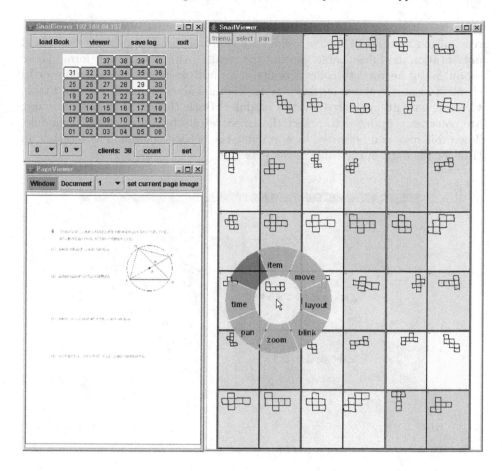

Fig. 2. Note-browsing interface in the AirTransNote manager

teacher can easily zoom in on part of the answer sheet in each student's panel by selecting a shortcut. Panning, zooming, and switching operations are performed with smooth animated transitions in the note browser.

In addition to the notes, a timestamp of stroke can also be used for a time-based presentation. AirTransNote can replay notes at different speeds, which enables time-based visualization of notes. The teacher can draw students' attention to a particular answer by using a time-line bar.

AirTransNote can be used to present ideas and solutions through note-sharing and it is particularly useful in the classroom. This system can be used, for example, in geometry class, helping the teacher evaluate students' drawings. The teacher can zoom in on a particular answer, explain solutions, and comment on student answers and drawings.

Although the interface of the manager is fairly sophisticated, there is still not enough time for the teacher to check the work of all students during a class period. We thus added an analysis function to AirTransNote. This function provides automatic recognition and presentation of results. We implemented the recognition module based on a simple region-matching algorithm; two visual presentation modules enable viewing the results in table or graph form. These modules can be used to collect results of a multiple-choice questionnaire or to check students' progress on paper tests. Figure 4 shows a graph view and table view of a result generated by the modules. Both the graph and table views are constantly updated to reflect the latest results in the recognition module. The table rows can be sorted by specifying the needed column. The teacher can transfer the data in the table into a CSV file.

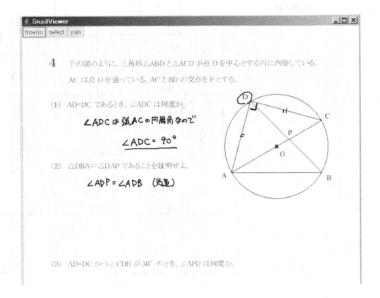

Fig. 3. Zoomed-in view of notes overlapped with a printed-paper image

The analysis function is useful because it helps the teacher quickly understand the progress of each student. Based on the responses, the teacher can control the speed of the lecture. Also the manager can issue commands to play sounds at the transmitter's side. This function can be used to inform students of test results as soon as they become available.

2.3   Advantages

Advantages to Students. The most useful feature of the paper-centric approach is that it frees the student from the need to use digital devices while preserving the traditional style of teaching with paper and pen. The goal of computer-mediated learning is to maximize the efficiency of the learning process and facilitate the acquisition of knowledge by using technology, not to make the student acclimate to the devices. Most conventional PC- or PDA-based learning technologies require that students use electronic devices. As a result, students who are not familiar with such devices may be at a disadvantage. Our system based on the paper-centric approach provides collaborative learning functions with a natural interface that is easy to use.

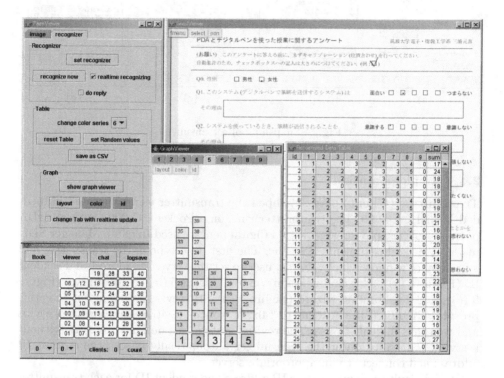

Fig. 4. Summary of questionnaire results presented in graph and table forms

Advantages to Teachers. We respect the traditional way of teaching and at the same time believe that it should be enhanced. Our system is designed to supplement the traditional teaching style with real-time collaboration. Teachers can use our system to supplement the more conventional instruction tools such as paper-based lecture materials.

In a classroom with many students, it may not be possible for the teacher to pay close attention to every student. Our system solves this problem by providing the teacher with a means to check students' work. By viewing test results presented in graph form, the teacher can see which students failed to solve which problems and can direct his/her attention to those students. A detailed log can be used to categorize test mistakes and problems so that the class could go over them in the future. This is also advantageous to students.

The system consists of a digital pen device with a PDA, a wave-LAN station, a projector, and a PC for the teacher. Assuming that both the digital pens and PDAs have been distributed among the students, and the wave-LAN station has been installed in the classroom, the system can be set up very quickly.

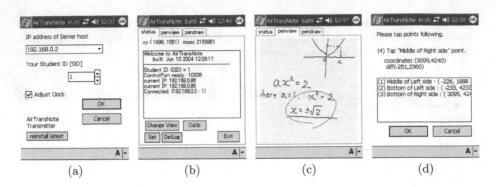

Fig. 5. Snapshots of a transmitter

2.4   Implementation

Transmitter (Client). We developed the transmitter using Microsoft eMbedded Visual C++ 4.0. The transmitter runs on a Pocket PC 2003 with an IrDA port. To collect notes created with a digital pen, we used InkNote Manager SDK made by Seiko Instruments USA Inc. The first prototype of the transmitter had a preference window which allows a user to set the server IP address and student ID (Figure 5 (a)), a log confirmation window (Figure 5 (b)), a note viewer (Figure 5 (c)), and a calibration wizard (Figure 5 (d)). However, we found out that this prototype required the student to tap the touch-sensitive screen with a stylus and was thus difficult to use. The revised system was designed to work without a stylus. The software of the transmitter automatically checks the current IP address and connects to an appropriate server.

It is difficult to setup a server IP address and student ID for each transmitter via the preference window. We therefore implemented an administration tool. We added the transmitter to the server port for initial configuration. The administration tool first finds the transmitter, then connects to the port and configures the devices in a remote operation. It also performs version control of the system and re-installment of transmitters. The server IP address and student ID are stored in the system registry key of PocketPC.

Manager (Server). The manager is implemented on Java2 with zooming toolkit Piccolo [5]. We designed the interface for both the pen and the mouse, because large displays with a touch sensor panel may become more common in the near future.

In order to show notes in paper sheet images, the teacher needs to prepare the sheet images in advance. An arbitrary image file such as JPEG or PNG can be converted into a "book file" format. The book file also stores some marks for recognition purpose. If the sheet image includes pixels of non-gray colors, the editor generates default marks in the corresponding areas of the pixels. The marks can also be generated manually, with reference to actual notes. After generating and grouping the marks, the teacher sets values for each mark and stores them in the book file. When the teacher opens the book file, the recognition module activates the marks.

3   Related Work

Much of the previous work on sharing handwritten notes and their applications in e-learning has been based on a device-oriented approach. NotePals[6, 7] is a

(a)

(b)

Fig. 6. Feasibility study

PDA-based note-sharing system that captures, and provides access to, hand-written notes and documents of interest to a work group. Notes in the shared repository can be reused by other people. Landay [8] integrated CrossPad[1] with NotePals but the system requires synchronization to upload notes. In addition, CrossPad is not the best system for daily use in current Japanese classrooms because of its size and weight. SEGODON-PDA [9,10] also uses a PDA as a medium for note-sharing. SEGODON-PDA provides both keyboard input and tap-based input for efficient note-taking. Students download class materials using a PDA connected to a wireless LAN, and to share a window of text editor with a cursor for presentation. SEGODON-PDA promotes overall learning including class preparation and review, but it requires a higher level of PDA operating skills than AirTransNote. Tamura and colleagues developed an e-learning system based on TabletPC and tested it in elementary schools [11]. This was done as part of a project initiated by the Center for Educational Computing (CEC) in Japan. The system provides an automatic recognition engine that recognizes both numbers and Japanese characters. The system enables interactive responses to digital content. But this system also implies a matter of deployment in classroom environment.

The system most similar to ours was described by Maruyama and colleagues [12]. This system was developed by Hitachi Public System Service Co., Ltd., in another CEC project. The system uses Anoto Pen[2] to record student answers, and the data are synchronized among computer cradles. This system is also based on a paper-centric approach and does not require the use of PDAs to transfer note data. However, it requires the use of paper with a special dotted pattern, and the data are not updated continuously. In addition, the task of connecting many cradles to the teacher's PC can be difficult and time-consuming. Bayon and colleagues [13] also point out that the cost of connecting devices together is high in a real-world school environment. AirTransNote has the following three advantages: (1) it enables real-time updates, (2) it minimizes the set-up time, and (3) it can be scaled to accommodate a different number of clients.

4   Preliminary Feasibility Study

To investigate the effectiveness and practicability of our system, we performed a preliminary feasibility study with 40 subjects. All subjects were first-year high school students (16 males and 24 females). We chose a math class (each class period is 45 minutes). The students first worked on printed questions with digital pens, and then the teacher explained each question.

At the beginning of the class, we distributed digital pens and PDAs, and explained how to use them. The instructions were given in five minutes because of limited class time. We used a 3.2-GHz portable notebook PC as a server and 40 PDAs (Pocket PC 2003, IEEE802.11b wireless LAN-enabled) as transmitters.

---

[1] http://www.research.ibm.com/electricInk/
[2] http://www.anotofunctionality.com/navigate.asp

Table 1. Questionnaire items

Q1. Did you enjoy the system?
Yes <5,4,3,2,1 >No
Q2. Did you mind the system sending notes?
Yes <5,4,3,2,1 >No
Q3. Did you feel stress while using the system?
Yes <5,4,3,2,1 >No
Q4. Do you want to use the system again?
Yes <5,4,3,2,1 >No
Q5. Do you think that replaying notes using a time-line bar can be helpful to you and the teacher?
Yes <5,4,3,2,1 >No
Q6. Do you think that this system improves the quality of learning?
Yes <5,4,3,2,1 >No

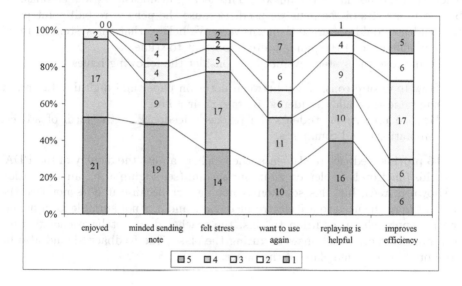

Fig. 7. Questionnaire results

The server was connected to a local private network by using a 100-base-TX LAN interface.

We asked the students to respond to a questionnaire in the last five minutes of the class. The questionnaires included both multiple-choice and open-ended questions (see Table 1).

Result. None of the 40 students had any trouble using the system, except for the initial connection set-up. One of the students drew doodles, but he stopped after the teacher erased the doodles on the screen.

We were worried about the bandwidth of the wireless network—whether it was sufficient to cope with note data from 40 transmitters. But the system worked without any problem. It is a benefit of the stroke data size which is relatively small. Figure 6 (a) and (b) show scenes from the class. The teacher showed individual students' answers to the class and explained solutions. However, contrary to our expectation, the teacher seldom used the computer display for browsing. The teacher preferred to look at the students and their answer sheets to specify typical answers for explanation. This means that the browsing interface in our system is still difficult to use in the real world. Although improving the browser interface is one solution, we should also look for ways of focusing on to the student panel in a natural way.

The questionnaires (see Figure 7) showed that most of the students were interested in the system and enjoyed the session. Some students were surprised by the system and digital pen devices. However, more than half of the students in the class said they were not comfortable with sharing their notes, particularly when they did not know the answer. This feeling of uneasiness was emphasized by the properties of the pens we used. Because the pens were ball-point pens, the students could not erase their answers. We believe that the system is useful but the difference of the pen is quite important to students.

To improve the system, we need to consider the following issues.

- How to ensure consistency between notes on paper and digital data and at the same time allow students to erase their notes.
- How to present to students the teacher's feedback in the form of advice, annotations, and comments.

To provide feedback to students, the teacher can use the display of the PDA, and this function is implemented in our system (see Figure 5 (c); an annotation is shown in red), but this solution is not perfect because it does not free the student from the need to use electronic devices and it is not suitable for a paper-centric approach. In addition to this, the teacher does not have enough time to manually reply to all answers during the class. The feedback should also be presented in the same place of the paper.

5   Conclusion

We developed a paper-centric collaborative learning system called AirTransNote. AirTransNote is designed to augment the traditional classroom instruction and enhance student-teacher interaction through note-sharing. Using this system, teachers can closely monitor their students' process. The system has a recognition module that helps the teacher summarize class progress as well as activities of each student. The system is also useful to students because it improves the quality of the learning process by making it possible for students to share ideas, solutions, and activities. Our preliminary study indicates that this approach to learning in the classroom is feasible. We believe that the paper-centric approach is appropriate because the pen minimizes the amount of cognitive effort required by the use of specific devices and maximizes collaboration through note-sharing. In the future, we want to improve the recognition module to better support teachers.

Acknowledgment

We would like to thank Hiroyuki Sakamoto for his comments and arrangements for our experiments. This work was supported in part by a grant-in-aid for Scientific Research (15020216, 14780187).

References

1. http://www.manabinet.jp/it_ed.pdf (in Japanese).
2. Jun Rekimoto, Yuji Ayatsuka, Hitoraka Uoi, and Toshifumi Arai. Adding Another Communication Channel to Reality: An Experience with a Chat-Augmented Conference. In *CHI 98 conference summary on Human factors in computing systems*, pages 271–272, April 1998.
3. Seiko Instruments USA Inc. InkLink. http://www.siibusinessproducts.com/support/discsupp.html.
4. François Guimbretière and Terry Winograd. FlowMenu: Combining Command, Text, and Data Entry. In *Proceedings of ACM User Interface Software and Technology 2000 (UIST 2000)*, pages 213–216, November 2000.
5. Benjamin B. Bederson, Jesse Grosjean, and Jon Meyer. Toolkit Design for Interactive Structured Graphics. Technical Report HCIL-2003-01, CS-TR-4432, UMIACS-TR-2003-03, Institute for Advanced Computer Studies, Computer Science Department, University of Maryland, January 2003.
6. Richard C. Davis, James A. Landay, Victor Chen, Jonathan Huang, Rebecca B. Lee, Francis Li, James Lin, Charles B. Morrey III, Ben Schleimer, Morgan N. Price, and Bill N. Schilit. NotePals: Lightweight Note Sharing by the Group, for the Group. In *Proceedings of the SIGCHI conference on Human factors in computing systems*, pages 338–345, May 1999.
7. Richard C. Davis, James Lin, Jason A. Brotherton, James A. Landay, Morgan N. Price, and Bill N. Schilit. A framework for sharing handwritten notes. In *Proceedings of the 11th annual ACM symposium on User interface software and technology (UIST98)*, pages 119–120, November 1998.
8. James A. Landay. Using Note-Taking Appliances for Student to Student Collaboration. In *Proceedings of the 29th ASEE/IEEE Frontiers in Education Conference*, pages 12c4–15–20, November 1999.
9. Takashi Yoshino and Jun Munemori. SEGODON: Learning Support System that can be Applied to Various Forms. In Claude Ghaoui, editor, *E-Education Applications: Human Factors and Innovative Approaches*, pages 132–152. Information Science Publishing, February 2004.
10. Tomohiro Shigenobu, Takahiro Noda, Takashi Yoshino, and Jun Munemori. SEGODON-PDA: Flexible Lecture Support System Using Wireless LAN and PDAs. *IPSJ Journal*, 45(1):255–266, January 2004. (in Japanese).

11. Hiroaki Tamura, Naomi Iwayama, Hiroshi Tanaka, Katsuhiko Akiyama, and Kazushi Ishigaki. An Implementatin of Handwriting Learning Materials on Tablet-PC and its Practical Studies in an Elementary School. In *Proceedings of Interaction 2004*, pages 47–52. IPSJ Symposium Series Vol. 2004, No. 5, March 2004. (in Japanese).

12. http://www.cec.or.jp/e2a/other/04PDF/b1.pdf (in Japanese; the URL of the project page is http://www.hitachi-ks.co.jp/cec/index.html).

13. Victor Bayon, Tom Rodden, Chris Greenhalgh, and Steve Benford. Going Back to School: Putting a Pervasive Environment into the Real World. In *1st International Conference on Pervasive Computing (LNCS 2414)*, pages 69–83, August 2002.

EnhancedTable: An Augmented Table System for Supporting Face-to-Face Meeting in Ubiquitous Environment

Hideki Koike[1], Shinichiro Nagashima[1], Yasuto Nakanishi[2], and Yoichi Sato[3]

[1] Graduate School of Information Systems, University of Electro-Communications,
1-5-1, Chofugaoka, Chofu, Tokyo 182-8585, Japan
`koike@acm.org, naga@vogue.is.uec.ac.jp`
[2] Faculty of Technology, Tokyo University of Agriculture and Technology,
2-24-16, Nakamachi, Koganei, Tokyo 184-8588, Japan
`yasuto@cc.tuat.ac.jp`
[3] Institute of Industrial Science, University of Tokyo,
4-6-1, Komaba, Meguro-ku, Tokyo 153-8505, Japan
`ysato@iis.u-tokyo.ac.jp`

Abstract. This paper describes our design and implementation of an augmented table system for face-to-face meetings. The system was designed to be used by multiple users in the ubiquitous environment, where people do not need to bring their laptop PCs. With effective use of the advantage of computer vision, we implemented the concept of *ubiquitous desktop* as personal workspace and *virtual Chinese table* as shared workspace. User can share/personalize files by drag-and-dropping icons to/from the shared workspace. The system also provides capabilities for interactive image capturing and finger position sharing, both of which would be useful for the meetings.

1 Introduction

As personal computers become more and more and popular, changes have occurred in the style of small group meetings. Traditionally, paper documents and white boards have been the main elements in such small meetings. On the other hand, people often bring their laptop PCs to the meeting in order to take notes and to show presentation slides to other participants. In addition, people also download electronic files, such as PDF documents, from the Internet during the meeting. Other participants may copy these files from his/her PC by using file transfer tools such as FTP.

Although such digitally enhanced meetings have succeeded in introducing efficiency, we often feel a little inconvenienced. For example, laptop PCs brought by the participants require a relatively large area of the space assigned to each participant on the meeting table. Little space remains in which to place other objects such as paper documents, and it is sometimes hard for participants to write memos in their notebooks.

H. Murakami et al. (Eds.): UCS 2004, LNCS 3598, pp. 117–130, 2005.

When exchanging electronic files, people need to know the IP address of the computer from which the files are downloaded They have to make a connection to the computer, and copy the files onto their own PCs.

On the other hand, much research is being conducted to realize the ubiquitous computing environment proposed by Mark Weiser[20]. In the ubiquitous environment, a large number of computers are embedded in the environment and will support users' activity implicitly and/or explicitly by enabling communication with each other. If such environments were to be established, users would not need to carry their laptop PCs, which are heavy but contain important data. The users' data would be stored in network file servers which are in a safe place, and would be retrieved when necessary. It is, moreover, expected that the environment would recognize the user's position and show appropriate information at the appropriate position. However, the traditional interaction framework such as GUI, which uses a keyboard and mouse as standard input devices will not be appropriate in such a ubiquitous environment. Then the Perceptual User Interface (PUI) [17] which utilizes several recognition technologies such as image recognition and speech recognition is focused on as the next generation interaction framework.

Fig. 1. Typical scene of a current small meeting. Each attendant brings his/her own laptop PC. As a result, most of the table surface is occupied by those laptops

We previously developed a vision-based augmented desk system named *EnhancedDesk* [5]. In this project, we developed a method for real-time finger recognition [12] and a method for interactive object registration and recognition based on color information [9]. Our system, however, was designed to be used by a single user like other augmented desk systems [1, 6, 8, 21]. The vision-based interaction such as used in our system could be easily extended to multi-user environment.

This paper describes our design for an augmented table system in a ubiquitous and augmented environment and its implementation in the near future. The system aims to support effective face-to-face meeting by allowing users natural and intuitive operation of digital files. The next section describes the key features of our design. Section 3 shows interactions in our system. Section 4 describes implementation details. Section 5 discusses advantages and disadvantages of our prototype. Section 6 concludes the paper.

2   Meeting in Ubiquitous and Augmented Environment

To date, many augmented systems have been developed. Most of them were designed for being used by a single user or for sharing one screen by multiple users. On the other hand, our interest is in integrating each user's personal workspace and a shared workspace on one screen. The key features of our system are as follows.

2.1   Integrating Ubiquitous Personal Workspaces and Shared Workspace on the Table

In the ubiquitous environment that we imagine, the user do not need to carry heavy laptop PCs which contain important files. When a user puts an object (e.g., a mobile phone) which identifies him/her on the table, the system identifies the user and displays his/her desktop with his/her personal files, which are stored in a networked file server, at that user's position. The user directly manipulates the displayed objects by using his/her own hand and fingers instead of using a mouse or trackpad.

At the center of the table, a special shared workspace is projected. When a user drags his/her personal file from his/her workspace to the shared workspace, the file becomes a shared file. Other users can copy this shared file just by drag-and-dropping the file from the shared workspace onto their own personal workspaces. Moreover, this shared workspace serves as a presentation screen when the user previews particular file as we describe later.

2.2   Enhancing Paper Documents Using Vision-Based Augmented Reality

As we described in [5], paper documents and digital documents will co-exist for the time being. The paper documents are easier to carry, easier to read, easier to add notes to, and so on. However, it is much more difficult to make copies and send them to other people quickly.

By effective use of the advantages of vision-based augmented reality, we implemented the following features which enhance the paper documents. One is interactive image capturing. The user can make a digitized image of a part of or all of a paper document just by showing a rectangle gesture. Another is finger position sharing. When the users enable the finger position sharing mode, each user's finger position is projected on the document.

3 EnhancedTable

3.1 Overview

In order to explore the interaction framework described above, we developed an augmented table system, named EnhancedTable, which allows parallel interactions by multiple users (Fig.3). The system uses a normal white table as a screen and interaction space. On top of the table, there are two LCD projectors (PLUS V-1080) for displaying images, two CCD cameras (SONY EVI-D100) for finger/hand tracking, and one CCD camera (SONY EVI-D30) for image capturing. A LCD projector, a CCD camera (EVI-D100), and a PC (Pentium 4 2.80MHz: 512Mb memory: Linux) with an image processing board (HITACHI IP5005) make a unit. Currently we have installed two units. Each unit covers a half of the table. The reason why we use two units is to get enough resolution for displaying and capturing image.

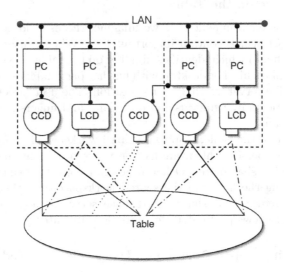

Fig. 2. System architecture of EnhancedTable

One of the important features of our system (and this feature is essential to support meeting) is the ability to allow parallel interaction by multiple users. Traditional touch panel systems do not allow such multiple interaction. Although some recent touch panel systems can detect multiple pointing, they still do not allow users to put some objects such as mug cups on the panel. It is also difficult or expensive to make a much larger table. On the contrary, our system naturally allows multiple interaction and could be extended to accommodate larger displays.

Fig. 3. EnhancedTable in use

Fig. 4. A private workspace. The mobile phone, the top-right position in this example, defines a reference point. The three icons on the left are operational icons. The four icons on the right are data icons

3.2 Personal Workspace: Ubiquitous Desktop

When the user sits at the table and put his/her mobile phone on the table, the system recognizes the mobile phone and identifies the user. Then it automatically projects the user's personal workspace such that the mobile phone is on the top-left (or top-right) corner of the workspace. Unlike other meeting systems which have embedded displays, the users can sit anywhere they want to because the projection coordinate is decided based on the position of the mobile phone.

There are data icons and operational icons in the personal workspace (Fig. 4). The data icons represent text files, image files, or audio files owned by the user. Users can drag these icons by using their fingers. The operational icons include trash icon, preview icon, etc. The users can perform a certain operation by drag-and-dropping the data icon on the operational icon.

3.3   User Identification

To recognize a mobile phone, we used a method for object registration and recognition using an RGB color histogram[9]. We first capture the image of an object by 60x60 pixels. The registration system scans each pixel and calculates RGB values of the pixel in 256 colors. If the value of the pixel is (r, g, b), where $0 \leq r, g, b \leq 8$, the system increments the value $H(r, g, b)$ by one. After scanning all the pixels in the image, this three dimensional matrix H is registered as a model of the object (Fig. 5). In the recognition process, the system looks for an object which has the size of usual mobile phones. When the system find the object, it calculates the RGB histogram of the object by using the same algorithm described above, and compares this histogram to those registered in the system. If the system finds a model whose histogram is close enough to the object's histogram, the object is regarded as matched to the model.

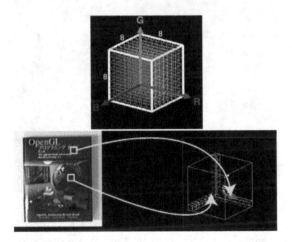

Fig. 5. RGB histogram (top) and an algorithm to make the RGB histogram. The system scans each pixel and calculates RGB values of the pixel in 256 colors. If the value of the pixel is (r, g, b), where $0 \leq r, g, b \leq 8$, the system increments the value $H(r, g, b)$ by one. After scanning all the pixels in the image, this three dimensional matrix H is registered as a model of the object

3.4   Shared Workspace: Virtual Chinese Table

On the center of the table, a circular shared workspace is always displayed (Fig. 6). When a user drags his/her personal file from his/her workspace and drops onto the shared workspace, the file becomes a shared file. Other users can copy this shared file just by drag-and-dropping the file from the shared workspace to their own personal workspace.

The user can rotate the circular shared workspace by hand as with a Chinese dining table in a Chinese restaurant (or with a lazy susan in a regular restaurant). The user in any position can reach every file in the shared workspace by rotating that space.

Fig. 6. A shared workspace. Each user can download shared files displayed in the shared workspace by drag-and-dropping these icons onto his/her personal workspace. The user can also upload his/her personal file to this shared workspace by using his/her hand. The user can also rotate this shared workspace by his/her finger

The shared workspace also plays a role as a presentation screen. When a user drags-and-drops any image file on the preview icon, that file is magnified at the shared workspace and all users can see and rotate the image (Fig. 7).

When we use the traditional presentation screen, if one user wants to point to the presentation slide, he/she needs to stand up and go to the presentation screen. On the other hand, the users of our system can point to the slide without leaving their seats. However, all users cannot see the slide from the right angle simultaneously.

3.5 Finger Recognition

To detect hand regions, the system calculates the difference between the initial image and the current image of the tabletop. After the binarization operation, objects which are larger than a threshold are recognized as hand regions. Since the hand regions must cross the edge of the image, the system investigates every pixel of the four edges and determines the direction of finger tips.

After the hand regions are detected, a certain area from the fingertips is recognized as the palm. By repeating the shrink operation to the palm region, the final pixel is determined to be the center of the palm. Then, using template matching with a circle template, the system finds the fingertips.

Fig. 7. The user can preview text or image files on the shared workspace by putting the icon on the "Preview" icon

Currently the system can detect and track eight hands in 20 frame/sec. If the CPU becomes much faster, the system can track more hands faster.

After detecting the hands on the table, it is necessary to decide to whom each hand belongs. To do this, the system currently uses the distance between the identified object and the center of gravity of the hand region and the center of the palm.

1. If the center of gravity of hand region is in the personal workspace, the hand is recognized as the owner of the personal workspace.
2. If the center of palm is in the personal workspace, the hand is recognized as the owner of the personal workspace.

Fig. 8. Interactive image capturing. When the user makes a rectangle gesture with the thumb and index finger of both hands and waits for three seconds, the area is digitally captured and saved

Fig. 9. When the finger sharing mode is enabled, other users' finger positions are projected onto the desktop. If each user aligns the paper document on the grid which is also projected on the personal workspace, the user can see what other users are focusing on

The reason why we need the first rule is that the center of the palm goes outside of the personal workspace when the user moves his/her hand to the shared workspace.

3.6   Interactive Image Capturing

In the current meetings, we sometimes want to digitize a part of or all of the paper document and send it to all participants during the meeting. In order to

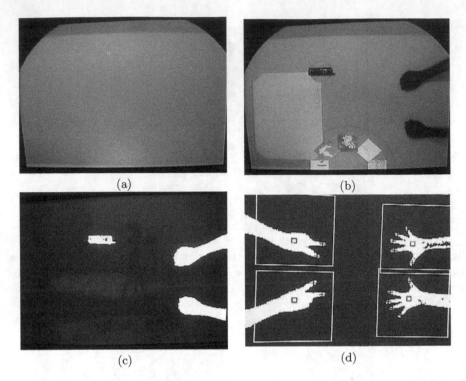

Fig. 10. Hand detection. (a) An initial image of the table. (b) The image when the user's hands and the object are on the table. (c) The difference between (a) and (b). The projected image can be eliminated in this calculation. (d) Four hands are successfully detected and recognized

do this in the current meetings, we need to go to a PC connected to an image scanner, scan the file, and send it as an attachment file. It is a time-consuming task.

On the other hand, our system provides interactive image capturing. When the user makes a rectangle with the thumb and pointing (index) finger of both hands and waits for three seconds, the CCD camera on the ceiling zooms into the rectangle area, and saves its image in JPEG format (Fig. 8). The reason why we used the third CCD camera is to obtain high resolution images when capturing the image.

3.7   Finger Position Sharing

When a user enables the finger position sharing mode, a grid is shown in the personal workspace. If the user aligns a paper document on the grid, other users' finger positions are projected on the document (Fig. 9). Different colors are assigned to each user to identify whose finger position they belong to.

4   Discussion

We have not yet done any formal user studies. It is rather difficult to evaluate the system by comparing it with any existing systems since some elemental technologies, such as user identification, which are essential to our system are not reliable enough. However, through the experimental use in our laboratory and the demonstrations to the visitors, we found that most of the people want to use the system in the real meetings.

The first reason is its natural and intuitive interface for exchanging digital files. In particular, our users preferred to use the virtual Chinese table. However, some people claimed that it is unnatural to use fingers during the meeting because they usually hold a pen. So it might be better to use pen instead of finger to manipulate digital objects, such as seen with tablet PCs. In our framework, it is relatively easy to use a pen instead of a finger to manipulate objects projected on the desk just by exchanging the template image.

The second reason is that people felt much closer to each other during the meeting because there is no physical fence or barrier (i.e., LCD displays of the laptop PCs) between users. In the current meetings, we do not know what other users are doing because of these barriers. Although this is nice to keep our privacy, it sometimes interferes with our mutual understanding.

4.1   User Identification

We used color information of the mobile phones to identify users. This object recognition system gave 92 % correct answers for a hundred different images in our experiment. If the number of users is small and they use phones with different appearances, this identification works. However, if the number of users is larger and they use phones with similar appearance, this identification system would fail.

For the better identification, there are some alternative methods.

1. face recognition
2. RFID tag

The former method is already practically used in some applications. This method works fine when the system can get almost full face of the user in high resolution. However, the image captured by a relatively remote camera would not be good. The latter method is accurate for detecting who is in the environment. However, it is not appropriate for detecting where the user sits. One solution would be to use an object sensor behind the table to detect the precise position of the user.

5   Related Work

There are several works which should be mentioned related to interactions in ubiquitous environment. "Office of the future"[14] proposed an augmented office with some projectors. The users can see information on the desk or on the wall of the office. However, the developers did not mention how to interact in such a ubiquitous environment. "EasyLiving"[2] proposed an intelligent living room in the future. The environment always tracks users in the room and displays the users' desktop at appropriate screens. The interaction, however, is done using the traditional mouse and keyboard.

Our work is mostly inspired by Rekimoto's Augmented Surface[10], which smoothly integrates the desktop of laptop PCs and augmented table surface and wall. Users do not need to know the IP address of computers to exchange digital information with each other. The concept of personal workspace and shared workspace is similar to ours. Augmented Surface is, however, a design prototype based on the current framework. It assumes an environment where people carry their own PCs. On the other hand, our system is a design prototype based on the ubiquitous environment of the near future. In particular, the ubiquitous desktop is a unique concept. Augmented Surface's vision system, called DeskSat, takes 30 seconds to scan the table surface. On the other hand, our vision system processes eight hands and other object in 20 frame/sec (i.e. 0.05 sec).

Another related work which should be mentioned is the "I/O bulb" concept in [18]. Unlike the normal bulb which has just the ON/OFF state, the "I/O bulb" has the ability of data projection and image capturing. As we described previously, EnhancedTable consists of two unit which includes a LCD, a CCD camera, and two PCs. This unit is a concrete implementation of the I/O bulb concept. We carefully designed our hardware and software so that each unit works by itself and is extensible. As a result, it is easy to add other units to the system in order to make a larger table (or room).

There are many systems that project digital information on the desk. The pioneering work of an augmented desk interface was done in Digital Desk [21]. Digital Desk proposed a basic hardware setup which has been used in later research. Digital Desk also experimented with basic finger recognition. Kruger [6] and MacKay [8] also experimented with augmented desk systems. MetaDesk [4] used real objects (Phicons) to manipulate digital information such as electronic maps. These systems are designed to be used by one user.

PDH[19, 13] is a circular table top display system. It is designed to be used by multiple users from any direction of the circular table. However, it is equipped with a touch panel and cannot detect simultaneous pointing by users. Recently, the touch panels which allow simultaneous, multi-user interaction have been developed (e.g., [3]). They still do not allow users to put some objects. It is also difficult or expensive to make much larger table.

6   Conclusion

This paper described our design and implementation of an augmented table system, called EnhancedTable. The system was designed to be used in the ubiquitous environment in the near future, where people do not need to carry laptop PCs. We proposed and implemented the ubiquitous desktop as personal workspace and the virtual Chinese table as shared workspace. Users can easily exchange their files via the shared workspace in a natural and intuitive manner. We also implemented interactive image capturing and finger point sharing capabilities.

We are currently interested in integrating mobile phones to our system. The mobile phones are used not only for identification but also for browsing files in the personal desktop. We are also interested in developing an intelligent smaller unit which automatically calibrates its camera and its LCD.

References

1. Arai, T., Machii, K, and Kuzunuki, S.: Retrieving electronic documents with real-world objects on InteraciveDesk. In Proceedings of the ACM Symposium on User Interface Software and Technology (UIST'95), ACM (1995) 37–38
2. Brumitt,B., Shafer, S.: Better Living Through Geometry. Personal and Ubiquitous Computing, Vol.5, Issue 1 (2001)
3. Dietz, P.H., Leigh, D.L.: DiamondTouch: A Multi-User Touch Technology, ACM Symposium on User Interface Software and Technology (UIST) , ACM (2001), 219-226
4. Ishii, H., Ullmer, B.: Tangible bits: Towards seamless interface between people, bits and atoms. In Proceedings of the ACM Conference on Human Factors in Computing Systems (CHI'97), ACM (1997) 234–241
5. Koike,H., Sato, Y., Kobayashi, Y.: Interactive Textbook and Interactive Venn Diagram: Natural and Intuitive Interfaces on Augmented Desk System. In Proceedings of the ACM Conference on Human Factors in Computing Systems (CHI 2000), ACM (2000) 121-128
6. Kruger, M.: Artificial Reality. 2nd edn. Addison-Wesley, (1991)
7. Lange, B.M., Jones, M.A., Meyers, J.L.: Insight Lab: An Immersive Team Environment Linking Paper,Display,and Data. In Proceedings of the ACM Conference on Human Factors in Computing Systems (CHI'98), ACM (1998) 550-557
8. MacKay, W.: Augmenting reality: Adding computational dimensions to paper. CACM, ACM (1993), Vol.36 No.7, 96–97
9. Nishi, T., Sato, Y., Koike, H: SnapLink:Interactive Object Registration and Recognition for Augmented Desk Interface. In Proceedings on IFIP INTERACT'01, (2001) 240-246
10. Rekimoto, J., Saitoh, M.: Augmented Surfaces:A Spatially Continuous Work Space for Hybrid Computing Environments. In Proceedings of the ACM Conference on Human Factors in Computing Systems (CHI'99), ACM (1999) 378-385
11. Robinson, P.: Animated paper documents. In Proceedings of HCI'97(21B) (1997) 655–658
12. Sato, Y., Kobayashi, Y., Koike, H: Fast Tracking of Hands and Fingertips in Infrared Images for Augmented Desk Interface. In Proceedings of IEEE Face and Gesture Recognition (FG 2000), IEEE (2000) 462-467
13. Shen, C., Lesh, N., Bardsley, R.S.: Personal Digital Historian:User Interface Design. In Proceedings of the ACM Conference on Human Factors in Computing Systems (CHI 2001), ACM (2001) 29-30
14. Raskar, R., Welch.G, Cutts, M, Lake, A, Stesin, L, Fuchs, H.: The office of the future: a unified approach to image-based modeling and spatially immersive displays, In Proceedings of the 25th annual conference on Computer Graphics and interactive techniques, ACM (1998)

15. Streitz, N.A. et al.: i-LAND:An Interactive Landscape for Creativity and Innovation. In Proceedings of the ACM Conference on Human Factors in Computing Systems (CHI'99), ACM (1999) 120-127
16. Streitz, N.A., et al.: Roomware - The Second Generation. In Proceedings of the ACM Conference on Human Factors in Computing Systems (CHI 2002), ACM (2002) 506-507
17. Turk, M.: Moving from GUIs to PUIs. In Proceedings of Fourth Symposium on Intelligent Information Media, (1998)
18. Underkoffler, J., Ishii, H.: Illuminating light: An optical design tool with a luminous-tangible interface. In Proceedings of the ACM Conference on Human Factors in Computing System (CHI'98), ACM (1998) 542–549
19. Vernier, F., Lesh, N. Shen, C.: Visualization techniques for circular tabletop interfaces. In Proceedings of Advanced Visual Interfaces (AVI 2002), (2002) 257-265
20. Weiser, M.: The Computer for the 21st Century. Scientific American, Sep. 1991.
21. Wellner, P.: Interacting with Paper on the DigitalDesk. CACM, ACM (1993) 86-96
22. Yamashita, J. Kuzuoka, H., et al.: Agora:Supporting Multi-participant Telecollaboration. In Proceedings of HCI 1999, (1999) 543-547

Agents That Coordinate Web Services in Ubiquitous Computing

Akio Sashima, Noriaki Izumi, and Koichi Kurumatani

Information Technology Research Institute (ITRI),
National Institute of Advanced Industrial Science and Technology (AIST),
Aomi 2-41-6 Koto-ku, Tokyo, 135-0064, Japan
{sashima, niz}@ni.aist.go.jp
k.kurumatani@aist.go.jp

Abstract. The paper describes an agent-based web service coordination framework in ubiquitous computing. It is called *context-mediated web service coordination*. In the framework, all service processes in ubiquitous computing environments are wrapped in web services that have standard communication protocols. The framework coordinates sensor devices wrapped in web services, web services on the Internet, and web services that manage user profile, etc. In addition, these web services are wrapped in specific types of agents. Giving a standard agent communication protocols to the heterogeneous web service processes, the framework introduces a new agent-based service coordination layer in ubiquitous computing. Coordinating these agents based on the user's intention and their physical contexts, we can seamlessly coordinate the heterogeneous service components over the digital and real world in a human-centered manner. We also show a prototype application of the framework, context-aware information retrieval services in a museum.

1 Introduction

Recently, Ubiquitous computing [1] has received much interest in both research and application. Although ubiquitous computing is a promising domain/area for intelligent services like context-aware information assistance, many research issues remain. A fundamental issue is coordination of devices, services, and users. Numerous heterogeneous devices (e.g., terminals, RFID tag systems, cameras, information appliances, etc.), various information services that use those devices (e.g., navigation aids, guides, information retrievals, controlling devices, etc.), and users who have different intentions are physically situated in a ubiquitous computing environment. In such a situation, how can we coordinate services and devices to assist a particular user in receiving a particular service and thereby maximize the user's satisfaction? In other words, how can we dynamically coordinate the heterogeneous services and devices physically situated in a ubiquitous environment according to a user's intention?

In this research, to solve this human-centered coordination issue in Ubiquitous computing, we focus on *web Services* [2] and *semantic web agents* [3]. Web services are software components that have standard communication protocols, such as SOAP and HTTP. Semantic web agents are autonomous programs that choose proper contents out

H. Murakami et al. (Eds.): UCS 2004, LNCS 3598, pp. 131–145, 2005.

of numerous web contents on the Internet on behalf of users. The semantic web agents coordinate web services for the users, and assist the users in accessing the contents derived from the web services.

Inspired by this ability of the semantic web agents with web services, we have been developing an agent-based web service coordination framework. It is called *context-mediated web service coordination*. In the framework, all service processes in ubiquitous computing environments are wrapped in web services that have standard interface and uniform communication protocols. The framework includes web services interfaces of sensor devices, web services on the Internet, and web services that manage user profile, etc. In addition, the web services are wrapped in specific types of agents. Giving a standard agent communication protocol to the heterogeneous service processes, the framework introduces a new agent-based service coordination layer in ubiquitous computing. By coordinating these agents based on user's intention and their physical contexts, we can seamlessly coordinate the heterogeneous service components in the digital world (e.g. Google Web service API [4]) and real world (e.g., sensor devices having Web services interfaces).

Although various web services coordination framework for the business process, such as BPEL4WS [5], WSFL [6] etc., have been proposed so far, the dynamic coordination of the web services in the context of the ubiquitous computing have not been considered yet.

In this paper, we first describe some functional requirements to realize the web service coordination in ubiquitous computing. Then, we propose context-mediated web service coordination as the framework to fill the requirements.

2   Coordination Issues in Ubiquitous Computing

We have shown a question: how can we dynamically coordinate the heterogeneous services and devices physically situated in a ubiquitous environment according to a user's intention? In this section, we address two functional requirements to answer this question. We call the requirements *context-aware matchmaking* and *representation alignment*.

2.1   Context-Aware Matchmaking

Services in ubiquitous computing environment should be selected according not to the service provider's assumption, but also to the user's intention. Thereby, we require a service selection mechanism on behalf of users.

Service selection is easy if the provided services are few and the users clearly recognize their own intentions. However, user selection of a service that matches an intention from among myriad information services (e.g., navigation, guide, information retrieval, controlling device, etc.) becomes difficult when those services are physically co-located.

To surmount this issue, we require a coordination mechanism that assists users in selecting and accessing appropriate services based on their contexts. This study refers to the mechanism as *context-aware matchmaking*.

2.2   Representation Alignment

Recently, many localization-devices, such as GPS, RFID tag system, Infrared sensors, etc., have been adopted. Each device has a certain communication speed, memory capacity, and sensing accuracy. Therefore, their output data formats are usually ad hoc raw information about the locations. For example, while GPS device output shows latitudes and longitudes, output of infrared sensors shows the presence of a user near the devices.

Similarly, many context-aware services that use location-information have been proposed. The services are designed to engage for some tasks, such as navigation. The task usually requires its own spatial representation representing a certain task-oriented view of the environments. For example, to provide some information based on the user's location, the agents should understand the user's location as *"the user is in a museum now,"* rather than as *"the user is at Longitude: 140.38.54 E, Latitude: 35.77.44 N at Mon., Jan 13 12:47:06 2003 JST."* In other words, we require representation alignment between device-oriented information like *"longitude"* and service-oriented information like *"in museum."*

In addition, each user has their own spatial representation about surrounding environments. Users have a personalized, embodied view of environments, sometimes called a *"personal space"* in Social Psychology. Such perceptions of space differ idiosyncratically based on body size, social background, etc.

Most context-aware services that use location-information ignore this difference in spatial representations. They are designed for a specific device and are tightly bound to device-oriented spatial representation. For that reason, it is difficult to place a presupposed device into a different context. For example, a location service that has presupposed RFID-sensor-data cannot be applied to a location service that has presupposed infrared sensor or GPS data.

To surmount this issue, we require a coordination mechanism that manages such diversity of context representation in ubiquitous computing. This study refers the mechanism as *representation alignment*.

3   Context-Mediated Web Service Coordination

We introduce an agent based coordination framework to realize context-aware matchmaking and representation alignment in ubiquitous computing. It is called *context-mediated web service coordination*. Although each agent manages a specific type of web service, their coordination enables users to access heterogeneous web services as a seamless service. The coordination framework is an agent-based extension of *web service architecture* [7] proposed by W3C. The web service architecture is a framework that provides the service that matches service provider agents to service requester agents, and initiates their communication. We extend the web service architecture so as to fill the functional requirements that we have discussed at section 2, context-aware matchmaking and representation alignment. An important extention of the proposed middle agent is an ability managing physical contexts based on a spatial model of an environment, where the services and the users are located.

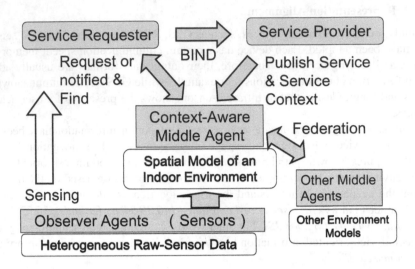

Fig. 1. Context-Mediated Web Service Coordination

Fig. 1 shows an outline of context-mediated coordination. The context-mediated web service coordination framework consists of the following types of agents.

Service Provider (Service Agent) the agent, a proxy-agent of a web service, manages a contents on the Internet. A service Provider asks a middle agent to register not only their capabilities, but also constraints of physical contexts to provide the service (service contexts). They provides requesters with services when the requesters asks them.

Service Requester (Personal Agent) the agent asks a middle agent to register their physical appearance, such as sensor signal ID, and requires service provider agents to perform some service (e.g. web services) on behalf of a human user.

Context-aware Middle Agent the agent plays matchmaker between Service Providers and Service Requesters by considering their locations, capabilities and requirements; it then initiates their communication. They manage the spatial model of environments and reason about service contexts, such as spatial relations of objects, users and service areas.

Observer Agent the agent is a proxy-agent of a sensor device having web service interfaces; it provides sensor information, derived from the sensor device, to the middle agent. Typical observer agents provide the location data of the objects (e.g., paintings, users, etc.).

3.1   Context-Aware Matchmaking

The middle agent plays matchmaker between service providers (e.g., proxy-agents of web services) and service requesters (e.g., personal agent on behalf of a user) by considering their locations, capabilities and requirements. It then initiates their communication. The coordination process is as follows:

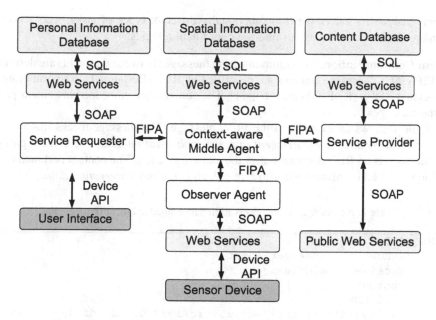

Fig. 2. Context-Mediated Web Service Coordination with Web Services

1. Service providers (e.g., proxy-agents of web services) advertise their capabilities and service contexts, such as service areas, to middle agents;
2. Service requesters request the middle agents to store their public properties that include sensor-based appearances (e.g., RFID tag signal);
3. Observer agents (e.g., proxy-agents of localization sensor devices) request the middle agents to store their sensor specifications and physical settings (e.g. locations of the devices));
4. The middle agents have a world model of the environments. They integrate the received information into the model. They also monitor the sensor data received from observer agents, map the sensor data on the world model. They check the service requesters that match the stored service contexts. If they detect such a requester, they offer the requester to access the service;
5. If the service requester accepts the offer, it asks the service provider to provide the requested services.

Agents with Web Services. Fig. 2 shows relations between the proxy-agents and web services. Each agent in Fig. 1 is a proxy of a web service in Fig. 2. The proxy-agent plays the role of an interpreter between FIPA Agent Communication Language (FIPA-ACL) [8] and Simple Object Access Protocol (SOAP) [9]. FIPA (Foundation for Intelligent Physical Agents) is a organization to standardize agent communication languages and protocols. FIPA-ACL is a well-known agent communication language. SOAP is a specification of communication protocols for the web services. By speaking both communication protocols, it receives requests form other agents, retrieves requested-contents by taking with the web services, and send the contents to the agents. Thus, agents and web services perform functionally different types of tasks; web services manage service contents; agents manage coordination logics.

Agent Communication. All communication messages between the agents are described by FIPA-ACL. Message contents are described by RDF (Resource Description Framework) and RDFS (RDF Schema) [10][11]. The contents are embedded in content parts of the messages.

Table 1 shows an example of the FIPA message. The message means that *an observer agent requests a middle-agent to register observation-data*. The content part of the message is an RDF document after the :content tag. The content part means an action requested by observer-agent, which is *register observation-data*.

Table 1. An example of the observation data embedded in a FIPA message

```
(REQUEST
    :sender      observer-agent
    :receiver    middle-agent
    :content
    "<rdf:RDF
       xmlns:rdf=\"http://www.w3.org/1999/02/22-rdf-syntax-ns#\"
       xmlns:fipa=\"http://localhost/2004/fipa-rdf0#\"
       xmlns:ubis=\"http://localhost/2004/ubicomp-schema#\">
       <fipa:Action  rdf:about=\"#register\"
                     fipa:actor=\"#middle-agent\">
       <fipa:argument
                     rdf:resource=\"#observed-id108028818467\"/>
       </fipa:Action>
       </rdf:RDF>"
    :language    JenaRDFCodec
    :ontology http://localhost/2004/ubicomp-schema
)
```

3.2   Representation Alignment

Fig. 3 shows outline of communications between a context-aware middle agent and other agents. Because a context-aware middle agent should coordinates various formats of spatial information using meta information from devices and services, the context-aware middle agent performs following intelligent tasks;

- management of contextual information based on a world model;
- reasoning about contextual information;
- storing observation data in an information repository;
- interpreting meta-information, such as sensor specifications.

Observation Data. The repository stores a history of sensor data, which we call *observation data*, received from observer agents. Table. 2 is an example of the observation data. The observation data consist of an observer (ubis:observer), an observed-object (ubis:observed), and a observed time (ubis:timestamp). The example

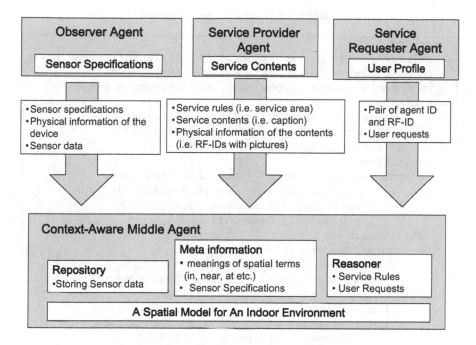

Fig. 3. Communication between a context-aware middle agent and other agents

describes a observation data that means *An RFID-Signal is detected at a 2-dimensional point (13, 6) by RFID-Sensor*. The data is embedded in a content part of a communication messages sent by a observation agent.

An RDF document can be represented by a graph representation that humans easily understand. Fig. 4 is a graph representation of the same observation data described in Table 2. In the figure (and other figures in this paper), oval boxes represent RDF resources; arrows represent RDF and RDFS properties; rounded rectangles represent RDFS classes; rectangle represent literals.

Meta Information for Interpreting Observation Data. Because context-aware middle agents integrate received observation data into a world model, they require meta information to interpret the observation data, such as sensor specifications, data formats, and sensor settings.

Fig. 5 illustrates an example of sensor data meta information sent from an observer agent. The example means that an observer agent, named `rfid-receiver-agent`, send a meta information about an RFID-receiver, named `ex:rfid-receiver-id1080288113454`. The meta information is as follows:

– data formats (`dataType` and `dataUnit`)
– sensor range (`range`)
– location (`at` and `orientation`)

Table 2. An example of observation data

```
"<rdf:RDF
    xmlns:rdf=\"http://www.w3.org/1999/02/22-rdf-syntax-ns#\"
    xmlns:fipa=\"http://localhost/2004/fipa-rdf0#\"
    xmlns:ubis=\"http://localhost/2004/ubicomp-schema#\">
    <ubis:Fact
        rdf:about=\"http://localhost/2004/cyber-
                museum#observed-id1080288113959\"
        ubis:timestamp=\"1080288197468\">
    <ubis:observer
        rdf:resource=\"http://localhost/2004/cyber-
                museum#rfid-receiver-id1080288113454\"
        rdf:type=\"http://localhost/2004/ubicomp-
                schema#RFID-Sensor\"/>
    <ubis:observed>
        <ubis:RFID-Signal
            ubis:id=\"id1080288113463\"
          rdf:about=\"http://localhost/2004/cyber-
                museum#signal-id1080288113463\">
        <ubis:detectAt
          rdf:resource=\"http://localhost/2004/cyber-
                museum#output-id1080288113958\"
          rdf:type=\"http://localhost/2004/ubicomp-
                                schema#Point2D\"
          ubis:x=\"13\"
          ubis:y=\"6\"/>
        </ubis:RFID-Signal>
    </ubis:observed>
    </ubis:Fact>
    <fipa:Action
      rdf:about=\"http://localhost/2004/cyber-
                                museum#register\"
      fipa:actor=\"http://localhost/2004/cyber-
            museum#middle-agent@tokyo.agentcities.net\">
    <fipa:argument
      rdf:resource=\"http://localhost/2004/cyber-
                    museum#observed-id1080288113959\"/>
    </fipa:Action>
</rdf:RDF>"
```

In this framework, the location (ex:floor-segment_3_4), is represented by an RDF resource. We have developed a spatial ontology to describe locations as resources.

Mapping Information Between Agents and Sensor Signals. The middle agents also require mapping information between sensor signals (e.g. RFID tag signals) and users to integrate users' locations into a world model. For that reason, service requester agents request the middle agents to store the mapping information of them. Fig. 6 shows a mapping information between a service requester agent (ex:personal-agent-

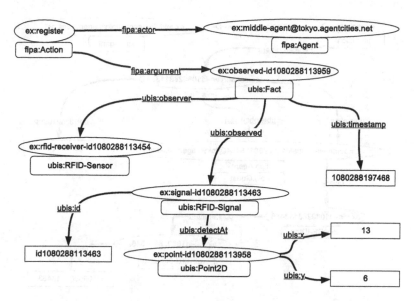

Fig. 4. An example of observation data (Graph Representation)

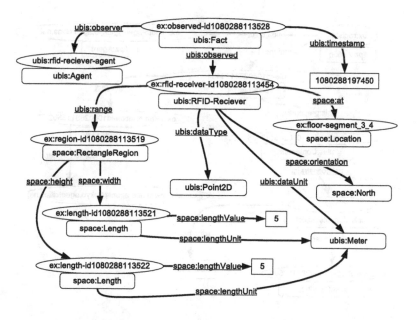

Fig. 5. An example of sensor data meta information sent from an observer agent

id1080288113454@tokyo.agentcities.net) and a sensor device which emit a signal (signal-id1080288113463). Thus, the middle agent can regard the sensor signal as a unique id of the agent. Sensing locations of the sensor signal, the system can keep track of locations of the agent.

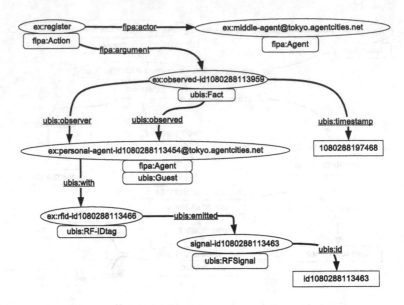

Fig. 6. An example of a mapping information between a sensor-ID and a personal agent

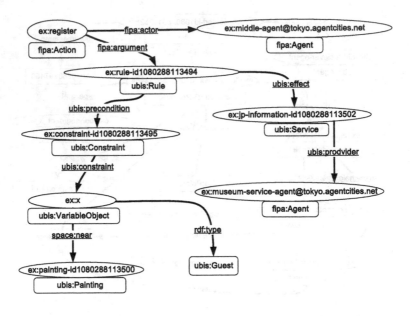

Fig. 7. A service rule (a description of a service context)

Service Context. Context-aware middle agents store service contexts, which is received from service provider agents, as service rules. Fig. 7) shows a example of a service context sent from a service provider agent. A rule consists of a precondition and an effect, like OWL-S [12]. The rules are described by service-oriented qualita-

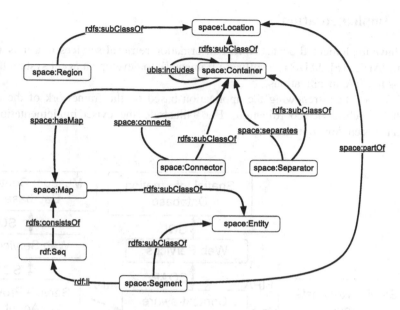

Fig. 8. A part of a spatial ontology

tive representation, such as "near the painting". The middle agent understand physical constraints in precondition based on spatial ontology that we have developed, and periodically checks the applicability of the rules into the observation data.

To understand physical meaning of "service contexts," the middle agent require mapping information between sensor signals and services. In other words, the middle agent needs to know where the services are available. For that reason, service provider agents also request the middle agents to store the mapping information of them.

World Model. The world model, a basic spatial representation to describe observation data and service contexts, consists of the relation of spatial regions, and their properties. The model is described by a spatial ontology that we have developed to describe an indoor space using a tree representation and a grid representation [13]. Fig. 8 shows the spatial ontology.

The tree representation is based on the human understanding of a spatial concept generally called mereological thinking [14], or reasoning about "part-of" relations. The tree-structure represents the relation of 2-dimensional spatial regions and their properties in the spatial ontology. *container* is a spatial region (e.g., room, building, etc.), which is a node of the tree representation. *includes* property represents a "part-of" relation of two *container* nodes.

We also use a grid representation to show the shapes and locations of spatial regions in the spatial ontology. We define *Map* and *Segment* in the ontology. A *Map* is a set of *Segment*s; A *Segment* is a primitive square segment referred by a 2-dimensional location on a *Map*. *partOf* relations represent that the segment is a part of a *Region* represented in a tree-representation.

4   Implementation

We have implemented context-aware information retrieval services in a museum [15] using JADE [16]. JADE is a software framework to develop an agent system that conforms to FIPA specifications.

We have been renewing the application based on the framework of the context-mediated web service coordination, . Fig. 9 illustrates the revised implementation which we have been developing.

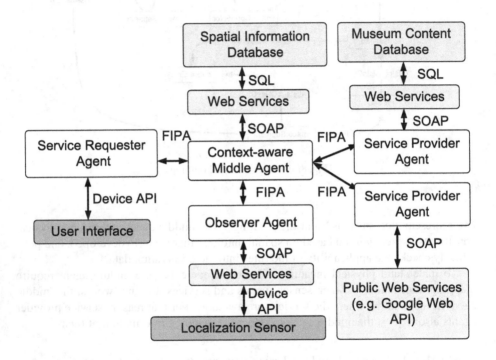

Fig. 9. Agents with web services in the museum system

In that application, agents are aware of the distance between a user and the paintings in the museum. When a user is located near a painting in the museum, the user can receive information about the painting via the user's portable display device. By using our coordination framework, this services can be easily integrated with the web services on the Internet. We have been implementing the service accessing the Google Web Services [4] on behalf of the user in the museum. If the user needs more information about the painting, the user should push the "tell me" button of the portable device. The agents notice the user's request, make a search query about the painting with the necessary information they have already had, e.g., the painting's name and user's preference.

The agent communication process in the revised system is as follows:

1. the service provider agent and the service requester agents inform the middle agent of their profiles and request the middle agent to search for a matched agent based on their service contexts;
2. the are described as some rules. The middle agent stores the service contexts as rules, and watches whether users who matched the rules are located in an environment;
3. the observer agent informs the middle agent where a user with a unique id is located;
4. when the middle agent notices that a user is located on a service region, the agent tells the service requester agents available services;
5. the service requester agent requests a service provider agent to send the service, and receives the service from the service provider agent.

5   Related Work

Numerous studies have addressed context-aware information assistance under the vision of ubiquitous computing [17][18][19]. However, the researches have not applied open distributed environment, such as agentcities networks, handling the context-awareness in ubiquitous computing environments. Thus they lack open connectivities that our agent architecture realized.

CoBrA [20] is a context broker architecture based on software agent system. The broker manages contextual information described by OWL and RDF/RDFS. The broker architecture is similar to our middle agent architecture. However, the broker architecture does not provide interaction frameworks between the broker and the clients, such as observers. The present paper describes the context-mediated web service coordination that provides abstract interaction frameworks between service providers, middle agents, service requesters, and observers, and implements them as context-aware information retrieval systems in museums.

Although some standardized spatial ontologies exist, such as SUMO [21] and Open-Cyc [22], we adopt a newly created spatial ontology on top of RDF/RDFS as a basic representation in spatial repository because SUMO and OpenCyc are not suitable for describing an indoor space, but an outdoor space.

The web service architecture proposed by W3C is regarded as a kind of middle agent architecture [23][24][25] , which have been developed in multi-agent research community. As mentioned previously, the work in this paper is an extension of web service architecture. Hence, results from those studies, such as integration of OWL-S [12], must be useful for our future research. Next steps of our research may be providing a framework for designing coordination logics or scripts described by OWL-S.

6   Conclusion

The paper showed a possibility of an agent-based service coordination layer in ubiquitous computing. We proposed concepts of context-aware matchmaking and representation alignment to realize the service coordination layer in ubiquitous computing. We also proposed an agent-based coordination framework, context-mediated web service coordination, inspired by semantic web agents and web services. We have confirmed the simplest framework of the coordination by applying agents to the context-aware information systems. Using the agent-based coordination framework, we have rapidly developed context-aware information systems. New services can be added to the system by defining the service agents and their ontologies.

References

1. Weiser, M.: The computer for the 21st century. Scientific American (1991) 94–104
2. Web Services Activity. http://www.w3.org/2002/ws/ (2004)
3. Berners-Lee, T., Hendler, J., Lassila, O.: The semantic web. Scientific American (2001)
4. Google Web APIs. http://www.google.com/apis/ (2004)
5. Business process execution language for web services (bpel4ws). http://www.siebel.com/bpel/ (2003)
6. Web service flow language (wsfl). http://www-306.ibm.com/software/solutions/webservices/pdf/WSFL.pdf (2001)
7. Web Services Architecture. http://www.w3.org/TR/ws-arch/ (2004)
8. The Foundation for Intelligent Physical Agents (FIPA). http://www.fipa.org/ (2004)
9. SOAP Specifications. http://www.w3.org/TR/soap/ (2003)
10. Resource Description Framework (RDF). http://www.w3.org/RDF/ (2004)
11. RDF vocabulary description language 1.0: RDF Schema (RDFS). http://www.w3.org/TR/rdf-schema/ (2004)
12. OWL-S 1.0 Release. http://www.daml.org/services/owl-s/1.0/ (2003)
13. Sashima, A., Izumi, N., Kurumatani, K.: Agents that coordinate devices, services, and humans in ubiquitous computing. In: Proceedings of the Eighth International Workshop CIA 2004 on Cooperative Information Agents (LNAI 3191), Springer (2004) 167–182
14. Casati, R., Varzi, A.C.: Parts and Places: The Structures of Spatial Representation. The MIT Press, Cambridge, Massachusetts (1999)
15. Sashima, A., Izumi, N., Kurumatani, K.: Consorts: A multiagent architecture for service coordination in ubiquitous computing. In: Multiagent for Mass User Support (LNAI 3012). Springer (2004) 190–216
16. Java Agent DEvelopment framework (jade). http://sharon.cselt.it/projects/jade/ (2004)
17. Garlan, D., Siewiorek, D., Smailagic, A., Steenkiste, P.: Project AURA: Toward distraction-free pervasive computing. IEEE Pervasive computing 4 (2002) 22–31
18. Chen, G., Kotz, D.: Solar: An open platform for context-aware mobile applications. In: Proceedings of the First International Conference on Pervasive Computing (Short paper). (2002) 41–47 In an informal companion volume of short papers.
19. Roman, M., Hess, C., Ranganathan, A., Madhavarapu, P., Borthakur, B., Viswanathan, P., Cerquiera, R., Campbell, R., Mickunas, M.D.: GaiaOS: An infrastructure for active spaces. Technical Report UIUCDCS-R-2001-2224 UILU-ENG-2001-1731, University of Illinois at Urbana-Champaign (2001)
20. Chen, H., Finin, T., Joshi, A.: Semantic Web in in the Context Broker Architecture. In: Proceedings of PerCom 2004. (2004)
21. Suggested Upper Merged Ontology (SUMO). http://ontology.teknowledge.com/ (2004)

22. OpenCyc. http://www.opencyc.org/ (2004)
23. Decker, K., Sycara, K., Williamson, M.: Middle-agents for the internet. In: Proceedings of the 15th International Joint Conference on Artificial Intelligence, Nagoya, Japan (1997)
24. Sycara, K.P., Klusch, M., Widoff, S., Lu, J.: Dynamic service matchmaking among agents in open information environments. SIGMOD Record **28** (1999) 47–53
25. Paolucci, M., Kawmura, T., Payne, T., Sycara, K.P.: Semantic matching of web services capabilities. In: Proceedings of the 1st International Semantic Web Conference. (2002) 333–347

Realizing a Secure Federation of Multi-institutional Service Systems

Yu Enokibori and Nobuhiko Nishio

Department of Computer Science, Ritsumeikan University,
1-1-1 Noji-Higashi, Kusatsu, Shiga 525-8577, Japan
vori@ubi.is.ritsumei.ac.jp, nishio@cs.ritsumei.ac.jp
Tel: +81 77 561 2741

Abstract. Today, many organizations and individuals are creating a large variety of services. However, even if these services are connected through a network, there are very few examples where such services operate in an interconnected way. One reason for this is the lack of systems that are able to coordinate multiple systems, with different schemes for user management, in a safe way with adequate authorization. Furthermore, the same problem arises when users carrying mobile terminals wishes to connect to and use services at location that they are visiting. In this paper, we are proposing an extended framework for service provision based on Kerberos, allowing groups of services and information about ordinary users that are managed on an organizational or personal level to be combined, handling service systems with different management bases as units of gSpaceh, while defining the security relations between different spaces.

1 Introduction

The prices of various IT equipment has been gradually reduced and a large number of organizations and individuals are constructing a variety of services. At the same time, following the growth of the Internet, a broadband environment that makes it unproblematic to use such services even from long distances is gradually becoming available. However, even if such services were connected through the network, there are still few examples where such services are interconnected in a mutual way. We regard one of the reasons for this to be because the governing bodies/individuals managing users, are different between organizations, and it is necessary to offer mutual security between the different parties. As an example of this, in the case that a user only is authorized in one service system, if such a user is to take advantage of services in another service system, how should the capabilities of the user be handled, and if the user is visiting another organization, how should the user be recognized when the user is to connect to the visited system with their own terminal?

The amount of processing, the complexity, and the difficulty in negotiation, is obstructing the interconnection between separate management bodies, and is a large hurdle for the realization of the ubiquitous society. For distributed

H. Murakami et al. (Eds.): UCS 2004, LNCS 3598, pp. 146–156, 2005.

file systems, Andrew File System [1] (AFS) is an example of a solution to this problem. AFS allows for mutual secure interconnections between distributed file systems managed by different organizations, and is successful in creating a global route with this facility covering the all of the globe. With this paper, we are solving the same problem for the ubiquitous service world, proposing a framework that allows the services and terminals of each individual to be connected freely and mutually in secure and pluggable way in the course of our *United Spaces* Project.

In chapter 2 we discuss technology that is already available, in chapter 3 we discuss our definition of secure, chapter 4 presents the algorithms and frameworks that we used in order to realize the secure system, discussing the unit of gSpaceh, and the use of this definition. In chapter 5 we discuss the user management framework, in chapter 6 the service management, while chapter 7 we discuss the management of each space as a whole, and the inter-space operations of combination and fusion. In chapter 8 we look at applications, before the conclusion in chapter 9.

2   Related Work

There are a number of systems that realize ubiquitous spaces. The Gaia Project [2], IROS [3], Roomware [4] Aware Home, [5] and other projects all realize ubiquitous system. However, they only take into account one institution. Thus, they can not realize secure combination between separately managed institutions.

Mobile Gaia [6] is derived from the Gaia. It creates a personal space that consists of nearby devices, and those devices provide ubiquitous services by co-operated operation that is under the control of a personal space. When the owner moves, a personal space modifies its set and it continues to provide services. A personal space is a unit that provides a ubiquitous system for a person, so personal spaces are managed by separate institutions (individuals). Services and users are able to contact each other between personal spaces. For an individual personal space, Mobile Gaia defines some security schemes. Inside of personal spaces, those owners are able to create simple security policy that identifies which devices are able to connect the space. For devices, those owners are able to define access control that identifies what information or resources a device can share with a specific space name. However, for inter-personal space interactions, this does not define permissions for how to use each securely.

3   Defining Secure Systems

In order to define what we can regard as secure, we regard systems fulfilling the following five points as secure.

1. Systems that have some sort of authorization framework, such that only accepted users can use the system.
2. Systems that can maintain a state where accepted users are only able to use resources that they are authorized to use.

3. Systems where user privacy is not compromised depending upon contents of usage as well as utilization conditions, and where the contents of communication is not interfered with, even by the system administrators of the different systems.
4. Each user contents is protected from third parties with encryption etc.
5. All connections are protected against eavesdropping, imposters, and falsification of contents.

In the same fashion as AFS, by embedding Kerberos [7, 8] as the basic framework, for communication between service and user, and service and service , complete encryption is realized. Furthermore, Kerberos allows for transfer of user authority as a basic login feature, and login timeout can be set, fulfilling several necessary security aspects. By embedding the features that cannot be realized by Kerberos alone, management of the authorities of accepted uses, the method for adapting these to the group of services, as well as the achieving completeness between the service systems, we are realizing a system that is secure according to our premises.

4   System Overview

We regard the set of service systems that is managed by a singular organization or user, as a gSpaceh unit, and we enable mutual secure interconnectivity between these spaces by achieving safety over the communication paths, and by defining the user authentication between each space. gSpaceh is a logical unit, and is not limited to physical spaces such as real rooms or buildings. Service systems located in different rooms can be grouped, and organized as one space. One the other hand, mobile terminals that are carried around by users and their laptop computers can also be regarded as one space, and the secure connection between the mobile terminal and the service system is realized through the connection between the small space and the larger space in this situation. Basic service access model of our system bases on Jini and we have made many secure extensions. When an entity wants to access services, it should be authenticated by a space management mechanism, and obtain a list of available services for it. Afterward, it selects a service from the list and submits an access request to the space manager and establishes a secure connection to the service. Space manager wonft care for this connection basically. Space manager won't care for this already-established connection basically ever after.

As a space indicates the range of a service system managed by a singular subject, user information management and service information management become necessary.

Furthermore, the spaces should be adaptable to diverted information from existing sources. However, there are few cases where information can be adapted as-is, and we use Adapter Interfaces *User Directory Adapter (UDA)* and *Service Directory Adapter (SDA))* in order to bridge the gap between existing user/service information directories and the space management. Also, as it is conceivable that one organization maintains several user information directories and service information directories, multiple Adapter Interfaces might be necessary, and in order to group several Adapters, we use an Integrated Directory for User and Service respectively (*Integrated User Directory (IUD)*, *Integrated Service Directory (ISD)*). Finally, a framework managing the User and Service, handling the two Integrated Directories, as well as offering control of the services to the user, is offered in order to manage the relationship between the different spaces (*Space Server (SS)*). An example of the system with a singular management subject is showed in Figure 1.

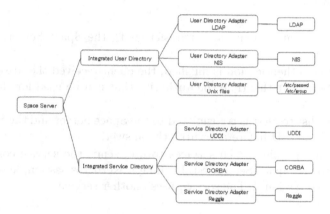

Fig. 1. An Example of Single Space Management System

The components that form the space in Figure 1 are in a tree structure, so that the distinction between all components can be carried out by domain names. Name distinction is carried out in the following way.

$$[UDA/SDAname].[IUD/ISD].[SSname] \tag{1}$$

SS name is usually regarded as the space name. For instance, if the space name is ubi.is.ritsumei.ac.jp, the UDA name is users_ldap, the name becomes users_ldap.IUD.ubi.is.ritsumei.ac.jp. The subject that dynamically uses the resources of the space, are of three categories, clients, the components that forms the space management and Service Providers that provide services. All communication between each component that forms the space, is encrypted using Kerberos, and certification for each entity as well as secure communication links are maintained. These components and Service Providers are set up with a Kerberos Master Key upon deployment. The keys are transmitted and stored in Service Providers by the administrators using an out-of-band mechanism. Basically clients would not be given Master Key so as to accommodate conventional user information directory services (NIS, LDAP, etc.) which are not conscious with Kerberos. Although clients have no Master Key, extending the Kerberos login part, the login transaction is entrusted with the UID, while all communication paths remain secure. For actually using the resources inside a space there are two different procedures. One procedure is that gthe client operates resources inside the spaceh and the other is that ga service manipulates (uses) another serviceh. For the latter in particular, there are two patterns of usage; using a service that is within the authority of a client that is already using another basic service, and a service that uses another service within its own authority. When the authority of the user is used, the authority delegation that is implemented in Kerberos is used. This avoids service usage accidents with authorities that were not intended. The basic flow when the client uses a service inside the space, and when a routed service uses a service is outlined below. ? The client uses resources inside a space.

1. An authentication request is transferred to the Space Server, where it is processed.
2. When the authentication is finished, the client received the session key used by Kerberos. At this time the authority that can be used for this session is fixed.
3. A service list request is transmitted to the Space Server and the Space Server inquiries the ISD before it returns the answer.
4. The client specifies which services to use, sends the service connection requests to the Space Server, establishing a Kerberos session, and establishes the service session. ? The service uses another service.

1. In the case the service is used by a client (the service is not operating autonomously), authority transfer processing is requested to the client.
2. If transfer processing is carried out, the transferred authority is used, and if not, the service uses its own authority, and transmits a connection request for the target service to the Space Server.
3. Upon completing the Kerberos session setup, a session towards the service is established.

In order to establish inter-space security, inter-space communication is basically using the Kerberos framework as well. The spaces that are to be combined creates a space user for the partner space in its user information management module. As the space management server logs in to the target space using this space user, it is confirmed that the space is allowed for space combination in advance, and encryption of the communication links is established.

Furthermore, a space combination is accomplished when an inter-space combination is established with each space on an equal term, while on the other hand a space fusion occurs when one space is absorbed into another space; from the outside of the absorbed space it looks as if one space has disappeared.

After the security of the inter-space communication pathways have been established, the flow is different between the space combination, and the space fusion, as described in later sections of this paper. Below we will discuss the three management frameworks, user management, service management and space management.

5 User Directory Management

User directory management is done by an IUD (Integrated User Directory) which integrates multiple UDAfs (User Directory Adapter) that interpret conventional user management systems to accommodate them into our space management.

5.1 Role

Service access control in a space is done by using gRoleh. When a user is successfully authenticated by a UDA, UDA determines which role should be assigned to the user. This role has a unique name represented by the UDAfs name + Role name. This unique name appears on the Service ACL of SDA shown below in order to judge whether service request is valid or not.

5.2 Key

The authentication information required by UDA includes conventional username/passphrase pair, biometrics features, RFID related ones and so forth depending on UDA-implemented facilities. Therefore, when user tries to get authenticated, he/she has to submit specific information on authentication method, e.g. specific UDA implementation. gKeyh is used for this specification including the following two items: a unique name for UDA which this key should be applied, and authentication information such as username/passphrase, finger print, etc. IUD collects a set of roles which are obtained via UDAfs after authentication processing using this key.

5.3 Key-Ring

Users who have registered to multiple user information directories will require some of such roles simultaneously, while some role should not be in work in an ordinary case. For example, administrator role should be used to the least limit.

Key-Ring is introduced for such case that users want to make an appropriate set of keys occasionally. This set of keys is passed to IUD, and IUD tries to authenticate this user via all the keys passed to all the UDAfs. Afterward IUD preserves all the collected roles for this newly generated session.

6 Service Directory Management

User directory management is done by an IUD (Integrated User Directory) which integrates multiple UDAfs (User Directory Adapter) that interpret conventional user management systems to accommodate them into our space management.

Role
    Service access control in a space is done by using *Roles*. When a user is successful y authenticated by a UDA, UDA determines which role should be assigned to the user.
Key
    The authentication information required by UDA includes conventional username/passphrase pairs, biometrics features, RFID and so forth depending

on UDA-implemented facilities. Therefore, when user tries to get authenticated, he/she has to submit specific information on authentication method, e.g. specific UDA implementation. *Key* is used for this specification including the following two items: a unique name for UDA which this key should be applied, and authentication information such as username/passphrase, finger print, etc.

Key-Ring

Users who have registered to multiple user information directories will require several roles simultaneously, while other role might not be used in ordinary cases. For example, the administrator role should be used as little as possible. *Key-Ring* is introduced for cases where users want to use an appropriate set of keys occasionally. This set of keys is passed to the IUD, and the IUD tries to authenticate this user via all the keys passed to all the UDAfs. Afterward IUD preserves all the collected roles for this newly generated session.

7   Service Directory Management

In order to accommodate conventional service directory systems, we prepare SDA (Service Directory Adapter) interface. For integration of multiple service directory systems, ISD (Integrated Service Directory) is introduced for merging multiple SDAfs and providing an integrated service usage interface. The SDA interface hides protocol difference among multiple service lookup systems like UDDI, Jinifs lookup server or etc. As for the services which donft preserve session information like ones using HTTP, SDA offers them a session management so that they can utilize encryption feature of Kerberos. Each SDA maintains the service-wise ACL information between service and required role for its access. Table 1 illustrates an example of this information table.

Table 1. Service ACL in SDA

Service	Required Role
WebDAV	Bob@UDA.name.IUD.SS.name, ...
Light Control	admin@UDA.name.IUD.SS.name, ...
...	...

8   Space Management

A space consists of a pair of IUD and ISD and the space is maintained by Space Server.

8.1   Space Server

Space Server functions as a KDC of Kerberos, and it also manages user authentication, session initiation between components, space combination/fusion control.

Kerberos specification does not care for a malicious host which pretends as KDC. It does not offer a secure processing before establishing logging-in. Therefore, Space Server and users utilize PKI and digital signature issued by the third party to justify the server and obtain secure logging-in processing. Both of digital signature and PKI are also applied for logging-in among spaces.

8.2   Space Combination

To establish combination between spaces, one space should log into another space. At this moment, any user/resource which belongs to the former space can utilize resources which belong to the latter one in the right of the role which is assigned to the former space from the latter one. When Space A is logging in Space B and has received a role as Bob, all users logging in Space A are capable of utilizing resources in Space B in the right of the role as Bob. Since this is done without any authentication for users in Space A, they donft even have to be registered to Space B. Administrators of Space B only have to take care of the role of space A which represents all the users logging in Space A. This is also secure against imposters who impersonate users logging in Space A. Administrators are free from managing users logging in other spaces. Figure 2 illustrates role handling in space combination.

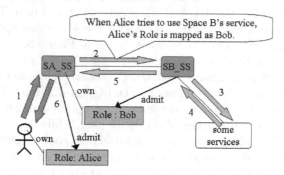

Fig. 2. Example of Using Resource in Two Space Are Combined

Meanwhile, the case shown above is relatively rare because it needs agreement among administrators beforehand. Suppose a certain space which resides in a Note PC has mobility. When this space visit somewhere, it will try to cooperate with spaces there, which have never known it. In such cases, guest role will be assigned, although it depends on the IUDfs administrative policy. Some might prohibit such guest role assignments.

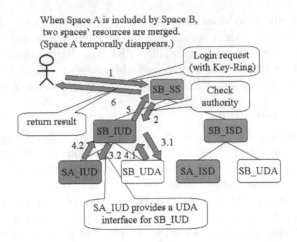

Fig. 3. Example of Using Fusion Space

8.3   Space Fusion

Whereas a union makes a combination on equal terms possible, there is a power relation in a fusion. The space that wishes to go into a fusion, logs in to the other space in order to prove that it has the necessary permissions in order to enter a fusion. Upon a successful login, the ISD and IUD of the space to be fused, is absorbed in the SDA and UDA of the space it is fused into. This framework is realized in a service to service form, where the absorbing space IUD uses the IUD of the absorbed space. The flow is shown in Figure 3.

The name for this space inside the other space at this time becomes g[UDA/SDA distinction name].[IUD/ISD].[absorbed SS name (Space name)] .[Absorbing SS name (Space name)]h. The biggest difference between combination and fusion is that whereas the authorities upon establishing a combination is mapped from the authorities of the space user, while for a fusion the authorities for each individual user can be used across spaces. Due to this, when a service is established across spaces, leveling of authorities does not occur. Also, a feature of the system is that for users that are not familiar with the absorbed space, the space looks reinforced, and they are not even aware that the absorbed space existed (exists) as a separate entity. Because of this, there is no particular need to be conscious about the absorbed space in itself, and the resources of the absorbed space can be used. At this time clients or other spaces in combination, even if they are using services separated by several spaces, only need to carry out identification between client and space, or between several spaces at one time.

9   Application Examples

In the case that ones own mobile terminal constructs its own space, this space is fused with the service system at a visited location, and files inside the mobile host can use presentation services in the visited space. Alternatively, the screen shown by the presentation service can be transferred to ones own screen by a presentation viewer service. By using screen viewer, sound input, and sound system services for service systems at separate locations, secure video conferencing systems can also be constructed.

By establishing and interconnecting spaces in each department of a company, a large space covering all of the company can be constructed, and while distributing the management responsibilities, safe service systems that are available from outside of the company can be constructed. In this case, it is also possible to mount a voice input service in a space that one has authorization, and then find out whether there are any people nearby, for so taking contact with these people. Also, for companies that already have established service systems can be connected securely, and mutual combinatory services can be offered by broker services, or new spaces can be constructed by fusing already fused spaces more, user information and service information can be weaved into a tree structure inside an organization, for so to express the authority level of all organizations inside a larger organization in one policy. Again, by repeating the tree structure, finally even a worldwide root, that expresses roles and service information in the same fashion as AFS can be constructed.

10   Conclusion and Future Work

In this paper, we have proposed a framework to allow separate management subjects to be combined in a secure fashion. Allowing plural ubiquitous environments to be combined, vastly increases the possibilities for existing systems, and we are currently involved in several experimental and research activities towards this goal. Among these, a large number of ubiquitous spaces with differing management subjects are being realized, and we have great expectations towards the improvement of security and practicality for such interconnected systems. In the future we plan to conduct space combination/fusion experiments that traverse network segments and firewalls, as well as conducting evaluations of our current system. Also, for laptops and other small spaces that will frequently traverse between several spaces (and thereby cause combinations/fusions), searching and establishing communications with these mobile spaces will be necessary in order to provide roaming and other services. Even for spaces that are not mobile, we are planning to develop a distributed directory following a P2P approach in order to offer adequate space searches for an increasing number of

Acknowledgments

We would like to thank the Advanced Solution R&D Center at Uchida Yoko, for providing the necessary experimental facilities and personnel in order to realize and verify the system in this paper. We would also like to thank the members at the Ubiquitous Computing and Networking Laboratory at Ritsumeikan University.

References

[1] Satyanarayanan, M.: Scalable, secure, and highly available distributed file access. IEEE Computer May 1990 **23** (1990)

[2] Roman, M., Hess, C.K., Cerqueira, R., Campbell, R.H., Narhstedt, K.: Gaia: A middleware infrastructure to enable active spaces. IEEE Pervasive Computing Magazine **1** (2002) 74–83

[3] Johanson, B., Fox, A., Winograd, T.: The interactive workspaces project: Experiences with ubiquitous computing rooms. IEEE Pervasive Computing Magazine **1** (2002)

[4] Kidd, C.D., Orr, R., Abowd, G.D., Atkeson, C.G., Essa, I.A., MacIntyre, B., Mynatt, E.D., Starner, T., Newstetter, W.: The aware home: A living laboratory for ubiquitous computing research. In: Cooperative Buildings. (1999) 191–198

[5] Johanson, B., Fox, A., Winograd, T.: The interactive workspaces project: Experiences with ubiquitous computing rooms. presented at CoBuild'99 (1999)

[6] Chetan, S., Al-Muhtadi, J., Campbell, R., Mickunas, M.: A middleware for enabling personal ubiquitous spaces. UbiSys '04: System Support for Ubiquitous Computing Workshop at Sixth Annual Conference on Ubiquitous Computing (UbiComp 2004) (2004) Nottingham.

[7] Neuman, B.C., Ts'o, T.: Kerberos: An authentication service for computer networks. IEEE Communications Magazine **32** (1994) 33–38

[8] : (KTH Heimdal) http://www.pdc.kth.se/heimdal/.

Middleware Supporting Various Input/Output Devices for Networked Audio and Visual Home Appliances

Tatsuo Nakajima, Nobuyuki, Kobayashi, and Eiji Tokunaga

Department of Computer Science,
Waseda University
tatsuo@dcl.info.waseda.ac.jp

Abstract. In this paper, we propose universal interaction for networked home appliances, which provides a simple mechanism to fill the gap between traditional user interface systems and advanced user interaction devices. Our middleware enables us to control appliances in a uniform way at any places, and the system allows us to select suitable input and output interaction devices according to our preferences and situations. Our middleware has based on the stateless thin-client system, and translates input and output interaction events according to user interaction devices. Therefore, our system allows us to use a variety of interaction devices without modifying applications using existing GUI toolkits.

1 Introduction

Our daily life will be dramatically changed due to a variety of objects embedding computers. These objects behave intelligently to extend our bodies and memories. These computing environments are widely called *ubiquitous computing*[13]. In *ubiquitous computing environments*, a variety of objects are augmented by containing computers. Since any programs can be executed on the computers, there are infinite possibilities to extend these objects by replacing the programs. Also, these objects have networks to communicate with other objects, thus respective objects will behave more actively by replacing programs at each other according to surrounding situations. For example, our environments may memorize what is going on in the world instead of us, or each object tells us where it currently exists.

There are a lot of researches for realizing ubiquitous computing environments. Some research groups have been working on building prototypes of ubiquitous computing environments[2, 7]. These projects show the impact of ubiquitous computing to our life. Also, recently, several standard middleware specifications are proposed for realizing ubiquitous computing. Jini and UPnP provide mechanisms to discover a variety of services in distributed environments. Also, HAVi(Home Audio/Video Interoperability) enables us to develop networked home appliances. Therefore, ubiquitous computing in home environments will be realized in the near future, and the ubiquitous computing environment is called home computing. This is a very interested field since home computing is

H. Murakami et al. (Eds.): UCS 2004, LNCS 3598, pp. 157–173, 2005.

directly related to our daily life. Also, it is a good candidate to show the effectiveness of ubiquitous computing because every person expects radical advances in home computing environments.

In these environments, one of the most important problems is how to interact with a variety of objects embedding computers. The interaction between us and computers embedded in various objects has been developed by several research groups[5, 11]. These devices enable us to interact with embedded computer more naturally. However, current standard middleware components for networked home appliances have adopted traditional standard graphical user interface systems such as Java AWT or GTK+. Therefore, it is not easy to control home appliances from advanced interaction devices such as PDAs, cellular phones, or a variety of research prototypes described above. Also, natural interaction is changed according to a user's current situation. For example, if a user is cooking a dish. He likes to control appliances via voices, but if he is watching TV on a sofa, a remote controller may be better. This means that the most appropriate interaction device should be dynamically chosen according to a user's current situation and preference, and the selection of interaction devices should be consistent whether he is living in any spaces such as at home, in offices, or in public spaces.

In this paper, we propose universal interaction for networked home appliances, which is a user interface middleware to fill the gap described above. Our middleware allows us to control various appliances in a uniform way at any places, and the system enables an application to use traditional standard graphical user interface systems such as Java AWT or GTK+, but a user can navigate the interface through a variety of devices such as PDAs, cellular phones, or advanced technologies. We show that it is possible to realize the goal very easily based on the stateless thin-client system such as Citrix Metaframe[1], Microsoft Terminal Server[6], and AT&T VNC(Virtual Network Computing) system[10]. We have built a prototype system, and shown that a user can use a variety of interaction devices carried by him. The prototype system is currently integrated with our home computing system[8, 9] that have implemented HAVi(Home Audio/Video Interoperability), which is a standard distributed middleware specification for home appliances, and shows that our system is useful to control home appliances.

The remainder of this paper is structured as follows. In Section 2, we describe desirable user interface systems for home appliances. Section 3 presents the design and the implementation of our user interface system for home appliances. In Section 4, we show how our system works in our home computing system. Section 5 presents the current status of our system, and several experiences with building our system, and we describe related work in Section 6. Finally, in Section 7, we present future work and conclude the paper.

2   Interaction with Networked Home Appliances

Distributed middleware components such as HAVi enable us to control multiple networked home appliances in an integrated fashion. For example, HAVi defines

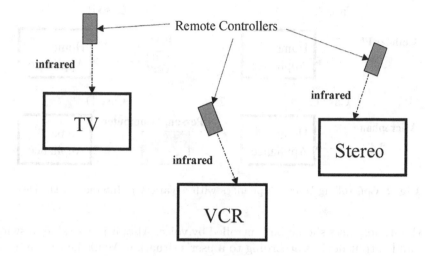

Fig. 1. User Interaction with Home Appliances

API for controlling respective audio and video home appliances. A portable application is able to be created by using the standard API without taking into account the differences among vendors. However, the system gives us a traditional way to interact us with home appliances as shown in Figure 1. As shown in the figure, each home appliance has a different remote controller device to control itself. The approach is not good to support future home appliances since we may have a lot of appliances in our houses, and it will confuse us to use the remote controllers. For example, to control an appliance, we usually need a special remote controller, therefore we need to control several appliances independently, and we need to learn how to use appliances even if the same type of appliances is used. Also, when a user controls an appliance, a system does not understand the situation of a user. Therefore, a user needs to take into account which appliance he likes to control, where the appliance is currently located, and the differences among appliances such as vendors.

We believe that the following three issues are important to realize better interaction with future networked home appliances.

- The appliances can be controlled with a variety of interaction devices such as PDA and cellular phone. Also, input events and output events may be processed in separated devices.
- It is possible to control multiple devices as one appliance.
- The user interface should be customized according to each user's preferences.

The most desirable interaction device to control home appliances should be changed according to a user's preference, currently available interaction devices from him, or his current situation as shown in Figure 2. For example, when both hands of a user are used for something, he cannot control appliances by traditional remote controllers, PDAs, or cellular phones. In this case, it is desirable

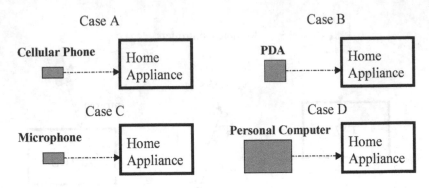

Fig. 2. Controlling Home Appliances with a Variety of Interaction Devices

that these appliances should be controlled by voice. Also, it is desirable to switch input and output devices according to a user's situation. While he sits on a sofa in a living room, he likes to use a universal remote controller to control TV, but while he is cooking, he likes to control TV via his voice. The situation is suddenly changed according to a variety of reasons such as a change of his feeling. This means that flexible interaction should be realized to control home appliances, for example, it is better to switch interaction devices dynamically according to a user's situation.

Also, the user interface system for networked home appliance should provide a mechanism to select input and output devices independently, and change them dynamically even if these devices are connected to different appliances. For example, a display device where user interface is displayed is dynamically changed according to the location of a user. If a large display device is not available in the current room, it is better to show the user interface on the screen of a user's PDA.

As the number of home appliances is increased, the control of these appliances will be difficult due to the complexities. In the future, we will have a lot of home appliances in our houses. Therefore, a mechanism to virtually reduce the number of home appliances is required. One of promising approaches is to compose multiple appliances into one appliance as shown in Figure 3. It makes possible to deal with these multiple appliances as one appliance. Currently, distributed middleware components like HAVi allow us to use respective functions such as tuner, amplifier, display and speaker in different appliances separately. Therefore, it is possible to compose these multiple functions to build a new appliance since a small function makes it easy to compose multiple functions.

Future home appliances will provide rich functionalities. However, if the number of functionalities is increased, this makes it difficult to use these home appliances by most of usual users. To support rich functionalities is important since each user's preference requires to use various optional functions. Therefore, it is important to customize user interface according to the user's preference. Also, it is desirable to use context information of a user to customize user interface. For example, the location information is useful to select a suitable appliance for the user as shown in Figure 4, and the information acquired by monitoring usual behavior of a user is useful to customize the user interface.

3   Design and Implementation

3.1   Design Issues

There are several ways to realize the goals described in the previous section. The most important issue is how to support a variety of interaction devices. Traditional user interface systems assume a few types of interaction devices. For example, mouses, track points, and touch screens are used as input devices. In this section, we describe three alternative approaches to build a flexible user interface system as shown below, and present why our approach is chosen.

- Builds a new user interface system from scratch.
- Builds a new device independent layer that invokes respective traditional user interface systems for a variety of interaction devices.
- Captures input and output events of traditional user interface systems, and transforms the events according to interaction devices.

In the first approach, a new user interface system that can be used with a variety of interaction devices from scratch. The approach is able to survive when a new interaction device appears because the system takes into account to accommodate new interaction devices. However, we need to modify existing applications and middleware components for incorporating the new user interface system, and the development needs to take a long time. Many home computing systems already have adopted existing solutions, therefore it may be impossible to replace the currently used user interface systems.

In the second approach, there are two alternatives to support a variety of interaction devices by adding a new layer on traditional user interface systems.

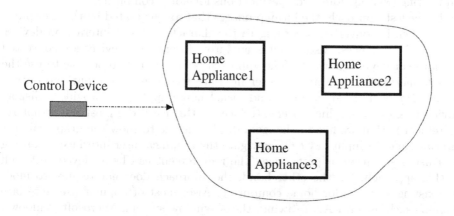

Fig. 3. Composition of Home Appliances

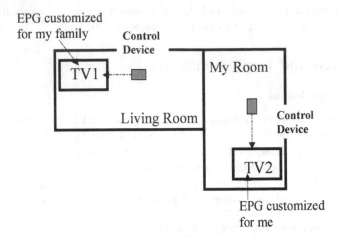

Fig. 4. Context Awareness

In the first alternative, an interaction device independent layer translates the standard requests of applications to the requests for respective user interface systems. For example, in document based approaches[3, 7, 12], each application specifies a document containing how to interact between a user and an appliance. The device independent layer renders the document for respective existing user interface systems. In multiple user interface approaches, which is the second alternative, each appliance provides the *getUI()* method. The method returns a reference to a multiple user interface support service, and the service offers the most suitable user interface for respective interaction devices. The both approaches are very promising, but they require to modify existing applications like the first approach, and the device independent layers should be implemented for respective interaction devices. Therefore, the approach is not suitable for supporting existing standard specifications for home computing.

In the last approach, the bitmap images that are generated by the user interface system is converted according to the characteristics of interaction devices to control appliances. Also, input events from interaction devices are converted to mouse or keyboard events. The approach is limited not to be able to use the layout information in graphical user interface to convert the input and output events. However, most of audio and visual home appliances provide a display device to show a graphical user interface. In this case, the most important requirement is that we like to change a display device to show the graphical user interface and an input device to navigate the graphical user interface according to a user's situation or preference. The requirement can be achieved very well in this approach. On the other hand, the approach does not require to modify existing software for home computing. Also, most of popular user interface systems such as Java AWT/Swing, the X window system, Microsoft Windows, which have been adopted in traditional home computing standard middleware, can be adopted very easily in this approach.

In this paper, we have chosen the third approach since our home computing system implementing HAVi requires to use Java AWT, and we like to use various home computing applications developed on HAVi in the near future without modifying them. Recent interests in the use of embedded Linux to build home appliances make our approach more practical since Linux usually adopts the X window system as its basic user interface system, and our system enables a variety of applications on embedded Linux to be controlled by various interaction devices. The approach makes the development of a variety of embedded applications very easy since the applications can use traditional and familiar user interface toolkits.

3.2   Universal Interaction

In our approach, we call the protocol that can be universally used for the communication between input/output interaction devices and appliances *universal interaction*. *Universal interaction* enables us to control a variety of home appliances in a uniform way. This means that our behavior is not restricted according to where we are or which appliance we like to control. Therefore, our approach provides very natural interaction with home appliances.

In our approach, the output events produced by appliances are converted to *universal output interaction events*, and the events are translated for respective output interaction devices. Also, input events generated in input interaction devices are converted to *universal input interaction events*, and the events are processed by applications executed in appliances. We also define a universal interaction protocol which is a protocol to transfer universal input and output events.

A *universal interaction proxy* that is called the Unit proxy described in the next section plays a role to convert between the universal interaction protocol and input/output events of respective interaction devices in a generic way. The proxy allows us to use any input/output interaction devices to control appliances if the events of the devices are converted to the universal interaction events. This approach offers the following three very attractive characteristics.

The first characteristic is that input interaction devices and output interaction devices are chosen independently according to a user's situation and preference. For example, a user can select his PDA for his input/output interaction. Also, the user may choose his cellular phone as his input interaction device, and a television display as his output interaction device. The user may control appliances by a his gesture by navigating augmented real world generated by a wearable device.

The second characteristic is that our approach enables us to choose suitable input/output interaction devices according to a user's preference. Also, these interaction devices are dynamically changed according to the user's current situation. For example, a user who controls an appliance by his cellular phone as an input interaction device will change the interaction device to a voice input system if his both hands are busy for other work currently.

The third characteristic is that any applications executed in appliances can use any user interface systems if the user interface systems speak the universal interaction protocol. In our approach, we currently adopt keyboard/mouse events as universal input events and bitmap images as universal output events. The approach enables us to use traditional graphical user interface toolkits such as Java AWT, GTK+, and Qt for interfacing with a variety of interaction devices. In fact, a lot of standards for consumer electronics like to recently adopt Java AWT for their GUI standards. Thus, our approach will allow us to control various future consumer electronics from various interaction devices without modifying their application programs. The characteristic is very desirable because it is very difficult to change existing GUI standards.

3.3   System Architecture

Our system uses the thin-client system to transfer bitmap images to draw graphical user interface, and to process mouse/keyboard events for inputs. The usual thin-client system consists of a viewer and a server. The server is executed on a machine where an application is running. The application implements graphical user interface by using a traditional user interface system such as the X window system. The bitmap images generated by the user interface system are transmitted to a viewer that are usually executed on another machine. On the other hand, mouse and keyboard events captured by the viewer are forwarded to the server. The protocol between the viewer and the server are specified as a standard protocol. In the paper, we call the protocol the *RFB(Remote Frame Buffer) protocol*. The system is usually used to move a user's desktop according to the location of a user[2], or shows multiple desktops on the same display, for instance, both MS-Windows and the X Window system.

In our system, we replace the viewer of a thin-client system to the Unit(Universal Interaction) proxy that forwards bitmap images received from a Unit server to an output device. In our approach, the server of a thin-client system can be used as the Unit server without modifying it. Also, Unit proxy forwards input events received from an input interaction device to the Unit server.

Our system consists of the following four components as shown in Figure 5. In the following paragraphs, we explain these components in detail.

- Home Appliance Application
- Unit Server
- Unit Proxy
- Input/Output Devices

Home appliance applications generate graphical user interface for currently available home appliances to control them. For example, if TV is currently available, the application generates user interface for the TV. On the other hand, the application generates the composed GUI for TV and VCR if both TV and VCR are currently available.

The Unit server transmits bitmap images generated by a window system using the RFB protocol to a Unit proxy. Also, it forwards mouse and keyboard events received from a Unit proxy to the window system. In our current implementation, we need not to modify existing servers of thin-client systems, and

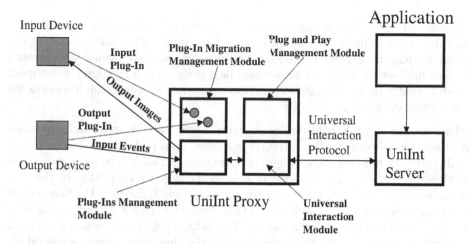

Fig. 5. System Architecture

any applications running on window systems supporting Unit servers can be controlled in our system without modifying them.

The Unit proxy is the most important component in our system. The Unit proxy converts bitmap images received from a Unit server according to the characteristics of output devices. Also, the Unit proxy converts events received from input devices to mouse or keyboard events that are compliant to the RFB protocol. The Unit proxy chooses a currently appropriate input and output interaction devices for controlling appliances. Then, the selected input device transmits an input plug-in module, and the selected output device transmits an output plug-in module to the Unit proxy. The input plug-in module contains a code to translate events received from the input device to mouse or keyboard events. The output plug-in module contains a code to convert bitmap images received from a Unit server to images that can be displayed on the screen of the target output device.

The last component is input and output interaction devices. An input device supports the interaction with a user. The role of an input device is to deliver commands issued by a user to control home appliances. An output device has a display device to show graphical user interface to control appliances.

In our approach, the Unit proxy plays a role to deal with the heterogeneity of interaction devices. Also, it can switch interaction devices according to a user's situation or preference. This makes it possible to personalize the interaction between a user and appliances.

3.4 Implementation of Unit Proxy

The current version of Unit proxy is written in Java, and the implementation contains four modules as shown in Figure 5. The first module is the RFB protocol module that executes the RFB protocol to communicate with a Unit server. The replacement of the module enables us to use our system with different thin-client systems. The module can use the same module implemented in a viewer of a thin-client system. The second module is the plug-in management module that receives input and output plug-in modules from interaction devices, and dynamically links the modules in the Unit proxy. The third module is the plug-and-play management module that detects currently available input and output interaction devices. The last module is the plug-in migration management module that manages the migration of input and output plug-in modules between interaction devices and a Unit proxy.

Management for Available Interaction Devices. The plug and play management module detects the currently available input and output devices near a Unit proxy. In our system, a unique ID is assigned for each type of input/output devices. The Unit proxy broadcasts beacon messages periodically. In the current prototype, interaction devices are connected via IEEE802.11b, Ethernet or infrared networks. When each interaction device receives a beacon message, it replies an acknowledgement message. The acknowledgement message contains the unique ID to identify the device type. If the Unit proxy receives several acknowledgment messages from multiple interaction devices, it chooses one device according to the preference determined by the Unit proxy. Also, when a newly detected device replies an acknowledgement message, the device may be chosen as a currently used interaction device, if the device is more preferable than the currently used device.

When a Unit proxy chooses a new device after the detection of the device, it sends an acknowledgement message before using the device. Then, the Unit proxy sends a terminate message to the device that is used until now. Finally, the Unit proxy waits for receiving a plug-in module from the new device. The preference to select input and output devices is registered in a Unit proxy for each user. If the system cannot detect who likes to use an appliance, a default preference is chosen. Also, each plug-in module supports an event to switch the currently used input and output devices. For example, a user can send a command to change a currently used output device to a Unit proxy. The Unit proxy switches the current output device to the next one until the user selects his favorite output device.

Migration Management of Plug-In Modules. When receiving an acknowledgement message from the Unit proxy, the input/output devices send plug-in modules to the Unit proxy. After the plug-in modules are downloaded in the Java virtual machine executed in a Unit proxy, the plug-in migration module sends a migration complete message to the input/output devices. The MobileSpaces system supports hierarchical agents, and the agents can be communicated when they reside at the same hierarchical level. Therefore, we also implement a Unit proxy as a mobile agent, but the agent does not be migrated to other hosts. However, the feature may be used to move a Unit proxy to a near computer from input and output devices.

Currently, we are using a mobile agent system written in Java, but we consider that the assumption to use Java in every device has a limitation since some devices cannot have Java virtual machines due to several limitations. We are working on building a very small runtime written in the C language to send agents to other computers. The runtime does not execute agents, but can trans-

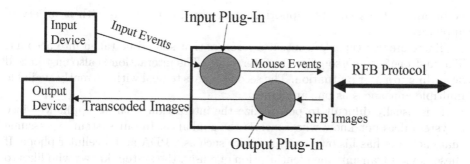

Fig. 6. Plug-In Modules

mit the agents to other runtimes. We believe that such a small runtime is desirable to support a variety of interaction devices. Also, the approach allows us to universally adopt Java based mobile agent systems that provide rich functionalities. This means that it may be possible to build a standard mobile agent system that can be used in any devices that have extremely different requirements.

Life Cycle Management of Plug-In Modules. Figure 6 shows a plug-in management module. The module contains an input and an output plug-in module. The input plug-in module receives events from an input device that is currently selected. The event is converted to a mouse or a keyboard event, and the event is transferred by the RFB protocol to a Unit server. For example, if a user touches a button drawing a right arrow, the event is transmitted to the input plug-in module delivered from a PDA device. The event is translated to a mouse movement event to the right, and the event is finally forwarded to a window system.

Also, after bitmap images are received by the RFB protocol module in a Unit proxy from a Unit server, an output plug-in module processes the images before transmitting to an output device. For example, a color image received from a Unit server is converted to a black and white image. Also, the size of the image is reduced to show on a PDA's screen.

The current version provides three output plug-in modules and four input plug-in modules. The first output plug-in module draws bitmap images on a standard VGA screen, the second one is for a Compaq iPAQ, and the third one is for monochrome display. Also the respective four input plug-in modules process events from a keyboard and a mouse, iPAQ, a game console, and a NTT Docomo's i-mode cellular phone that has a Web browser supporting compact HTML[4].

3.5 Context-Awareness in Home Computing Applications

The role of home computing applications is to allow us to control home appliances easily. The interaction between a user and home appliances will become more complex since the functionalities of appliances will be richer and richer. Also, the number of appliances will be increased in the future. Therefore, future home applications should support context aware interaction with a variety of appliances.

There are two types of context awareness that should be taken into account. The first one is to personalize the interaction. The interaction is also customized according to a user's situation. The second type is to deal with currently available multiple appliances as one appliance.

It is usually difficult to personalize the interaction with an appliance since a system does not know who controls the appliance. In our system, we assume that each user has his own control device such as a PDA and a cellular phone. If these devices transmit the identification of a user, the system knows who likes to control the appliance. However, in our system, there is no direct way to deliver such information to a home computing application from interaction devices since we assume that the application adopts traditional user interface systems that do not support the identification of a user. Therefore, in our current implementation, each user has a different Unit server that executes personalized applications for each user. The application provides customized user interface according to each user's preference. The Unit proxy chooses an appropriate Unit server according to the identification of a user acquired from an input device.

Our system needs to know which appliances are currently available according to the current situation. In the current system, we assume that an application knows which appliances can be available. For example, if the application supports three home appliances, the application needs to provide seven graphical user interfaces with the combination of the three appliances. The user interfaces are selected according to the currently available appliances. In our system, we assume that each home appliance is connected via IEEE 1394 networks. Since IEEE 1394 networks support a mechanism to tell which appliances are currently connected and whose power switches are turned on, it is easy that the application easily knows the currently available appliances, and selects the most suitable user interface.

The approach described in this section is not ideal, but we can show the effectiveness of context-awareness in our system. In the future, we need to improve the support of context-awareness in a more systematic way.

3.6   Input and Output Interaction Devices

In our system, a variety of interaction devices are available, and the input devices and output devices may be separated or combined. For example, a graphical user interface can be displayed on the screen of a PDA or a large display device on TV. The user interface displayed on TV can be navigated by a PDA device. Therefore, a user can choose a variety of interaction styles according to his preference. Also, these devices can be changed according to the current situation. For example, when the currently used interaction devices are unavailable, another interaction device may be selected to control appliances.

We assume that each device transmits a plug-in module to a Unit proxy as described in Section 3.4.3. However, some input devices such as a microphone may not be programmable, and it is difficult to support the communication to a Unit proxy. In this case, we connect the device to a personal computer, and the computer communicates with a Unit proxy to deliver a plug-in module. However, it is difficult to know when a program on the personal computer returns an acknowledgement message when a beacon message is received from a Unit proxy since the computer does not understand whether a microphone is currently available or not. Therefore, in the current prototype, we assume that the device is always connected and available. However, it is expected to embed a processor in a microphone, and implement our user interface system without a great effort.

4   How Does Our System Work?

4.1   Controlling AV Appliances with PDA

When an application recognizes that currently available appliances are a television and a video recorder, it shows a graphical user interface for controlling them. Since the current user does not interested in the TV program reservation, the application draws a user interface containing power control, TV channel selection, and VCR function to its Unit server. As described in Section 3.5, a Unit proxy selects a Unit server executing an application drawing a customized user interface for the user who likes to control these appliances, and the selected Unit server transmits bitmap images containing the interface to the Unit proxy.

Let us assume that the Unit proxy detects that the user has a PDA device. The PDA device delivers input and output plug-in modules to the Unit proxy. The Unit proxy transcodes bitmap images transmitted from the Unit server using the output plug-in module before transmitting the images to the PDA device. In this case, 24 bits color images whose image size is 640x480 are reduced to monochrome images whose size is 180x120. Also, input events on the touch screen of the PDA device are converted to mouse and keyboard events by the input plug-in module. However, we assume that the user likes to see the graphical user interface on a bigger display now. The user transmits a command to the Unit proxy by tapping on the screen. When the Unit proxy detects it, the bitmap images containing the graphical user interface are forwarded to the display system, and the images are converted by the output plug-in module provided by the bigger display before transmitting them. Also, the user interface will be displayed again on the screen of the PDA device by tapping the PDA's screen.

4.2   Controlling CD Player with Cellular Phone and Voice

In this section, we show a scenario where a user controls a CD player using his cellular phone, but it will be controlled by voice when the cellular phone is turned off.

A Unit proxy makes the input plug-in module for a cellular phone activated if it recognizes that a user has a cellular phone. Also, an output plug-in module is downloaded to use a TV display for showing a graphical user interface. Therefore, bitmap images transmitted from the Unit server are displayed on the TV display. If a user pushes a button on the cellular phone, the event is transferred to the Unit proxy. The Unit proxy converts the event to a mouse movement event, and sends it to a Unit server to simulate the movement of a mouse cursor. When a user pushes another button, the Unit proxy translates it to a mouse click event. Then, the Unit server forwards the event to an appropriate application, and the application recognizes that a button such as a play button is pushed.

Now, let us assume that the user turns off the power switch of his cellular phone. In this case, a voice recognition software on his personal computer is selected as an input interaction device since the user does not carry other currently available input devices. Thus, the Unit proxy needs to download the input plug-in module for voice control from the personal computer. The plug-in module translates texts converted by the voice recognition software to mouse and keyboard events to control the CD player.

4.3   Controlling a TV Appliance Using a Wearable Device

In this example, we like to show that our approach enables us to use advanced wearable devices to control various home appliances. Let us assume that a user wears a head-mounted display that cannot be distinguished from prescription lenses, and he wants to control a television. In this case, the graphical user interface of the television is displayed on his glass. The user navigates the graphical user interface via his voice.

The Unit proxy converts the image size that is suitable for displaying on the glass. If a user takes off the glass, the graphical user interface is automatically displayed the graphical user interface on the display near the user. The voice is also used to move the cursor on the graphical user interface. The voice is translated to keyboard/mouse events in the Unit proxy and these events are delivered to the application executed in the television.

In the future, our cloth will embed a display and a control panel, and the cloth can be used to control a variety of appliances. The future wearable computing is very attractive for using our system.

5   Current Status and Experiences

In this section, we first describe the current status of our prototype system, then we discuss several experiences with building our prototype system to control networked home appliances.

5.1   Current Status

Our system have adopted the AT&T VNC system[10] as a thin-client system, and the VNC server can be used as the Unit server without modifying it. The current prototype in our HAVi-based home computing system[8, 9], where HAVi is a standard specification for digital audio and video, emulates two home appliances. The first one is a DV viewer and the second one is a digital TV emulator. Our application shows a graphical user interface according to currently available appliances as described in the previous section. Also, the cursor on a screen that displays a graphical user interface can be moved from a Compaq iPAQ. However, if the device is turned off, the cursor is controlled by other devices such as a game console. It is also possible to show a graphical user interface on the PDA device according to a user's preference. Also, the current system has integrated cellular phones to control home appliances. NTT Docomo's i-mode phones have Web browsers, and this makes it possible to move a cursor by clicking special links displayed on the cellular phones. In our home computing system, Linux provides an IEEE 1394 device driver and an MPEG2 decoder. Also, IBM JDK1.1.8 for the Java virtual machine is used to execute the HAVi middleware component.

Figure 7 contains several photos to demonstrate our system. Currently, our home computing applications are executed on HAVi, and a control panel is written by using Java AWT. In the demonstration, if both a DV camera and a digital TV tuner are simultaneously available, the control panels for them are combined as one panel. As shown in the photo(Top-Left), the control panel can be navigated by both a cellular phone(Top-Right) and a game console(Bottom-Left). Also, the control panel can be displayed and navigated on a PDA(Bottom-Right).

Our middleware proposed in this paper enables us to use various interaction devices and to interact with the appliances in a context-aware way. By integrating home appliances with our middleware, a user is allowed to choose the most suitable interaction device according to his situation.

Fig. 7. Current Status of Our System

5.2   Experiences

In this section, we show three experiences with building the current prototype of a user interface system for networked audio and visual home appliances.

Limitation of Our System. In our system, a bitmap image that contains a graphical user interface is transferred from a Unit server to a Unit proxy. Since the image does not contain semantic information about its content, the Unit proxy does not understand the content. For example, it is difficult to extract the layout of each GUI component from the image. Therefore, it is not easy to change the layout according to the characteristics of output devices or a user's preference. Also, our system can deal with only mouse and keyboard events. Thus, the navigation of a graphical user interface can be done by emulating the movement of a cursor or pressing a keyboard and mouse buttons. If the limitation makes the usability of a system bad, other approaches should be chosen. However, navigating a graphical user interface from a PDA and a cellular phone provides very flexible interaction with home appliances. Our experiences show that home appliances usually allow us to use a large display and show graphical user interfaces on the display to control the appliances. Thus, we believe that our system has enough power to make future middleware components for home appliances flexible.

Better Control for Home Appliances. Our system can control any applications executed on standard window systems such as the X window system. In our home computing system, traditional applications coexist with home computing applications, and these applications can also be controlled in an integrated way by our system. For example, we can navigate an MP3 player or a Netscape browser running with home computing applications via our system. However, the overlapping window layout is painful to be navigated by our user interface system. We consider that the tiled window strategy is more suitable for controlling home appliances. Also, our experience shows that we can control both home appliances and traditional applications such as presentation software and web browsers by using our system in a comfortable way if our system supports the movement of a mouse cursor at a variety of speeds.

6   Conclusions

This paper has described a new user interface system to fill the gap between traditional graphical user interface systems and advanced input/output interaction devices for networked home computing. We have also described the effectiveness of our system by demonstrating our system to control our home computing system.

Our system does not analyze the content of bitmap images containing graphical user interface. Therefore, it is not easy to use our system unless bitmap images are translated for output devices, or input events are translated to mouse or keyboard events, but we believe that our system is enough to control networked audio and visual home appliances since these appliances are usually used with a large display device. Also, our system can be used to control a variety of applications running on Windows and Linux like Pebble.

References

1. Citrix Systems, "Citrix Metaframe 1.8 Background", Citrix White Paper, 1998.
2. Andy Harter, Andy Hopper, Pete Steggles, Andy Ward, Paul Webster, "The Anatomy of a Context-Aware Application", In Proceedings of the 5th Annual ACM/IEEE International Conference on Mobile Computing and Networking, 1999.
3. T. Hodes, and R. H. Katz, "A Document-based Framework for Internet Application Control", In Proceedings of the Second USENIX Symposium on Internet Technologies and Systems, 1999.
4. T.Kamada, "Compact HTML for Small Information Appliances", W3C Submission, http://www.w3c.org/TR/1998/NOTE-compactHTML-19980209.
5. N.Khotake, J.Rekimoto and Y.Anzai, "InfoStick: an interaction device for Inter-Appliance Computing", Workshop on Handheld and Ubiquitous Computing (HUC'99), 1999.
6. Microsoft Corporation, "Microsoft WIndows NT Server 4.0: Technical Server Edition, An Architecture Overview", Technical White Paper 1998.
7. M. Munson, T. Hodes, T. Fischer, K. H. Lee, T. Lehman, B. Zhao, "Flexible Internetworking of Devices and Controls", In Proceedings of IECON, 1999.
8. T. Nakajima, "Experiences with Building Middleware for Audio and Visual Networked Home Appliances on Commodity Software", In Proceedings of ACM International Conference on Multimedia, 2002.
9. T. Nakajima, "System Software for Audio and Visual Networked Home Appliances on Commodity Operating Systems", In Proceedings of the IFIP/ACM International Conference on Distributed System Platforms - Middleware 2001, 2001.
10. T.Richardson, et al., "Virtual Network Computing", IEEE Internet Computing, Vol.2, No.1, 1998.
11. I.Siio, T.Masui, K.Fukuchi, "Real-world Interaction using the FieldMouse", In Proceedings of the ACM Symposium on User Interface Software and Technology (UIST'99), 1999.
12. User Interface Markup Language, http://www.uiml.org/
13. Mark Weiser, "The Computer for the 21st Century", Scientific American, Vol. 265, No.3, 1991.

Bazaar: A Conceptual Framework for Physical Space Applications

Kaori Fujinami, Tetsuo Yamabe, and Tatsuo Nakajima

Department of Computer Science,
Waseda University, Tokyo, Japan
{fujinami, yamabe, tatsuo}@dcl.info.waseda.ac.jp

Abstract. In ubiquitous computing era, the notion of context-awareness will play an important role. An application should be aware of its operating context for supporting and enriching human activities. Such contextual information is required to be extracted as seamlessly as possible through interaction between users and surrounding environments. This leads to the need for dealing with a wide variety of contextual information from a physical world.

In this paper, we propose a conceptual framework, *Bazaar*, for modeling the physical world and for manipulating the model. It constructs the model with self-descriptive objects represented as a set of triples. Additionally, it provides a programming model for a developer so that he/she can intuitively manipulate the model and develop an application. We also report experiences with building a sample application.

1   Introduction

The advancement of technologies, such as wireless communication technologies and high performance downsized computation, allows intelligence to be spontaneously embedded into everyday living spaces and to be connected to networks[6]. Such a computing environment is often referred to as a ubiquitous computing environment[24], and has been investigated since early 1990's.

In ubiquitous computing era, the notion of context-awareness will play an important role and one of the exciting research topics[5][21][20]. A system that is aware of its operating situation, i.e. context, can adapt its behavior to a user. This can be considered to make two major contributions to our everyday lives. One is assisting us by extracting relevant information from flooding of information. For example, let us consider a case in which networked room lights are installed into an office and a user staying one room wants to move to another. The user then need not to be aware of the names or network addresses of the lights to turn off and on. Instead he/she should only move to the room, and context-aware room light controller should do the rest. The other is enriching our daily living with value added services. For example, if someone forgets to take an important thing that is required for him/her based on sensed context, a context-aware belongings checker is able to alert that it is left behind[9].

H. Murakami et al. (Eds.): UCS 2004, LNCS 3598, pp. 174–191, 2005.

Contextual information is required to be extracted as implicitly as possible through interaction between users and surrounding environments. This leads to the needs for handling a wide variety of contextual information from a physical world, e.g. the existence on particular location[12], co-locating[2], the state of use of everyday object[11], and so on. We have presented a notion of Sentient-Materials to extract contextual information implicitly through the use of sensor augmented everyday objects[25]. If collected information is more likely to the real situation and an appropriate interpretation facility is provided, a user will feel less burdensome because a system can act autonomously based on what the user might perceive. Applications in a physical space can often consume the same kind of contextual information. Such information should neither be extracted by one application nor used only by itself. Therefore, it should be managed apart from an application itself and shared with another with some system supports. This is often called a *world model*[12][17].

In this paper, we propose a conceptual framework, *Bazaar*, for modeling physical world ensuring that the extracted information from this model can be shared between applications and will help the developer to build space-based context-aware applications. The model is constructed with self-descriptive objects that are represented as a set of triples. It is expected that such objects will build the model flexibly because unified specifications are less required than rigid object-oriented modeling. Additionally, it provides a programming model for a developer so that he/she can intuitively manipulate the model and develop an application. This contributes to the developer in that it hides details on building the model like internal representation of a world and methods to collect data from sensors, instead it provides him/her with a unified interface. We also report experiences with building a sample application.

The structure of this paper is as follows. In section 2, roles of a world model and requirements for it will be introduced. Section 3 will examine related work. Section 4 will describe the proposed conceptual framework, *Bazaar*, as well as two key design points and their issues. In section 5, we will describe implementation of *Bazaar* and an example application. Section 6 will discuss on issues raised during the development, and finally, section 7 concludes the paper.

2   A World Model

In this section, we point out roles and requirements of a world model.

2.1   Roles of a World Model

In this section, we describe the roles of a world model.

- **Shared knowledge between applications:** An application uses the same or a part of contextual information which is used by other applications. Combining information from multiple applications can make the applications more reliable in inferencing contextual information as well as enables a developer to build new applications. Suppose a sensor augmented cellular

phone cradle which knows its state of use, the state "non-existence" of the
cellular phone on the cradle can be combined with the state "sit by none"
of a sensor augmented chair to infer the absence of its owner. In such a case,
sharing states of multiple objects, makes the inference of current context
more reliable. Therefore, a shared model of a world is required. Without
such a model, an application has to extract contextual information by itself even if another application that uses the same information exists. This
requires significant extra work for a developer.

– **Shared knowledge between a developer and an environment:** In
addition to the advantage of sharing information among applications, developers can be benefited from the intuitiveness of the world they live in.
They can easily find and use an appropriate component for building an application, e.g. physical object, sensor, and context, by physical attributes,
e.g. location, color, or state of object of interest. For example, if a query like
"select *states* from *chairs* where *in partition-1*" is put to the world model, it
is expected to return a software component which represents states of chairs
located in *partition-1*. This requires neither a knowledge of an IP address
nor an ID of the chair. Instead, this uses highly abstract information which
is familiar with a person living in a physical space. A developer can build an
application as if he/she were in the application space.

Thus, a world model is expected to be a basic infrastructure for a context-
aware application.

2.2   Requirements for a World Model

A list of requirements for a world model is as follows:

– **Semantically rich representation and flexible querying:** Many kinds
of information can be contextual information. This includes not only a state
of usage of an object, but also location, type, owner, and even color of it.
Moreover, their collection and combination can be the one. Let's suppose
"Context-aware Juke-box", a context-aware juke-box in a restaurant, which
can select the most suitable music according to the number of customers. It
has been noticed that there is a chemistry between size of a group and type
of a background music(BGM), e.g., a group of a few persons seems to like
slow and mild BGM, while a large group may prefer with up-tempo. Size
of the group can be obtained by the number of chairs whose state are "sit
by someone". This is the case with contextual information from collective
property of a group. Therefore, the model should manage such rich semantics
as well as providing flexible querying mechanisms.

– **Flexibility in handling heterogeneous elements:** In a real world, an
object like a chair, a cradle, or a door is to be made by a different manufacturer. So, it is hard to standardize all attributes of objects in advance.
Number of attributes that objects can have might be different even for the
same kind of object. Moreover, the semantics of an attribute of one object
can differ from that of another. Manufacturers can also produce new products of same type with different attributes. This heterogeneity is essential

for a ubiquitous computing environment. In order to be a practical model, the model has to be tolerant with the heterogeneity and deal with this appropriately.

- **Dynamicity of the model:** In an outdoor world model, the geographical and geometric feature do not change so often as in an indoor one. For example, a shape of a city or a building does not change in a short duration while the location of a chair can change in an hour. It may be cost effective to build outdoor model in a top down manner with rigid design because such a model can be shared with many applications for a period of time once it is built. In other words, it is hard to fix an indoor world model in advance. So, it should be built as autonomously as possible so that it can handle dynamicity of objects.

- **Intuitive manipulation:** A world model should not be only semantically rich and flexible to both heterogeneity and dynamicity as described above, but also should be manipulated as easy as possible. Since a world model plays the role of a bridge between a developer and an environment, it is useless if he/she cannot manipulate it without heavy cognitive burden.

In the next section, we examine related work.

3   Related Work

Existing works model a world in a top down manner based on object-oriented apporach. They provide basic types of objects as super classes and extend them if needed, which requires quite careful prior analysis on the types of super classes and attributes of them in advance. NEXUS[17] is a platform for mobile and spatially aware applications, which provides a common data model for location-related information called Augmented World(AW) Model. It provides a model of elements of world such as rooms, buildings, streets, areas, cities, or also mobile objects in a form of class file. It must be designed in a top-down manner. If a new class is required in some local AW, it is defined as a sub-class of appropriate one. In case of interoperation between different AWs, only methods and fields in common super-class can be accessed because each AW does not know domain specific information.

The Sentient Computing project[12] targets an indoor application with the Active Bat location system. It has limited numbers of physical object model like people, computers, keyboards and telephones. It was implemented using Common Object Request Broker Architecture(CORBA). We consider that purely object-oriented manner is not cost effective, especially indoor system, and it is not practical in use. However, this project also introduces a notion of *programming with space*, which allows a developer to use an event-driven style of programming that treats spaces on the floor as buttons on a traditional GUI display. In this case, mobile entities like people play a role of mouse pointers. To the best of our knowledge, it is not clear how to get the desired area or artefact and what kinds of API it provides beyond such a location focused API.

The MediaCups project[2] aims at augmenting everyday artefacts with sensors and establishing communication with each other based on contextual proximity. It has an inherent location model called the RAUM [3]. It requires no central information management facility, instead each artefact locally manages its own location information. However, it lacks of semantically richness other than location.

From the perspective of semantically richness of a world, Burnett et al. describe the importance of dealing with complex characteristics in a world model[4]. They present tree-based object model containing ID, communication specification of a device, type of device as well as location. There is no discussion on software infrastructure because they focus on building an ontology for location and context-aware environment.

The ContextToolkit[7] is well known for a context-aware application development environment. It offers fine component-based abstraction for both a sensor device and an entity that has many contextual information: *Widget* and *Aggregator*. These components are utilized to provide an application with an abstract view of contextual information. They can be managed in *Discovery* component, and queried from other component. However, since it provides quite low level APIs and there is no formal model of world, an application developer has to construct appropriate component repository by him/herself. Therefore, it is difficult to build a large scaled application which contains numerous and diverse kinds of physical object.

Based on these thoughts, we will introduce *Bazaar* conceptual framework for modeling and manipulating a world model.

4   *Bazaar* Conceptual Framework

4.1   Basic Design

Figure 1 shows overall architecture of this framework.

Bazaar conceptual framework consists of six major parts. This includes, 1) an identifiable object as a source of low level contextual information, 2) a sensor and actuator as interfacing functions, 3) Bazaar World Model Manager(BWMM) that constructs and maintains an appropriate area of world, 4) contextual extraction framework that interprets and makes the low level contextual information available to the application as highly abstract information, 5) application logic that a developer has to build, and 6) application programming interfaces(APIs).

Bazaar's core concept is representation of a physical world with self-descriptive objects. This is led by the requirements: flexibility and dynamicity. Each object constructing an application can provide its attributes to the model in its own semantics, i.e. different vocabulary. Each of these attributes can be considered as a metadata of the object. So, we think it is natural to adopt the Resource Description Framework (RDF)[15] which is getting much attention in semantic web technology[23] to provide interoperability between computational entities. In addition, third party software for handling RDF, e.g. IsaViz[14] as visualization tool and Jena[13] as semantic web application framework, allows a developer to concentrate on his/her own tasks. We expect RDF to meet the above requirement: semantically richness of description and flexible querying.

A unique identifier (ID) has to be assigned to each object so that the object can link itself to descriptive information and to represent its presence in cyber space. The ID with location may be 1) detected automatically by some kinds of technologies such as radio frequency identifier system (RFID), ultrasonic location system and so on, 2) reported by itself from self-positioning like the Global Positioning System (GPS), or 3) registered manually. This means an object is able to be a part of a world if the ID is registered with BWMM in any way. If a new ID is added to BWMM, IDResolver resolves the location of descriptive information where the information is retrieved. It is similar to Auto-ID's Object Name Service(ONS)[1].

The framework also provides a programming model for intuitive manipulation of the world model. It provides the developers seven familiar types of components on object and notion existing in physical environment, i.e. world, location, state, sensor, actuator, command, and artefact (physical object). We will describe two key design points and their issues in the following sections.

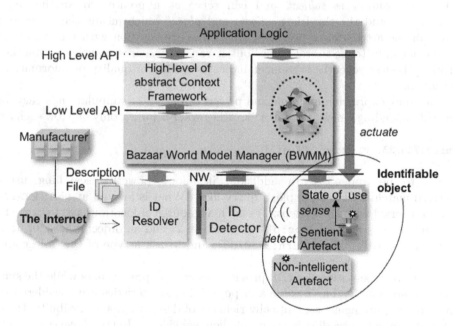

Fig. 1. Overall architecture of *Bazaar* conceptual framework

4.2 Flexible and Powerful Model with RDF

As described above, every object has self-descriptive attributes including name, type, manufacturer, type of sensor(s) it has, size, and so on. In addition to static ones, dynamic one can be included: current state of use, location, owner, etc.

Much more describable information like quality of information, e.g. accuracy and precision of extracted state, and format of time expression, can be applied, which is expected to provide an application with portability and reliability[9]. Not only a type of attribute, but also a vocabulary can vary even in the same type of object by different manufacturers.

In RDF, every attribute can be simply represented as a form of triples: *subject* (or *resource*), *predicate*, and *object*. For example, a statement like "a chair located at partition-1 is being sit by someone with accuracy of 0.8" can be represented as follows, where "1750733" in *subject* is the ID of the chair:

```
1: (urn:1750733, v1:type, "chair")
2: (urn:1750733, v2:location, urn:loc:p1)
3: (urn:loc:p1, v2:name, "partition-1")
4: (urn:1750733, v3:state, urn:state:s)
5: (urn:state:s, v3:meaning, "sitting")
6: (urn:state:s, v3:quality, urn:qoi:a)
7: (urn:qoi:a, v3:accuracy, "0.8")
```

The first column is *subject*, and can serve as a pointer to another one. The second and the third is *predicate* and *object* which means the name and value of the attribute, respectively. In RDF representation with triples, *object* needs not only to be literal value, but it can be *resource* pointing to another triple. The last(seventh) statement indicates a kind of quality of information, *accuracy*.

Not only expression is simple and powerful, but also manipulation is easy. In case of appending a new attributes like "the owner is Fuji.", only one row such as:

```
(urn:1750733, v1:owner, "Fuji")
```

needs to be appended. In addition, it allows powerful searching using pattern matching. For example, a query like, "What is located at partition-1?" can be queried with three steps: 1) search a resource of location "partition-1" and get the answer "urn:loc:p1" in this case, 2) find an object whose location is "urn:loc:p1" and get "urn:1750733", and 3) ask a type of the object and reach the final answer "chair".

Thus, representation by RDF provides a strong expressiveness while the syntax is quite simple. The flexible and powerful characteristics are considered to meet the requirements: semantically richness of description and flexibility. However, semantic transcoding is quite a challengeable issue. In the above statement, three vocabularies are used: v1, v2, and v3. They exist as a prefix in the *predicate* of each statement and indicate namespaces. If two same kind of objects have different vocabularies, for example v2:location and v4:place as location of an object, then a software entity should internally exchange one to another like a translator to encapsulate the difference. However, in our framework, the technique to encapsulating such a difference is an issue for future work.

4.3   Programming Model

As described in section 4.1, *Bazaar* provides a developer with seven basic elements of a world as a collection of classes in object-oriented language. BWMM maps all attributes of an instance of an appropriate class to "key - value" based table, for example `Hashtable` in Java. This seems to loose the benefit of object-oriented language and tools: inheritance and introspection by rigid modeling. However, as described in section 2.2, heterogeneity in a ubiquitous computing environment is hard to fully model in advance. So, we have modeled only seven types, and others are to be set to and get from the table. This design decision will be discussed later. Although RDF Data Query Language(RDQL)[22] provides environments for manipulating RDF data model using SQL-like query, we consider a developer should not concern about syntax of the model. *Bazaar* internally utilizes RDQL and maps it to APIs described below.

Three basic operations are provided for each type of class: 1) get an appropriate instance of a class by attribute(s) from BWMM, 2) poll a value from the instance by name, and 3) put a callback reference to the instance if he/she hopes to receive a change of value of the attribute as an event. The last operation is the same as that for a GUI widget and considered to be easily accepted by today's developers. We introduce these classes and some of interfaces below, where `attr` is the abbreviation for the term *attribute*.

- **World, a class of a world:** It provides interfaces for obtaining the basic types by varieties of attributes from BWMM. Especially, obtaining instances of `Artefact` by an instance of `Location` is intuitive because it is similar to the action of searching objects in physical space.

  ```
  Location[] getLocationsByAttrs(Hashtable a)
  Location[] getLocationsByID(String id)
  Artefact getArtefactByID(String id)
  Artefact[] getArtefactsByAttrs(Hashtable a)
  Artefact[] getArtefactsByLocation(Location l)
  Artefact[] getArtefactsByState(String type, String state)
  Sensor[] getSensorsByAttrs(Hashtable a)
  Actuator[] getActuatorsByAttrs(Hashtable a)
  ```

- **Location, a class of a location:** This class provides methods to set/remove a callback reference for event notification, `IDListener`. Also, it provides similar kinds of `getter`-style interface. The callback method is called when something has entered to or removed from the location. This can be easily understood.

  ```
  void addDetectionListener(IDListener il)
  void removeDetectionListener(IDListener il)
  ```

- **Artefact, a class of an artefact:** This class also provides two types of interfaces for callback reference setting/removing: `LocationListener` and StateListener. LocationListener is called when a location of a specific artefact is changed, while StateListener is invoked when a specific state-of-use is changed. Also, this class provides methods for obtaining objects representing state, sensor and actuator.

```
void addLocationListener(LocationListener ll)
void addStateListener(StateListener sl)
Location getLocationByAttrs(Hashtable a)
State getStateByAttrs(Hashtable a)
State getStateByType(String s)
Sensor getSensorByAttrs(Hashtable a)
Actuator getActuatorByAttrs(Hashtable a)
```

- **State, a class of a state :**   This provides interfaces to obtain current state of use and set a callback reference like the above ones.

```
String getCurrentState()
void addStateListener(StateListener sl)
```

- **Sensor, a class of a sensor:**   This provides interfaces to obtain a value from a sensor attached to an object directly as well as to set a callback reference.

```
void addDataListener(DataListener dl)
Object getCurrentValue()
```

- **Actuator, a class of an actuator:**   This class has an interface for controlling an actuator. So, it has a reference to Command object internally and provides a method for obtaining it.

```
Command getCommand(String name)
```

- **Command, a class of an actuation command:**   This class encapsulates processing of remote command execution from a developer by passing only contents as arguments. Here, Response indicates return value of the command.

```
Response execute(Hashtable params)
```

These APIs are primitive and referred to as low level API in Figure 1. With these API's, high level ones are to be developed, e.g. APIs for inferencing context based on the first order predicate.

5   Implementations and Sample Application

In this section, we describe implementation of *Bazaar* and a sample application using *Bazaar* and *sentient artefacts*[1].

5.1   *Bazaar*

BWMM is written in Java and many kinds of sensor can be integrated if they conform to Service Provider Interfaces(SPIs) shown in Figure 1. A change of state of use from *sentient artefacts* can also be reported to BWMM through such SPIs. Currently, BWMM is implemented on a single host, and each component to be accessed by applications is instantiated as a remote object for Java RMI.

An RDF model can be represented with simple triples as well as XML or directed graph. So, traditional relational database technologies can be adopted with some efforts. Although triples is simple and suitable for such a database system, it is hard for a person to understand. So, we have chosen an XML based representation of RDF and edit a text file written in XML-encoded RDF description. To parse and manipulate such RDF model, we utilized HP-Labs' Jena[13], which is a Java framework for building a semantic web application.

In current implementation, the context-extraction framework depicted in Figure 1, does not exit. So, the application to be described below is implemented using low level APIs shown in section 4.3.

We have utilized RFCode Inc.'s Spider RF-tag reader as a location detection system. However, as described before, any kind of location system that provides detected ID can be applicable. Moreover, thanks to flexible representation of RDF, other kinds of location representation like geometric model and hybrid one are expected to be adopted easily.

5.2   A Personal Workspace Application

We have developed a *personal workspace* application which is aware of presence of a person. Figure 2 shows the experimental environment. The application turns on and off the stand light based on a person's presence. It can also serve as a telepresence application like [10]. It assumed that a person does not have an RFID tag, therefore person's presence cannot be detected directly. Instead, two *sentient artefacts* provide their awareness of a person's presence, which is integrated to improve reliability of the information. We have developed three types: SentientCradle (Figure 2-(i)), SentientLight (Figure 2-(ii)), and SentientChair (Figure 2-(iv)). In case that both SentientCradle and SentientChair are detected by location detector, information from them is aggregated(OR operation): if none of them is indicating someone is there, the light is turned off. On the other hand, only one of them is detected or available, it is utilized individually.

- **SentientCradle:** SetientCradle[25] is a cellular phone cradle that is aware of three kinds of information: 1) the existence of the cellular phone on the

---

[1] We called it Sentient Materials in the past[25].

cradle, 2) number of call received until it is reset, and 3) the state, i.e. resetting or not. When a call is received, the cradle moves its legs based on the number of calls to notify its owner of the call-receiving. It utilizes two types of sensor connected to Phidget Interface Kit[19]: a force sensor and a touch sensor. A force sensor is attached at the back holder, which detects existence of a cellular phone and vibration at the time of arrival of a call. A touch sensor is attached at the front of the holder to detect the state of being reset by a person, possibly its owner.

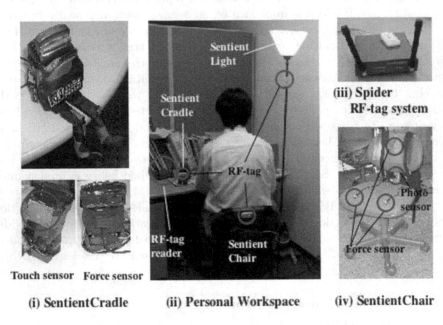

Fig. 2. Experimental Environment

- **SentientLight:** Sentient Light is a sensor augmented ordinary stand light. It senses environmental light-level using Phidget photo sensor as well as make surroundings bright as its own functionality, and can be controlled via X10 light module.
- **SentientChair:** SentientChair is a sensor augmented chair that is aware of its states of use, i.e. someone is sitting or not. It has four Phidgets sensors as can be seen in Figure 2-(iv): one photo sensor and three force sensors. The sensors are attached as follows: one of the force sensors is on the back of the chair, and the other two are on the seat of it to touch and detect human's back and both thighs. A photo sensor is also attached to the space between the seat and the back of the chair in order to sense coverage with something, a person, a baggage, etc. It can be used as a method for obtaining human presence at a certain location implicitly as well as for triggering a certain task. As a result of preliminary experiments, accuracy of the state of use

distinction was approximately 80%. This means that presence of a person can be inferred with accuracy of 80%.

Each sentient artefact is connected to a laptop individually for extracting context and controlling itself via USB or RS-232C, and they communicate with central server hosting BWMM and the application by HTTP over wireless LAN connection. In the future, a laptop should be replaced to embedded computers. In the experimental setting, only RF-tag reader is fixed in location, while the other sentient artefacts with RF-tags are movable and determined at runtime.

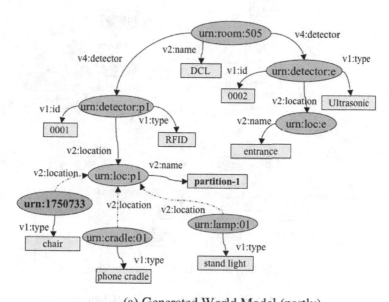

(a) Generated World Model (partly)

Fig. 3. Generated World Model (a part)

A part of generated world model is shown in Figure 3 with an RDF graph style[2]. At the root of the graph in this case, there is a resource "urn:room:505" whose name is "DCL". It is a whole room and has two ID detectors: "urn:detector:p1" and "urn:detector:e", which are located at partitioned area "partition-1" and an entrance, respectively. In addition, a dotted arc represents that it is variable at any time: for example, location of the chair("urn:1750733") can be varied after it removed to another area of detection.

---

[2] A circle, an arc, and a rectangle is a resource, a property, and a value in RDF, respectively.

Figure 4 shows self-description of the chair linked to detected location "partition-1" [3]. Entity, e.g. person, chair, etc., can have more than two states at a time. For example, a person is sitting while sleeping. To achieve this requirement, we utilized "rdf:Bag" type. This self-description is to be created by the manufacturer, where it is managed until the object is detected by a location detector in the room for the first time. Then it is to be retrieved from manufacturer side and cached locally.

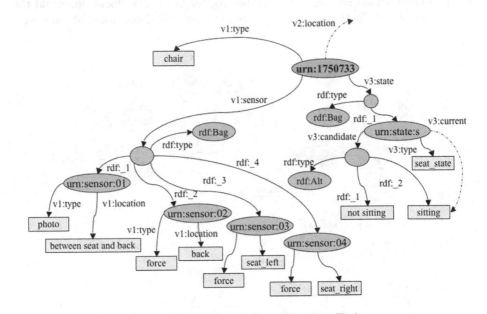

(b) Self-description of SentientChair

Fig. 4. Self-description of SentientChair

Let us walk through fragments of code for adding StateListener to a reference to object indicating "a chair located at partition-1". In the code, w is a reference to *Bazaar* local world model managing room505, and hn indicates a reference to a Hashtable object.:

First of all, artefacts for "chair" located at "partition-1" are retrieved. There can be multiple replies if there are more than two chairs in the area.

```
1: //Find Artefact for ''chair" located ''partition-1"
2: h1=new Hashtable();
```

---

[3] Blank node(*resource*)s are resources representing groups of resources. Properties like "rdf:_N" and "rdf:type" are predefined ones and both "rdf:Bag" and "rdf:Alt" are also predefined types.

```
3: h1.put("v2:name","partition-1");
4: h1.put("v1:type","chair");
5: Artefact[] a=w.getArtefactByAttrs(h1);
```

Next, reference to a type of state "seat_status" is obtained, and reference to an object that implements StateListener is added to each of them: in this case, the object itself (this).

```
6: State s[] = new State[a.length];
7: for(int i=0;i<a.length;i++){
8:   s[i]=a[i].getStateByType("seat_status");
9:   s[i].addStateListener(this);
10: }
```

It is ready for receiving change of state events: "sitting" and "not sitting". This is considered intuitive in that a developer can handle computational objects as if he/she were there and touched real objects located there. This is because of its semantically richness and a knowledge about the area being shared between a computer and a developer via *Bazaar* world model.

6   Discussions and Future Directions

In this section, we discuss on some findings through development of *Bazaar* and *Personal Workspace* application.

6.1   Support for Non-intelligent Physical Objects

Although we have developed an application using intelligent everyday objects, *sentient artefact*, objects do not always need to be intelligent so much. Since such descriptive information is linked to an ID assigned to each artefact, and it can provide rich context about itself, even static description can be useful. Collective attributes of such a non-intelligent tagged object can be also meaningful. As described in section 4.1, *Bazaar* is independent of an ID registration method. This means an object is able to be apart of a world if its ID is registered with BWMM in any way. Integration of non-intelligent objects with sentient artefacts and context representation by collective attributes will be examined in the future.

6.2   Model by Object-Oriented Design Versus Collections of Attribute

We have designed *Bazaar* World Model with collections of attribute, *triples*. However, we have partly implemented elements of a world model in an object-oriented manner. That is classes for manipulating the world model described in section 4.3. While a developer is provided with a collection of classes in Java, detailed attributes are acquired through getAttribute method of the classes. This is our design decision so that a developer can benefit from flexibility by the attribute based approach, however, it looses the benefit of object-oriented approach: robustness by strong type checking and introspection by IDE like Eclipse[8]. Previous work like Sentient Computing project[12] and NEXUS[17] fully adopted object-oriented approach. They provide a basic type of object as a super class and extend that if needed. It requires quite careful analysis on a type of super class and an attribute of it in advance. Although attribute based approach is flexible, it is impossible to detect mismatching and/or loss of required value in a specific application during compilation time. So, the issue should be addressed in another way, e.g., by an IDE that we will propose next.

6.3   Needs for IDE for Physical Space Programming

We strongly need an IDE for physical space programming to address issues pointed above. For example in the previous application, a developer must know the name of target location "partition-1". Moreover, when he/she integrates contextual information from two *sentient artefacts* into one, the type of state provided by each one is to be understood in advance, for example, by documents.

The idea is to use self-description of an object for development environment as well as for modeling a world. This is similar to the idea proposed in [16]. However, we can go beyond if a developer with location detector, e.g. RF-tag reader, goes to a place for programming and collect appropriate information for the application. Any attribute can be seen, and the developer can confirm what there is. A name of the personal workspace is turned out at the place. Types of states are also clarified and the developer is also able to decide which artefact to use for his/her purpose. This is distribution of responsibility between human and a computer: human is superior to a computer in decision making, while it is opposite in storing and processing huge amount of information effectively. "On-site" development like this is close to the notion of *bodystorming*[18] which shows effectiveness in understanding a domain of application, while the paper focuses on analysis and design phase.

Moreover such an IDE might be more useful for handling an actuator that often has complex command sequences. For example, in case of a radio receiver, there can be three steps: 1) turn it on, 2) select a band, and 3) adjust appropriate level of sound. Therefore, an IDE that shows the procedure when the device is detected is required. The issue on type mismatching can be detected through the IDE. Currently, we are developing the IDE as an Eclipse Plug-in.

6.4   Managing and Maintaining a World

Currently, BWMM manages all information about a world in one host machine. Namely, it cannot distribute parts of it. To avoid significant scalability drawbacks in practical use, any size of world should be created on a machine and communicate with others. A special server or stationary sentient artefact, e.g. ceiling, door, etc., should manage distributed BWMMs. Additionally, consistency management in a world model is a future work.

6.5   Supports for Various Location Model

The application presented in section 5.2 has interests in only one location, i.e. partition-1. So, another location does not need to be handled. Suppose a query like "What is the nearest partition from partition-1, which is reachable by a person? " is required to be processed. The answer should not be the one that is reachable by a person, e.g. along a path. So, relationship between locations from the perspective of human activities as well as information of each location needs to be considered. Let's suppose a new property of a resource like "v2:reachable", which indicates "reachability", provides such topological representation. In the situation described in section 4.2 or depicted in Figure 3, if the entrance is reachable, then it could be simply represented with a form of triples as such:

(urn:loc:p1, v2:reachable, urn:loc:e)

6.6 Installation Policies of RF-Tag Reader

As described above, we have utilized an RFID location system to identify approximate position of a tagged object. In installing the location system, there can be two options: 1) installing at fixed location with no intention, and 2) installing around fixed furniture or into very closed space where an significant activity can occur. The former means RFID readers are located in a certain order, e.g. lattice. We have utilized the latter one, namely, installation into a closed space "partition-1". We consider location is a primary contextual information, and therefore we may choose appropriate area in response to application's requirements rather than installing everywhere with no intention.

6.7 Toward Reliable Context Extraction

Semantically rich model of a world allows an application to utilize reliable contextual information. For example, lets suppose that a chair is detected in two location which are 20 meters away almost at the same time, e.g. in one second. In this case either or both of them is considered to be incorrect detection. This can be detected if the world model has topological relationship and geometric value between detectors and a knowledge representing it is impossible to move so fast is utilized. However, we consider such knowledge should not handled within a world model since it can change in application context. In addition, in case that a sentient artefact extracts contextual information with low confidence, it can improve this by asking appropriate one(s). This time world model is utilized to search suitable one(s) with many kinds of attributes. Thus, a world model is expected to provide an application with reliable context-awareness, and *Bazaar* supports this. We will further investigate this through various complex application developments.

7 Conclusions

We presented two roles of world model: shared knowledge between applications, and between a developer and an environment. Then, we described four requirements for a world model: semantically richness, flexibility, dynamicity, and intuitiveness. Based on these, *Bazaar* conceptual framework was proposed and implemented as well as a simple application named *Personal Workspace*. *Bazaar* encapsulates details on building a world model, i.e. internal representation of the model, context acquisition from sentient artefacts, and tracking of them, instead providing a developer with uniform interfaces. We also discussed some findings including future directions.

References

1. Auto-ID Center. Web site:. URL: <http://www.autoidcenter.org/>.
2. M. Beigl, H.-W. Gellersen, and A. Schmidt. MediaCups: Experience with Design and Use of Computer-Augmented Everyday Objects. *Computer Networks, Special Issue on Pervasive Computing*, 35(4):401–409, March 2001.
3. M. Beigl, T. Zimmer, and C. Decker. A Location Model for Communicating and Processing of Context. *Personal and Ubiquitous Computing*, 6(5–6):341–357, December 2002.
4. M. Burnett, P. Prekop, and C. Rainsford. Intimate Location Modeling for Context Aware Computing. In *Proceedings of the Workshop on Location Modeling for Ubiquitous Computing, in UbiComp2001*, pages 77–82, September 2001.
5. G. Chen and D. Kotz. A Survey of Context-Aware Mobile Computing Research. Technical Report TR2000-381, Department of Computer Science, Dartmouth College, 2000.
6. Computer science and telecommunications board. *Embedded, Everywhere, A Research Agenda for Networked Systems of Embedded Computers*. National Research Council, 2001.
7. A. Dey, G. Abowd, and D. Salber. A Conceptual Framework and a Toolkit for Supporting the Rapid Prototyping of Context-Aware Applications. *HUMAN-COMPUTER INTERACTION*, 16(2-4):97–166, 2001.
8. Eclipse Foundation. Web site:. URL: <http://www.eclipse.org/>.
9. K. Fujinami, T. Yamabe, and T. Nakajima. "Take me with you!": A Case Study of Context-aware Application integrating Cyber and Physical Spaces. In *Proceedings of ACM Symposium on Applied Computing(SAC) 2004*, pages 1607–1614, Mar. 2004.
10. H. Gellersen and M. Beigl. Ambient Telepresense: Colleague Awareness in Smart Environments. In *Proceedings of the 1st International Workshop on Managing Interactions in Smart Environments, MANSE'99*, pages 80–88, 1999.
11. H. Gellersen, A. Schmidt, and M. Beigl. Multi-Sensor Context-Awareness in Mobile Devices and Smart Artifacts. *Journal on Mobile Networks and Applications, Special Issue on Mobility of Systems, Users, Data and Computing (MONET)*, 7(5):341–351, Oct. 2002.
12. A. Harter, A. Hopper, P. Steggles, A. Ward, and P. Webster. The Anatomy of a Context-Aware Application. In *Mobile Computing and Networking*, pages 59–68, 1999.
13. HP Labs Semantic Web research group. Jena 2. URL: <http://jena.sourceforge.net>.
14. IsaViz. A Visual Authoring Tool for RDF. URL: <http://www.w3.org/2001/11/IsaViz/>.
15. O. Lassila and R. Swick. Resource Description Framework(RDF) Model and Syntax Specification. URL: <http://www.w3.org/TR/1999/REC-rdf-syntax-19990222/>.

16. R. McGrath, A. Ranganathan, R. Campbell, and M. Mickunas. Use of Ontologies in Pervasive Computing Environments. Technical Report UIUCDCS-R-2003-2332, Department of Computer Science, University of Illinois, Urbana-Champaign, Apri 2003.
17. D. Nicklas, M. Großmann, T. Schwarz, S. Volz, and B. Mitschang. A Model-Based, Open Architecture for Mobile, Spatially Aware Applications. In *Proceedings of the 7th International Symposium on Spatial and Temporal Databases: SSTD 2001*, pages 117–135, Jul. 2001.
18. A. Oulasvirta, E. Kurvinen, and T. Kankainen. Understanding contexts by being there: case studies in bodystorming. *Personal and Ubiquitous Computing*, 7:125–134, 2003.
19. Phidgets Inc. Web site. URL: <http://www.phidgets.com/>.
20. B. Schilit, N. Adams, and R. Want. Context-Aware Computing Applications. In *Proceedings of IEEE Workshop on Mobile Computing Systems and Applications*, 1994.
21. A. Schmidt. Implicit Human Computer Interaction Through Context. *Personal Technologies*, 4(2-3):191–199, June 2000.
22. A. Seaborne. RDQL - A Query Language for RDF. URL: <http://www.w3.org/Submission/2004/SUBM-RDQL-20040109/>.
23. W3C. Semantic web. URL: <http://www.w3.org/2001/sw/>.
24. M. Weiser. The Computer for the Twenty-First Century. *Scientific American*, pages 94–104, Sep. 1991.
25. T. Yamabe, K. Fujinami, and T. Nakajima. Experiences with Building Sentient Materials using Various Sensors. In *Proceedings of the the 4th International Workshop on Smart Appliances and Wearable Computing(IWSAWC)*, pages 445–450, Mar. 2004.

A Unified Application Service Model for ubiHome by Exploiting Intelligent Context-Awareness

Yoosoo Oh and Woontack Woo

GIST U-VR Lab,
Gwangju 500-712, S. Korea
{yoh, wwoo}@gist.ac.kr

Abstract. We propose a unified ubiHome application service model which provides user-centered services by exploiting intelligent context-awareness. Recently, most of research related to smart home focused on the infrastructure rather than a user, and did not consider effective use of context. Such approaches are not appropriate for a user-centered interface, intelligent home control, flexible extension of application service, etc. In this paper, we design a unified ubiHome application service model by exploiting ubi-UCAM (unified context-aware application model). The proposed model provides services corresponding to a user's intention and also supports flexible interaction between a user and ubiHome environment. It provides personalized ubiHome environment to each user. The proposed model contributes flexible interaction between a user and ubiHome environment. And it provides personalized ubiHome environment to a user and simplifies extension of various application services. Therefore, the proposed model helps ubiquitous applications obtain users' context and provide adaptive applications flexibly.

1 Introduction

Recently, computing technology has steadily developed. Ubiquitous Computing, called the forth revolution, is being reflected in our lives [1]. The future will be an environment that promotes interaction of human and computer by sinking many kinds of computing resources in our living space. Especially, intelligent user-centered services will play an important role in the future home environment [2]. And it is necessary to further develop context-aware technology and find out how context information can be applied to the design of various sensors and applications, for intelligent user-centered services [3][4][5].

Significant research related to smart home has been progressed. This includes Adaptive House (Univ. of Colorado) [6][7], AwareHome (GATECH) [8][9], Easy-Living (Microsoft) [10], and House_n Project (MIT) [11]. However, most of the related research mainly focused on the infrastructure rather than a user, and did not consider effective use of context for providing services corresponding to a user's intention. The existing research lacks thorough examination, which is about convenient user-centered interface and intelligent control of the smart environment. Moreover, it is difficult to extend application services flexibly by central management of application services. Also, it is difficult to generalize in real life because of their high cost

H. Murakami et al. (Eds.): UCS 2004, LNCS 3598, pp. 192–202, 2005.

and low-quality service. Furthermore, previous proposed system did not define effective integration model for a user-centered smart home application service [12].

In this paper, we propose a unified ubiHome application service model by exploiting ubi-UCAM, which employs intelligent context-awareness to overcome the limitation of the existing smart home [13]. We build a new kind of smart home and design a model which provides personalized service for each user. Also, we evaluate usability of the proposed model. It enables privacy protection and provides a user-friendly environment at low construction cost.

The proposed model has the following advantages. First, it provides flexible interaction between a user and ubiHome environment, and provides services corresponding to a user's intention. This is achieved by the user-centered design and intelligent context-awareness. Second, it provides personalized ubiHome environment by effective use of context. It is presented in which context is created by various kinds of sensors in 5W1H form. Finally, it simplifies extension of various application services through the distributed architecture for sensors and application services. In other words, it guarantees independence of sensors and application services. And it provides a user-friendly environment at low construction cost by employing inexpensive sensors such as On/Off switch, IR sensor and USB memory. It enables privacy protection by using ubiKey.

This paper is organized as follows: In Section 2, we describe intelligent context-aware model. In Section 3, we explain a unified ubiHome application service. Especially, we focus on user interface and discuss examples of ubiHome application services in detail. And the implementation and experimental results are explained in Section 4. Finally, conclusion and future works are presented in Section 5.

2 Intelligent Context-Aware Model

Many sensors and context-based application services have been embedded in smart home environment. It is necessary for context-aware technology to provide assistance for the particular work that a user wishes to do. Therefore, we use ubi-UCAM which provides application service through awareness of a user's intention and efficient management of context. ubi-UCAM is a model which efficiently integrates context and manages to provide the smart home application service that the user wants. The context is created by various kind of sensors in 5W1H (Who, What, Where, When, How and Why) form.

Fig. 1 expresses the structure of ubi-UCAM. The ubi-UCAM can have reasoned "Why" context, and grasp a user's intention by integrating preliminary 5W1H set. Therefore, a user-centered interface can provide the application service that the user wants by exploiting ubi-UCAM.

The ubi-UCAM consists of ubiSensor and ubiService. The ubiSensor creates preliminary context that all ubiServices can use. Preliminary context is the context of 5W1H form generated by single sensor. The ubiService consists of Context Integrator, Context Manager, Service Provider and Interpreter. Context integrator determines integrated context set by integrating preliminary contexts passed from several ubiSensors. Context Manager compares integrated context with context condition to execute

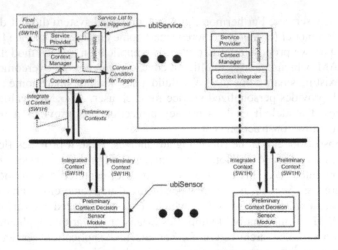

Fig. 1. ubi-UCAM structure, (a) ubiService (b) ubiSensor

specific service module. And then it generates final context and delivers final context to Service Provider. Service Provider triggers service module according to final context in service practice order. The user defines this order through Interpreter. Interpreter includes the defined context condition and service list that should be executed according to it. Context condition is registered in Context Manager. Information for service list, to be executed about each condition, is registered in Service Provider.

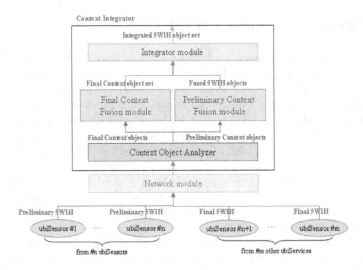

Fig. 2. Intelligent Context Integrator

Context integrator must make integrated context set, considering each preliminary context for intelligent context-awareness. And, Context integrator has intelligent structure that can infer a user's intention/emotion/sensibility and integrate various application services that are provided according to the user's request. Intelligent context integrator consists of Context Object Analyzer, Preliminary Context fusion module, Final Context Fusion module, and integrator module. Fig. 2 demonstrates the interior structure of intelligent context integrator.

Context Object Analyzer aggregates preliminary context objects from n sensors and final context objects from m services. Preliminary Context fusion module receives preliminary 5W1H context objects from n sensors. By using decision fusion method, each context is fused with the "Who" information. Preliminary Context fusion module reconstructs each element of 5W1H by efficiently fusing imperfect preliminary 5W1H context objects. Next, it creates fused 5W1H objects by merging reconstructed 5W1H contexts. At this stage, this module can infer the "Why" information, that corresponds to a user's intention/emotion/sensibility, from the fused 5W1H context. Final Context fusion module makes final context object set by binding each final context object according to "Who" information. Finally, Integrator module integrates fused 5W1H objects to the "Why" context and create integrated 5W1H set.

3 A Unified ubiHome Application Service

The unified ubiHome application service incorporates cMP, cMail checker and Camera monitoring. Application services such as cMP, camera monitoring and cMail checker are integrated to each other through the context's flow. Organized interaction between application services is ensured by intelligent context-awareness of ubi-UCAM and Context Integrator. For example, while sitting on a couch watching movie, a user can observe outsider scene through camera monitoring. Also, he can check his E-mail, and send reply using a PDA. Fig. 3 displays the concept of a unified ubiHome application service.

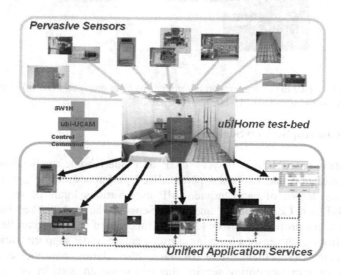

Fig. 3. Concept of a unified ubiHome application service

3.1 User Interface

User interface for a unified ubiHome application service model mediates among various kinds of application services distributed in smart home environment. A user can control several application services of smart home and can use personalized service based on his/her context. The user-centered interface plays an important role in creating context of a user's identification, location, action, emotion and intention etc. because the proposed model does not give inconvenience to the user to provide these services.

Fig. 4 shows user interface to efficiently control and use the proposed model. The user interface is embodied in order that a user is apt to use application service of movie appreciation, camera monitoring, and e-mail check. It is designed so that users can exploit indirect gesture commands through Space sensor [14] as well as direct control command through PDA.

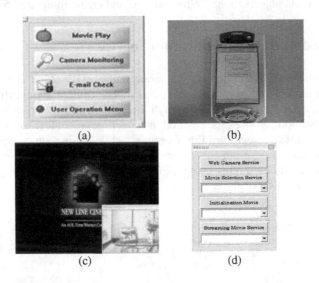

Fig. 4. User Interface (a) User menu on big screen (b) User menu on PDA (c) Camera Monitoring among movie screening (d) User Operation menu

3.2 ubiHome Application Service

cMP (Context based Movie Player). cMP is a smart home application service for movie appreciation that expresses personalized preference movie list, playing time and progress degree of each movie. cMP uses various kinds of sensors, such as ubiKey, ubiFloor, CouchSensor, and SpaceSensor. The personalized information is based on a user's profile in ubiKey [2]. Each function of cMP is controlled by context generated from each sensor observing a user's action. cMP supports various kinds of movie contents from cinema state database. Also, during a movie screening, cMP utilizes the camera monitoring service that can sense an outsider or confirm baby's state. Fig. 5 shows connection between cMP and each proposed sensor.

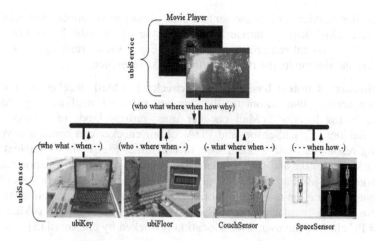

Fig. 5. Connection between cMP and each sensor

cMP starts with authentication of a user's ubiKey as he enters ubiHome environment. User profile is transmitted from ubiKey to ubiHome environment during the user authentication. When a user sits on a couch, he initiates application service cMP by selecting an appropriate menu. Fig. 6 instructs context flow between sensors and

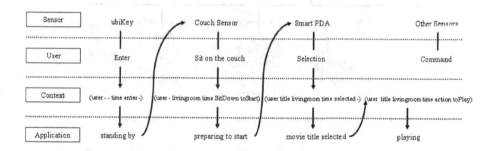

Fig. 6. Context flow of cMP

UsermovieDlg				
User : yoh	Current Time :	2003-01-25 22:00:48		
The Load of Ring2 :		Last Time :	2003-01-25 21:46:44	PLAY
Christie :		Last Time :	2003-01-25 21:51:11	PLAY
dvfuri :		Last Time :	2003-01-25 21:47:38	PLAY
Fifa Goal :		Last Time :		PLAY
KOF :		Last Time :	2003-01-25 21:49:17	PLAY
NBA 2003 :		Last Time :		PLAY

Fig. 7. Personalized movie information of cMP

the application service until a user enters smart home environment and receives the cMP service. cMP displays movie list that fits the user's taste. User's preference is determined by personalized profile information. Fig. 7 shows running times saved for each movie and the movie list reflecting the user's preference.

cMail checker (Context-based e-Mail checker). cMail checker is a ubiHome application service that automatically supplies received mail message to a user according to his location. cMail checker uses various kinds of sensors, such as ubiKey, ubiFloor, CouchSensor, and PDA. cMail checker can confirm e-Mail from computing resources close to each user in ubiHome. Fig. 8 shows context transfer between cMail checker and sensors that create contexts. User information such as ID or password for e-Mail account is supplied in ubiKey. When a user leaves ubiHome, his personal information is stored in ubiKey. Fig. 9 shows arriving mail messages and mail status for a particular user. cMail checker can display received e-Mail on large screen or PC close to the user. User's location is tracked by ubiFloor [15].

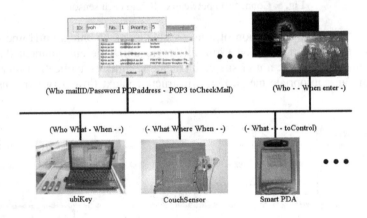

Fig. 8. Connection between cMail checker and each sensor

(a)   (b)

Fig. 9. Personalized information of cMail checker (a) Current status of cMail (b) Received mails

4   Experiments

As shown in Fig. 10, various kinds of sensors such as ubiKey [2], Couch sensor, IR sensor, USB camera, web camera, PDA, space sensor [14], ubiFloor [15], RF tag etc.

are deployed in ubiHome, the smart home testbed at GIST U-VR Lab. Each sensor individually is linked to a PC and acts as a smart sensor with inherent processing, networking, and sensing abilities.

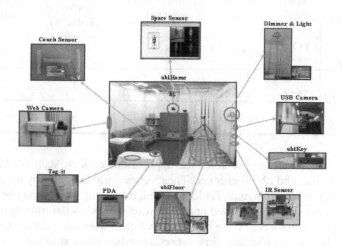

Fig. 10. ubiHome test-bed

All experiments are performed by using resources in ubiHome. We investigated the system's usability from 20 (10 adult, 10 child) ordinary people to evaluate the proposed model. The evaluation involved iterative experiment which provides application services in home environment. With an aim to achieve a user's satisfaction in the experiment, 4 general PCs (Pentium□ 800MHz, 512 GB SDRAMs), 1 Compaq PDA (iPAQ 5450), and proposed sensors were used.

About utilization of context, we quantitatively compared existing approaches with our application service model, such as cMP, camera monitoring service, and cMail checker. As shown in Table 1, we observed that the proposed model utilizes more rich context rather than existing methods. In Table 2, we analyze quantitatively provision of personalized service to users. We could know that users are satisfied with the proposed model because they can use service of their own.

Table 1. Quantitative analysis of context usage

Application service	The existing method	The proposed method
cMP	What (movie list)	Who(user name), What(movie title), When(entering time, play time), Where(living room), How(gesture), Why (ex. to play)
Camera Monitoring	Nothing	When (detection time)
cMail checker	Nothing	Who(user name), What(ID/PWD), Where(POP address), How(POP3), Why(ex. to check)

Table 2. Quantitative analysis of personalized service

Person (Age, sex)	ID/ PWD	Preferred service	Preferred light intensity	No. of Preferred movie (Total: 8)	Degree of satisfaction
User A (28, man)	YOh/ ****	cMP	20 %	4	85 %
User B (26, woman)	SjOh/ ****	cMail checker	100 %	1	75 %
User C (30, man)	SJang/ ****	cMP	40 %	3	80 %

We asked all 20 users to use ubiHome application services, such as cMP, camera monitoring service, and cMail checker. Then we estimate usability by averaging data formed from 20 users' average in Table 3. Average learning time means how long the user who does not use the proposed application service takes the time to perform the application service. As a result, we observed that each user achieved the task in average 17 seconds. Usage efficiency time represents when users who use more than one time reuse the application service. We also observed that the proposed model is efficient as a result of the usage efficiency time. In addition, we knew that users remember enough application service through system memory efficiency. Also, we estimated users' average rehabilitation rate about how frequently users have a mistake and return this when users use application service 1 time, with the following equation (1).

$$\text{Average rehabilitation rate}(\%) = (\frac{\text{Average No. of rehabilitation}}{\text{Average No. of mistake}}) \times 100 \qquad (1)$$

According to the experiment results, we can know the proposed model gives enough satisfaction to users through the practical use of context and user-centered personalized services unlike the existing smart home application. As shown in Table 3, we can know users can easily return the mistake in use for the proposed model. In other words, the proposed model is user-friendly in ubiHome environment. Table 4 expresses necessity of the proposed model by making up a question concerning users' satisfaction. The proposed model provides correct services in a user's preference and intention. Therefore, users could use the proposed model conveniently even if they do not care specially about any devices of smart home.

Table 3. Usability test of the proposed model

Average learning time	Average usage efficiency time	System memory efficiency	Average rehabilitation rate
17 sec	8 sec	95 %	66 %

Table 4. Qualitative evaluation of satisfaction degree of the proposed model

Personalized information protection	Personalized service expression	Home environment control	User Interface	Reaction of user's motion	Connectivity of application services
70 %	85 %	80 %	65 %	95 %	90 %

5 Conclusion

In this paper, we proposed a unified ubiHome application service model which provides user-centered services by exploiting intelligent context-awareness. We presented the proposed model in which context is created by various kinds of sensors in 5W1H form. Our proposed model helps ubiquitous applications obtain users' context and provide adaptive applications flexibly. In future works, we plan to develop free communication of context through networking between application services and between sensors. In addition, we will consider group context creation method and practical use. This will smooth the interaction between smart environments and multi-users. Also, we need to develop intelligent agent which can deduce person's will. With this continuous development, we will establish a firm infrastructure for smart home environment.

References

1. M. Weiser, "The Computer for the 21st Century," Scientific American, pp. 94-104, Sep. 1991.
2. Yoosoo Oh, Seiie Jang, Woontack Woo, "User Authentication and Environment Control using Smart Key," KSPC 2002, vol. 15, No. 1, pp. 264, Sep. 2002.
3. Anind K. Dey, "Understanding and Using context," Personal and Ubiquitous computing, Special issue on Situated Interaction and Ubiquitous computing, vol.5, no.1, 2001.
4. Anind K. Dey, Gregory D. Abowd, "Context Toolkit: Aiding the Development of ContextAware Applications," In Proceedings of Human Factors in Computing Systems: CHI 99. Pittsburgh, PA: ACM Press. pp. 434-441, May 15-20 1999.
5. T. Selker and W. Burleson, "Context-Aware Design and Interaction in Computer Systems," IBM Systems Journal 39, Nos. 3&4, 2000.
6. Mozer, M. C., "An intelligent environment must be adaptive," IEEE Intelligent Systems and their Applications, 14(2), pp. 11-13, 1999.
7. http://www.eurekalert.org/releases/ mozer-house.html
8. "Sensing the Subtleties of Everyday Life," It appeared in the Winter 2000 issue of Research Horizons, the research magazine of Georgia Tech.
9. "A Context-based Infrastructure for Smart Environments," Anind K. Dey, Daniel Salber and Gregory D. Abowd. In Proceedings of the 1st International Workshop on Managing Interactions in Smart Environments (MANSE '99), Dublin, Ireland, Dec. 1999.
10. S. Shafer, B. Brumitt, and B. Meyers, "The EasyLiving Intelligent Environment System," CHI Workshop on Research Directions in Situated Computing, Apr. 2000.
11. http://architecture.mit.edu/house_n/web/projects/projects.htm

12. Y. Oh, S. Jang, W. Woo, "User centered context-aware Smart Home Applications," Journal on Korea Information Science Society (KISS): Software and Applications, vol. 31, No. 2, pp. 111-125, Feb. 2004.
13. S. Jang, W. Woo, "ubi-UCAM: A Unified Context-Aware Application Model," LNAI (Context03), pp. 178-189, 2003.
14. D.Hong and W.Woo, "A Vision-based 3D Space Sensor for Controlling ubiHome Environment," HCI2003, vol. 12, No. 2, pp. 358-363, Feb. 2003.
15. S. Lee and W. Woo, "Music Player with the ubiFloor," KHCI2003, pp. 154-159, Feb. 2003.

A Behavior-Based Personal Controller for Autonomous Ubiquitous Computing

Takamitsu Mizutori, Yuta Nakayama, and Kenji Kohiyama

Keio University Graduate School of Media and Governance,
Design Studio B, 5322 Endoh Fujisawa, Kanagawa 252-8520 Japan
{mizutori, uta, kohiyama}@sfc.keio.ac.jp

Abstract. In this paper, we propose a way to retrieve and invoke ubiquitous objects within our living spaces by our behavior. Accumulations of GPS location information collected by a tiny program on a user's cellular phone are organized into a structure which represents the user's spatial behavior. This representation provides ubiquitous computing environment with assumptions about the user's movement in one-day duration, and allow them to act for the predicted future locations of the user. Since this knowledge representation about the user's daily route is a key to invoke ubiquitous objects by her/his current spatial behavior, we call it "Behavior-based Personal Controller" or "BPC".A learning algorithm to organize the Behavior-based Personal Controller and a mechanism of the BPC's invoking networked ubiquitous objects are detailed in this paper.

1 Introduction

Currently a large number of entities are having sensors, computations, and networks. The increase of ubiquitous functions, however, require us complex decisions to use them. Modern Approaches in resolving this problem is making ubiquitous computing environment to sense our context, and automatically provide us with their services.

In the researches on creating smart spaces and wearable computers a user' s position or action is associated with object actions [6], [5]. For example in [12], a display shows presentation visuals by the approach of the speaker. In addition to laboratory-level advanced smart spaces, we could see the similar ideas in our living space. For example automatics doors and faucets act by the user's action.

These approaches, however, limit their focus on the user's current position or action in providing corresponding services. Not only the current location or action of the user, but her/his spatial behavior in longer duration should provide ubiquitous computing environment with richer assumptions about the user's context.

Thus, in this paper, we describe the way computing environment senses a user's position in the duration of one day, and learns his/her routine spatial behavior. A feature representation of the user's frequented or routine spatial behavior is created from GPS (Global Positioning System) location information automatically collected in her/his everyday lives. By referencing this knowledge representation, ubiquitous computers can infer the user's future locations when the user took the same route again, and make service decisions for those movements beforehand. Since this repre-

H. Murakami et al. (Eds.): UCS 2004, LNCS 3598, pp. 203–213, 2005.

sentation can be seen as a controller for invoking ubiquitous computers by the user's behavior, we call it "Behavior-based Personal Controller" or "BPC".

The following section explains how to make a BPC. The experiment on two users' spatial behavior is described in Section 3. In Section 4, a mechanism to invoke ubiquitous objects by the BPC is described. We conclude this research work in Section 5 with the future direction of this work.

2 Representing Human Spatial Behavior for the Behavior-Based Personal Controller

2.1 Overview

Our internal knowledge representations about surrounding environment are called "Cognitive Maps" [3]. We create cognitive maps from partial sensory input (mainly visual input), and incrementally improve the maps by constant input of sensory information about environment. By reviewing the cognitive maps with sensory information, we can easily follow our familiar paths [8].

A Behavior-based Personal Controller, proposed in this paper, is an alternative knowledge representation for computing environments to recognize a user's familiar path. In this section, we describe a system and algorithm to create a BPC.

2.2 Related Work

Learning spatial context of a user has been explored in the following works.

MOST. Querying future positions of moving objects is modeled in "MOST" (Moving Objects Spatio-Temporal) [15]. MOST language defines an object with a current position and a set of temporal functions. This approach requires predefined temporal functions to calculate the future positions of the object.

Bayesian Filters for Location Estimation. Fox et al. statistically fused multiple sensor inputs, which include ultrasound sensors, infrared tags, and laser range finders, and achieved high quality of location estimation [4].

Com Motion. Com Motion automatically identifies a user's entrance to buildings from repeated losses of GPS signals [9].

Significant Location Learning. Ashbrook et al. conducted k-mean clustering on GPS location information collected over a period of time to learn the user's meaningful locations at two levels of cluster scales [1].

Among these works, the last one by Ashbrook is the closest approach to ours. In this work, after creating clusters of places where a user stays more than a certain time, a learning system has to again go back into the original data to organize transition probabilities between each pair of clusters. In addition, time of stay and transition are not concerned in this model. Our learning model, on the other hand, creates a structure where transition between locations and its time are automatically organized.

2.3   Organizing a Behavior-Based Personal Controller

A BPC is created by GPS location information automatically collected by the system shown in Figure 1.

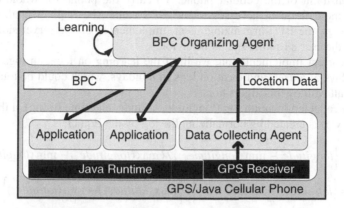

Fig. 1. A BPC organizing system

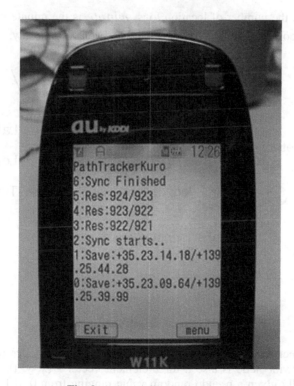

Fig. 2. A data-collecting agent

A tiny Java program on a GPS/Java capable cellular phone of KDDI corp. is sensing GPS location information every 10 minutes, and stores it on the storage of the cellular phone. Whereas, another thread of this program sends these stored location logs to the server (Figure 2). The 10-minute-interval of GPS collection is based on the battery constraint of the cellular phone. To carry the phone for whole day without recharge, more frequent accesses to the GPS cannot be implemented. From those collected logs, the BPC-organizing agent, implemented on the server side, learns the feature of the user's routine spatial behavior.

In the current implementation, we limit the learning on location logs collected in working days of a user, and location logs in holidays, which could be totally random, are not dealt with by this algorithm.

From a collected location log (longitude, latitude, and time of log), a three-element vector (x, y, t) is created by normalizing the log by the Eq.(1).

$$x_i = \left\{ longitude_i - \min_{j=1\ldots m}(longitude_j) \right\} / \left\{ \max_{j=1\ldots m}(longitude_j) - \min_{j=1\ldots m}(longitude_j) \right\}$$

$$y_i = \left\{ latitude_i - \min_{j=1\ldots m}(latitude_j) \right\} / \left\{ \max_{j=1\ldots m}(latitude_j) - \min_{j=1\ldots m}(latitude_j) \right\} \qquad (1)$$

$$t_i = minute_i / 1440$$

In Eq. (1), m is the number of location logs, $minute_i$ is the minute value of the time of log, and the constant number 1440 is the minute value of one day.

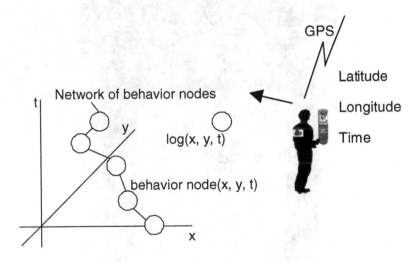

Fig. 3. A learning network and an input log

A learning network is constructed by a fixed number of nodes (called "behavior node"). A behavior node is also a three-element vector - (x, y, t), each element of which is initially given a pseudo random value ranging from 0 to 1. Behavior nodes are monotonically connected to represent, after learning, the sequence of behavior (i.e. transition) (Figure 3). The learning procedure is based on the self-organizing neural network [7]. For each log, every behavior node calculates the distance to that log. The distance between an input log vector I and an behavior node vector O, denoted as DIST(I,O), is calculated as,

$$DIST(I,O) = \sqrt{\alpha\left\{(x_{out} - x_{in})^2 + (y_{out} - y_{in})^2\right\} + \beta(t_{out} - t_{in})^2} \qquad (2)$$

where α and β are weights to define the relation between the distance in space and the distance in time (both α and β are set 1 in the experiment). After all the behavior nodes calculate their DISTs to the log, the behavior node with the minimum DIST value is selected as the "winner". The internal vectors of the winner behavior node and its neighborhood behavior nodes are updated (Figure 4) as,

$$O_i(t+1) = O_i(t) + \alpha(t)\beta_{ij}(t)(I(t) - O_i(t)) \qquad (3)$$

where j is the winner node id, and $O_i(t)$ is the vector of the behavior node i at iteration number t. $\alpha(t)$ is the learn rate at iteration t defined as,

$$\alpha(t) = \alpha(t_o)(\alpha(T)/\alpha(t_o))^{t/T} \qquad (4)$$

where $t_o = 0$, and T is the maximum iteration number. $\alpha(t)$ starts with the initial value $\alpha(t_o)$, at iteration $t = t_o$ or 0, and ends with $\alpha(T)$ at iteration $t = T$. The neighborhood learning rate $\beta_{ij}(t)$ defines how much the winner node j's neighborhood node i updates its weight vector. $\beta_{ij}(t)$ is given as the Gaussian function,

$$\beta_{ij}(t) = \exp(-|i - j|^2 / \sigma(t)^2) \qquad (5)$$

where $\sigma(t)$ is the size of the neighborhood nodes to be updated. Note that when $i = j$ means that i is the winner node, thus $\beta_{ij}(t) = 1$.

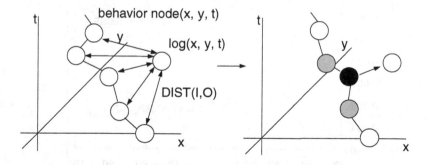

Fig. 4. Weight update of the "winner" behavior node

An epoch of learning is the process of Eqs.(2)-(3) through the all logs. This one epoch of learning is repeated T times, and finally, the network of behavior nodes represents a BPC, that is the feature of the user's spatial behavior in the duration of one day.

3 Experiment on Organizing Behavior-Based Personal Controllers

Two Behavior-based Personal Controllers were created from two different sets of spatial behavior. Two users (one is cafe stuff (User A) and the other one is college student (user B)) have carried GPS/Java capable cellular phones for two weeks, and the data collecting programs collected their location information in their working days. The GPS receiver is of the accuracy of 10 meters without any obstacles, 24-30 meters on arcaded streets, about 60 meters in concrete canyons, and more than 100 meters inside buildings [14].

876 logs from User A and 610 logs from User B were used for the learning. The iteration number T is set to make the network learn from 500 times larger inputs than the number of behavior nodes as,

$$T = num\_behaviornodes \times 500 / num\_log s \qquad (6)$$

The initial learn rate is 0.3 and the final learning rate is 0.1 in Eq.(4). The neighborhood size $\sigma(t)$ in Eq.(5) is set as,

$$\sigma(t) = \begin{cases} 5 & when \quad 0 \leq t < T/5 \\ 4 & when \quad T/5 \leq t < 2T/5 \\ 3 & when \quad 2T/5 \leq t < 3T/5 \\ 2 & when \quad 3T/5 \leq t < 4T/5 \\ 1 & when \quad 4T/5 \leq t \leq T \end{cases} \qquad (8)$$

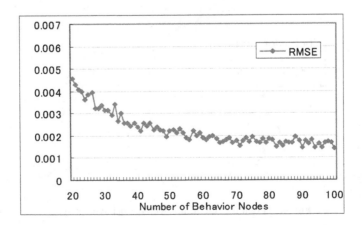

Fig. 5. RMSE values (User A)

BPCs were organized by different numbers of behavior nodes. RMSE values (defined in Eq.(9)) between each log and its nearest behavior node are shown in Figure 5 and Figure 6. In Eq.(9), m is the number of logs and n is the number of behavior nodes.

$$RMSE = \sqrt{\frac{1}{m}\sum_{i=1}^{m} \min_{j=1..n}\left\{ DIST(I_i, O_j)^2 \right\}} \tag{9}$$

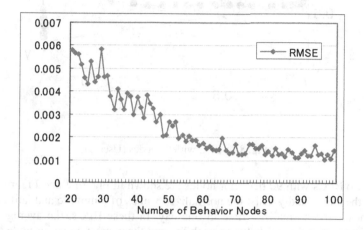

Fig. 6. RMSE values (User B)

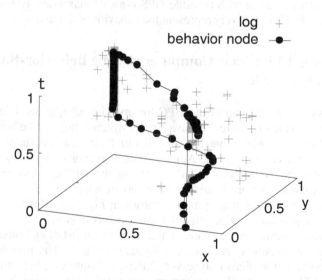

Fig. 7. A BPC with 90 nodes (User A)

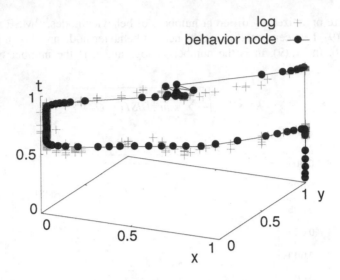

Fig. 8. A BPC with 90 nodes (User B)

The two BPCs with 90 behavior nodes are shown in Figure 7 and Figure 8. In these figures, the axis x and y insist the normalized values of longitude and latitude, and the axis t means the normalized time in one day. In these BPCs, the average error distances (in space and time) between each log and the nearest behavior node are respectively (180 meters, 16 minutes) for User A, and (305 meters, 11 minutes) for User B. This result shows that even with possible GPS error of maximum 100 meter (inside buildings), these BPCs effectively represent the behavior of the users.

4   Controlling Ubiquitous Computers by the Behavior-Based Personal Controller

Figure 9 shows the mechanism of the BPC for invoking ubiquitous objects. The 3D graphic on the left side of Figure 9 is Java Applet which expresses the behavior nodes of the BPC, ubiquitous objects, and the user all with their locations and time.

The white connected nodes in the Applet are the behavior nodes of the BPC. Location embedded pictures collected by the user via the GPS/Camera cellular phone through her/his daily lives are linked to the behavior nodes in the Applet. The location-embedded-picture-archiving system is shown in Figure10. Reader can see those pictures as ubiquitous information related to the user's behavior.

A sphere which located at the center in the Applet screenshot and linked to several behavior nodes represents a "networked ubiquitous switch". The networked ubiquitous switch consists of a micro web server "XPort" of Lantronix, Inc., an AVR micro controller of ATMEL corp., IR transmitters, and a solid state relay. The networked ubiquitous switch provides a controlling logic for ubiquitous computers – power controlling by the solid state relay and sending various commands by the IR transmitters.

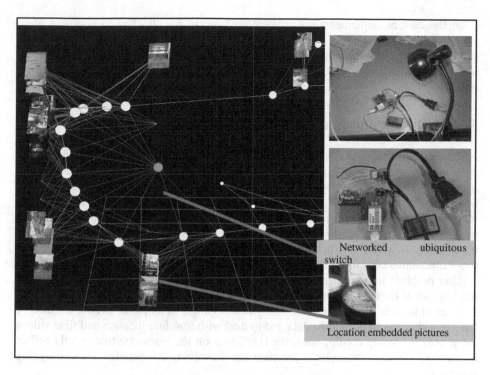

Fig. 9. A mechanism to invoke and retrieve ubiquitous objects from a BPC

One scenario the BPC and the networked ubiquitous switch draw is that, when leaving home, an air conditioner and lights turned themselves off, and latest train arrival time shows up on the user's mobile phone and automatically updated by the user's approach to the nearby station.

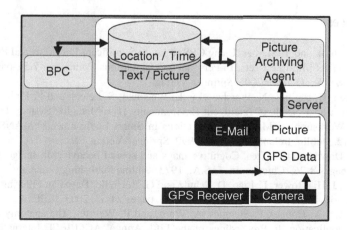

Fig. 10. A location embedded picture archiving system

In the current implementation, ubiquitous objects are attached location (or area) and time (or time interval), and related to the BPC by the k-nearest neighbor query [13]. Building general frameworks to define actions of ubiquitous computers and their relations to a BPC are needed to augment the BPC to wider ubiquitous computing scenarios.

5 Conclusion and Future Work

A representation of a user's spatial behavior is built from GPS location information collected by an on-mobile-phone agent in order to form a controller to retrieve or invoke ubiquitous objects by the user's behavior. The experiment on two users' location logs showed that the BPCs represented those users' behavior with the accuracy more than half a kilometer in location and half an hour in time. We show a prototype mechanism to invoke and retrieve ubiquitous objects by a BPC in Section 4. This mechanism - "invoke by behavior", will assist our everyday lives when more and more ubiquitous computers appear in the near future.

One problem in the current algorithm is to normalize the all location logs among the first set of logs. This means that the algorithm, after the learning is finished on the first set of logs, is not dynamic for newly coming logs. In addition, even if we modify the algorithm not to normalize data and to deal with absolute location and time values for managing newly coming logs, the regulation on the learn rate to correctly reflect changes of the user's behavior is not clear yet. Resolving this problem is our on-going research.

Designing human-readable descriptions, which define actions of ubiquitous objects, contexts of the BPC, and relations between them, are among the most important future works. Synthesizing the functions of distributed objects and describing ubiquitous computing services are deeply explored in [11], [10], and [2]. We believe ideas in these works will be great help in the augmentation of the Behavior-based Personal Controller.

References

1. D. Ashbrook and T. Starner. Using GPS to Learn Significant Locations and Predict Movement Across Multiple Users. In Personal and Ubiquitous Computing 7(5), pages 275-286, London, U.K., October 2003, Springer-Verlag.
2. M. Coen, B. Phillips, N, Warshawsky, L. Weisman, S. Peters, and P. Finin. Meeting the Computational Needs of Intelligent Environments: The Metaglue System. In 1st International Workshop on Managing Interactions in Smart Environments (MANSE'99), pages 201-212, Dublin, Ireland, December 1999, Springer-Verlag.
3. R. M. Downs and D. Stea. Cognitive maps and spatial behavior. In Image and Environment, pages 8-26, Chicago, IL, U.S.A., 1973. Aldine Publishing Company.
4. D. Fox, J, Hightower, L. Liao, D. Schulz and G, Borriello. Bayesian Filtering for Location Estimation, IEEE Pervasive Computing, 2(3), pages 24-33, 2003. IEEE
5. A. Harter, A. Hopper, P. Steggles, A. Ward, and P. Webster. The anatomy of a context-aware application. In Proceedings of the Fifth Annual ACM/IEEE International Conference on Mobile Computing and Networking, MOBICOM'99, pages 59-68, Seattle, WA, U.S.A., August 1999. ACM Press.

6. T. Jebara, B. Schiele, N. Oliver, and A. Pentland. Dy-PERS: A Dynamic and Personal Enhanced Reality System. Appeared in the Second International Symposium on Wearable Computing, Pittsburgh, PA, U.S.A., October 1999. IEEE Computer Society.
7. T. Kohonen, Self-Organizing Maps, Berlin, Germany, 1995. Springer-Verlag.
8. B. Kuipers. The Map in the Head Metaphor, Environment and Behavior, 14(2):202-220, 1982.
9. N. Marmasse and C. Schmandt. Location--aware information delivery with ComMotion. In Proceedings of International Symposium on Handheld and Ubiquitous Computing, pages 157-171, Bristol, UK, September 2000, Springer-Verlag.
10. M. Minami, K. Sugita, H. Morikawa, and T. Aoyama. A Design of Internet Application Platform for Ubiquitous Computing Environment. In IEICE Transaction, J85-B(12) pages 2313-1330, December 2002, IEICE.
11. S. Peters and H. Shrobe. Using Semantic Networks for Knowledge Representation in an Intelligent Environment, In 1st Annual IEEE International Conference on Pervasive Computing and Communications, Tg. Worth, TX, USA, March 2003, IEEE.
12. M. Roman, C. Hess, R. Cerqueira, A. Renganat. R. H. Campbell, and K. Nahrstedt. Gaia: A Middleware Infrastructure to Enable Active Spaces. In IEEE Pervasive Computing, pages 74-83, December 2002, IEEE.
13. H. Samet. Hierarchical representations of collections of small rectangles. ACM Computing Surveys (CSUR), 20(4):271-309, December 1988. ACM Press.
14. I. Sasaki, K. Goda, H. Tani, K. Kogawa, H. Tarumi. Evaluation of the Space Tag System. IPSJ SIG Technical Reports, GN47-5, 2003, Information Processing Society of Japan.
15. P. A. Sistra, O. Wolfson, S. Shamberlain, and S. Dao. Modeling and querying moving objects. In Proceedings of the Thirteenth International Conference on Data Engineering, pages 422-432, Birmingham, U.K., April 1997. IEEE Computer Society.

Scanning with a Purpose – Supporting the Fair Information Principles in RFID Protocols

Christian Floerkemeier, Roland Schneider, and Marc Langheinrich

Institute for Pervasive Computing,
ETH Zurich, Switzerland
{floerkem, langhein}@inf.ethz.ch
schneider_roland@student.ethz.ch

Abstract. Today's RFID protocols that govern the communication between RFID readers and tags are solely optimized for performance, but fail to address consumer privacy concerns by appropriately supporting the fair information practices. In this paper we propose a feature set that future privacy-aware RFID protocols should include in order to support the fair information principles at the lowest possible level – the air interface between readers and tags – and demonstrate that the performance impact of such an extension would be within acceptable limits. We also outline how this feature set would allow consumer interest groups and privacy-concerned individuals to judge whether an RFID reader deployment complies with the corresponding regulations through the use of a watchdog tag.

1   Introduction

When Mark Weiser envisioned computing capabilities everywhere, embedded in the environment in such a way that they can be used without noticing them, he also acknowledged that the invisible nature of the computing devices will make it difficult to know what is controlling what, what is connected to what, and where information is flowing [19]. The intended deployment of RFID-based tracking solutions in today's retail environments epitomizes for many the dangers of such an Orwellian future: Unnoticed by consumers, embedded microchips in our personal devices, clothes, and groceries can unknowingly be triggered to reply with their ID and other information, potentially allowing for a fine-grained yet unobtrusive surveillance mechanism that would pervade large parts of our lives. While industry standard bodies largely focus on optimizing the communication between RFID readers and tags for speed and cost at the expense of privacy, consumer interest groups consequently advocate the complete ban of RFID tags in the public part of stores [15]. Although the latter approach will naturally protect the privacy of the individual, it falls short of an optimal solution even from a consumer standpoint, since it is not just the retail store that can benefit from the use of RFID tags, but also the consumer. The magic medicine cabinet [18], the magic wardrobe [9], and the often-cited smart fridge are just some of

H. Murakami et al. (Eds.): UCS 2004, LNCS 3598, pp. 214–231, 2005.

the consumer applications that would benefit from post-point-of-sales item-level RFID tagging.

In this paper we argue for a middle ground, inspired by our everyday lives where we rarely encounter all-or-nothing tradeoffs, but rather engage in meaningful exchanges that conditionally lead us to disclose parts of our personal data to service providers in return for more or less tangible benefits. By incorporating the basic principles of the widely accepted fair information practices at the reader-to-tag protocol level, RFID-system operators will be able to deploy readers that only collect tag data relevant to the actual application, while small personal devices could additionally provide consumers with a detailed look at a reader's operator and its purpose for collecting data, potentially allowing for an explicit consent before any tag information is read out. Future tags might even be able to independently decide whether or not to reply to a reader's query, based on its stated ID, purpose, and target range. Having RFID readers explicitly declare the scope and purpose of the tag data collection, as well as disclosing the identity of their operators, will allow both consumers and regulators to better assess and control the impact of everyday RFID encounters.

The rest of the paper is organized as follows. After briefly restating the fair information principles and their role in today's privacy legislation, we describe some of the most important characteristics of RFID systems and show how the requirements put forth by the fair information principles could be embedded into the reader-to-tag communication of existing RFID standards. We then present an early prototype of a "watchdog" tag, a small personal device that can be used in conjunction with our protocol extensions to further increase the transparency of the identification process. We conclude with a discussion of our approach, giving special regard to its efficiency, as well as outlining future work.

2   Fair Information Practices

The Fair Information Practices (FIP), published by the Organization of Economic Cooperation and Development (OECD) in 1980 [14], are a well established set of guidelines for consumer privacy. They have their roots in a 1973 report of the "United States Department for Health, Education, and Welfare (HEW)" and were drawn up by the OECD to better facilitate the cross-border transfer of customer information as part of trade between its member states. The eight principles can be summarized as follows:

1. Collection limitation: Data collectors should only collect information that is necessary, and should do so by lawful and fair means, i.e., with the knowledge or consent of the data subject.
2. Data quality: The collected data should be kept up-to-date and stored only as long as it is relevant.
3. Purpose specification: The purpose for which data is collected should be specified (and announced) ahead of the data collection.
4. Use limitation: Personal data should only be used for the stated purpose, except with the data subject's consent or as required by law.

5. Security safeguards: Reasonable security safeguards should protect collected data from unauthorized access, use, modification, or disclosure.
6. Openness: It should be possible for data subjects to learn about the data collector's identity, and how to get in touch with him.
7. Individual participation: Data subjects should be able to query data collectors whether or not their personal information has been stored, and, if possible, challenge (i.e., erase, rectify, or amend) this data.
8. Accountability: Data collectors should be accountable for complying with these principles.

The FIP form the basis for many of today's privacy laws, such as the EU Directive 95/46/EC [6], which provides the framework for the national privacy laws of all EU-member states. For example, article 6 of the Directive requires data collectors to collect only as much information as necessary (also called the *proportionality principle* or the principle of *data minimization*) while article 7 requires them to obtain the unambiguous consent of the data subject before the collection.

It is undisputed that the act of reading out one or more RFID tags constitutes a data collection, meaning that existing privacy laws also apply to the communication between tags and their readers. This has also been recently pointed out by the international community of data protection and privacy commissioners [1]. At the outset, this would mean that RFID readers would need to be openly announced with the help of public signs and placards explaining the purpose and extend of the data collection, as well as the identity of the data collector [8]. While adequate from a legal point of view, presenting the necessary information in such a way easily suffers from being ignored by the consumer, as the ubiquitous privacy policy links on today's Web sites have demonstrated. This is because of two important drawbacks such an out-of-channel solution has: Firstly, data subjects need to actively seek out such information that might otherwise be easily overlooked. Secondly, even when accessible, reading and understanding this information puts an added burden on the consumer, as it is often written in dense legal prose.

On the Web, the Platform for Privacy Preferences Project (P3P) aims at alleviating these two drawbacks [4]. Developed under the auspices of the World Wide Web Consortium (W3C), P3P integrates machine readable privacy policies into the browser-to-server protocol, thus allowing the user's Web browser to automatically read the privacy policy of a Web site, compare it with the user's preferences, and subsequently take action on behalf of the consumer (e.g., facilitating or preventing a transfer of personal data, or advising the user in an easily understandable manner). Our goal is to implement a similar mechanism into the protocol between RFID tags and their readers, in order to lessen the burden on the consumer by having her tags (and optionally a personal mobile device carried with her) read and process privacy related information autonomously and support her in this task.

Some of these principles, such as individual participation or data quality, will need support primarily in the storage back-end, for example with the help of privacy-aware databases [2, 12]. However, the majority of the principles could be

Table 1. *Support for the FIP in our reader-to-tag air interface.* About half of the principles can be embedded directly at the protocol level

Principle	Support
(1a) collection limitation	through selection mask
(1b) consent	with watchdog tag (optional)
(2) data quality	out of scope (use privacy-aware DB)
(3) purpose specification	through purpose declaration
(4) use limitation	with collection types
(5) security safeguards	encryption (future work)
(6) openness	through reader and policy ID
(7) participation	out of scope (use privacy-aware DB)
(8) accountability	through reader and policy ID

supported directly at the point of data collection, i.e., when the reader interrogates the tags. Table 1 lists the level of technical support for the FIP that our extended reader-to-tag air interface offers. Obviously, most of this support can also be achieved through non-technical means, e.g., a notice about tag-reading taking place could also be simply announced through an easily noticeable sign. However, by incorporating such principles directly into the underlying protocol, both consumers and data collectors can more easily follow them, thus strengthening existing legal protection by providing the means to verify and thus enforce corresponding regulations.

3   RFID Primer

Before describing our planned extensions to existing RFID standards in detail, we give a brief overview on the functioning of an RFID system. RFID systems are composed of RFID tags, which are attached to the objects to be identified and an RFID reader, which reads from and possibly also writes to the tags. RFID tags consist of a coupling element and a microchip that stores, among other things, data including a tag identification number. The reader forms the radio interface to the tags and typically features some internal storage and processing power in order to provide a high level interface to a host computer system to transmit the captured tag data. Since RFID tags usually do not possess their own power supply, the reader supplies the tags with power through the coupling unit along with data and clock pulses.

While all RFID systems are made up of these two components, a wide variety of different RFID systems exist that address the requirements of individual application scenarios. Finkenzeller [7] provides a comprehensive classification of the various RFID systems commercially available. An overview of RFID systems that also addresses their privacy implications is available in [16]. For the purpose of this paper, the important differentiation features are the memory organization, read range and the methods that an RFID reader employs to detect multiple tags in its read range, the anti-collision algorithm.

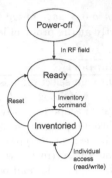

Fig. 1. *Simplified tag state transition diagram.* As soon as tags enter the reader's RF field, they move into the "ready" state and reply to the reader's "inventory" command. Once the reader has inventoried tags in its read range, it can access them individually

Protocol extension	Init round all	SUID flag	Round size	CRC-5
1 bit	6 bits	1 bit	3 bits	5 bits

Fig. 2. *The inventory command,* `Init_round_all`, as specified in ISO 18000-6 Type A. The command frame consists of a field that indicates the number of time slots that are available for a reply (round size), various flags, and a cyclic redundancy check (CRC) to detect transmission errors

In order to identify an individual tag in a group, tags usually store at least a unique ID (UID). One can generally distinguish the EPC approach [5], promoted by the Auto-ID Center (now EPCglobal), where a tag only carries a unique ID, but information about manufacturer and product type are encoded in this identifier, and the approach, where the memory is partitioned into a random serial number identifying the tag and additional memory to store information about the object to which the tag is attached.

Under ideal conditions, modern RFID systems in the UHF band (860-960 MHz) can achieve a read range of up to seven meters, though in reality the range is usually less. For HF and LF-based systems (13.56 MHz and 135 kHz, respectively), this comes down to no more than one or two meters, unless large tag antennas are used. While read range issues do not play any role in our protocol extension, it is nevertheless an important parameter for any privacy related discussion of RFID systems, as privacy concerns associated with the invisible nature of RFID increase with the achievable read range of an RFID system.

Once the tag is within the read range of an RFID reader, the tag is powered and is ready to communicate with the reader (cf. figure 1). When multiple tags respond simultaneously to a request from the reader, their signals can interfere with each other, resulting in a failed transmission. In order to inventory all tags within the read range, an anti-collision algorithm that controls access to the shared radio channel is employed by the reader.

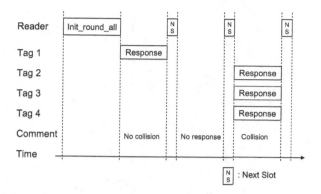

Fig. 3. *The inventory process*, as specified in ISO 18000-6 Type A. The reader initiates a round of tag replies by issuing an `Init_round_all` command. Energized tags respond by selecting one of the available time slots at random to transmit their ID

Figures 2 and 3 show examples of the inventory command (`Init_round_all`) and process, respectively, as defined in the ISO-Standard 18000 Part 6 Type A [10] (which is the standard we are basing our protocol extension on). This standard uses a probabilistic anti-collision protocol scheme, meaning that tags respond at randomly generated times, e.g., based on the Aloha scheme [7]. Deterministic algorithms, in contrast, typically use a binary tree-walking scheme to traverse the set of all possible tag numbers.

4 Supporting the FIP in Existing RFID Standards

In this section we outline how existing RFID standards can be modified to satisfy the principles of *collection limitation, purpose specification, openness, use limitation,* and *accountability*. The extensions are illustrated using the ISO-Standard 18000 Part 6 Type A as an example, though they can equally well be applied to other RFID standards.

4.1 Openness Through Reader and Policy Identification

None of today's RFID standards allow tags to identify the reader they are communicating with. The anonymous broadcast by the reader is certainly desirable from a performance point of view, since the reader's goal is to identify as many tags by their UID as possible in a certain period of time. The transmission of any additional data such as the identification number of the reader will thus reduce the speed at which tags can be detected. Without knowledge about the device that is collecting data, it is, however, impossible to satisfy the principles of *openness* and *accountability*. In order to address these FIP requirements also at the air interface, we include a unique reader policy ID (RPID) into the reader's inventory command, which both uniquely identifies the reader and its operator, as well as the policy in place. Having an explicit reference to the policy allows

Fig. 5. The UF performative partial order under Type A. The dotted lines are initial acts, dashed arrows are last acts, and the normal arrows are the-power of the actions of the actors might be undertaken in Type B.

Table 2. *RFID purposes declarations.* Data collectors can combine 15 different purpose declarations for RFID reader queries

Type (Pos)	Description
access control (0)	Tag IDs are scanned for the purpose of access control, e.g., by identifying a pass holder or by authorizing the validity of an access key.
anti-counterfeiting (1)	Readers read out data stored on the tags to assert the genuineness of a merchandise.
anti-theft (2)	Readers scan for tags that are attached to items that have not been paid for.
asset management (3)	Contrary to inventory purposes, tags are read to provide a picture of the whereabouts of assets, instead of monitoring changing stock quantities.
contact (4)	Tag contents are read out in order to determine a contact channel to the customer, e.g., a mobile phone number or email address.
current (5)	Tags are read to provide a service that was explicitly desired by the individual, e.g., when placing shopping items on a kiosk in order to calculate totals, or for disabling (killing) tags.
development (6)	This purpose should be used during system testing and development only.
emergency services (7)	The system is monitoring tags in order to provide rescue workers with occupancy information.
inventory (8)	A shelf monitoring its contents, e.g., in order to provide out-of-stock notices to a central system.
legal (9)	Law enforcement or other legal obligations require the system owner to read out tag IDs. Additional information on the legal grounds should be made available to the customer.
payment (10)	The current action involves payment, e.g., at checkout when tag IDs are read for billing purposes.
profiling (11-13)	Data is collected for profiling or ad-hoc personalization. See table 3 for individual values.
repairs and returns (14)	Warranty and manufacturing details are read out in order to facilitate or speed up a repair or return process.
other (15)	None of the above purposes fits. Further information should be accessible, e.g., in form of a sign or explicit contractual agreement.

RFID needs to be treated slightly different in the sense that in most cases the user will be unaware of the data collection taking place, as well as of the actual data being collected, many of the P3P purpose definitions can be equally well applied to the RFID domain.

Contrary to Web services, however, some purposes such as *admin* or *current* are much more difficult to assess in an RFID environment. For example, the current purpose is usually implicitly defined by the Web interaction the user is currently experiencing, e.g., the shopping cart checkout in a Web shop, while administration is usually defined by keeping Web server log files. In an RFID context, however, many different "current" or "admin" purposes can be envisioned: A smart shelf might issue read commands for inventory purposes (in a supermarket) or for asset tracking (e.g., for multimedia equipment that employees can check out from a central magazine), both of which could be called administrative purposes. "Current" purposes can equally vary, from a payment purpose at a self check-out station, to a repair and return purpose at a customer information station.

Consequently, we have expanded some of the existing P3P purposes while dropping others, in order to better reflect the more implicit interactions present in RFID systems. Table 2 lists the 14 purposes we identified as useful declarations in this context, even though additional purposes might become necessary in the future. This list is therefore only an initial suggestion that should be repeatedly validated by real-world prototypes, and subsequently standardized by an appropriate standardization body.

Apart from the "profiling" purpose, all purposes are encoded as single bit values that can be arbitrarily combined in our 16 bit number, indicating that data are collected for multiple purposes. The profiling purpose uses three bits to encode one of five possible profiling purpose types that are mutually exclusive (see table 3).

For example, a smart shelf application that monitors its contents for out-of-stock warnings, as well as provide data for anonymous in-store movement information (e.g., to see where consumers spend most of their time), would need to declare both the "inventory" and the "pseudo-analysis"-profiling purposes. A corresponding smart shopping cart that would provide customers with shopping suggestions, based on its contents, would declare "pseudo-decision"-profiling. And a self-checkout station that allows customers to wirelessly pay for their goods, while also associating the purchased items with the customer's loyalty card, would consequently declare the "payment," "anti-theft," and "individual-decision"-profiling purposes.

4.3   Use Limitation Through Collection Types

The principle of RFID reader-to-tag interactions (i.e., readers issuing an inventory command and tags replying with their IDs) makes it difficult to create privacy-friendly monitoring applications even if no identifying tag information needs to be collected as part of the envisioned application. Imagine an RFID system that tries to keep track of the number of people on a certain station platform, in order to avoid overcrowding. Even though RFID tags entering and exiting the area might reply to reader commands with their IDs, the application only needs to keep track of individual tags (e.g., an RFID-based train pass) without having to actually know their specific ID. Additionally, even when identifying information is collected, consumers will typically become much more concerned if this information is not only used locally, but also correlated across multiple readers in order to track an item's (or a person's) movements over time.

To allow data collectors to differentiate between the various collection needs, i.e., whether or not they actually require the serial number of individual tags,

Table 3. *Profiling purposes.* Profiling purposes are mutually exclusive, as profiling types lower in the table (i.e., with higher bit-codes) can potentially include all of the above types

Type (Bits)	Description
ad-hoc-tailoring (011)	This applies to immediate and anonymous tailoring, e.g., providing shopping recommendations based on the current content of a shopping basket, or suggesting accessories based on the clothing the customer has taken into the dressing rooms.
pseudo-analysis (100)	The collected data are used to learn about the interests or other characteristics of individuals. This may help to reveal the interests of visitors to different areas of a store. For example a store's shelves could be newly arranged based on the collected aggregated data.
pseudo-decision (101)	This information will be used to make customization decisions based on the interests of individuals, without actually identifying them. For example, a shop could suggest items to a customer based on his or her previous visits (without actually identifying that person).
individual-analysis (110)	The data collected is used in combination with identified data of an individual, allowing a profile of a certain customer to be generated. This could help to reveal the interests of visitors based on their age, social situation, or other relevant demographic data. Identification could occur in combination with a consumer or credit card.
individual-decision (111)	The information is used to determine individual preferences and to link them with identified data. This profile allows personalized suggestions, based on the individual's interests collected from previous visits, combined with personal information, e.g., from a consumer loyalty card.

or whether they intend to track multiple occurrences of the same tag across different location, we additionally define four distinct collection practices that must be declared as part of a reader's inventory command:

1. *Anonymous Monitoring:* Collecting state information about the items in the vicinity of a particular location, without the need to actual identify tags by their unique serial number. Examples would be simple sensor applications (e.g., an automatic door opener) or counting tasks (e.g., monitoring the number of items in a certain area).

2. *Local Identification:* Tag IDs are collected in order to provide a localized service, e.g., a smart medicine cabinet or smart fridge that monitors its contents. Although unique IDs are collected (e.g., for resolving them to human readable descriptions), the application does not require (nor attempt) the correlation of events across different locations.

3. *Item Tracking:* Collecting information about the location of an item for the purpose of monitoring its movements. Note that this potentially enables tracking people through constellations. However, in order to differentiate between these different intentions, the separate "tracking person" declaration should be used, if people are tracked by the items they carry.

4. *Person Tracking:* Collecting information about the location of a person. Note that although item-level tracking can potentially reveal the location of a person, data collectors will only need to declare this, if they actually collect RFID tag information for this purpose. It is up to legal frameworks to force data collectors to anonymize item-tracking data so that it cannot be used for person tracking.

Together with a corresponding purpose, collection declarations further facilitate the accurate assessment of any RFID scan event. This does not only help data subjects to better understand the *intentions* behind a data collection, but can also be used to selectively allow tags to remain *anonymous* whenever possible. Anonymous replies are already part of some RFID protocols, e.g., ISO 18000 Part 6 Type A, though the reason for using them is usually, again, efficiency, not data privacy. To detect collisions, a 64 bit or longer unique ID is usually not needed and just decreases the number of individual tags that can be successfully detected per unit of time. The anti-collision routine can thus first use the tag's random short identifier to single it out from the set of present tags, before requesting additional data, which might include the unique, but static serial number. We propose that this kind of an anti-collision protocol could become the default, whenever "anonymous monitoring" intentions are declared, thus explicitly providing tag anonymity and unlinkability.

Even without any specific support in the tags themselves: declaring, say, "local identification" would still provide the data subject with the additional level of assurance that her movements would not be tracked across different locations (though this might not preclude the keeping of log files that could be later combined, e.g., as part of a criminal investigation). Obviously, none of these declarations are a proof that the data collector stating them is actually following them. However, as with the purpose declarations, any explicit privacy policy declaration provides a lever to threaten wrongdoers with legal actions – just as it is the case with today's printed policies.

Keeping with the examples from the previous section, the smart shelf tracking inventory and performing anonymous movement analysis of customers within the store would thus need to declare a collection practice of "person tracking", even though these traces are anonymous (pseudo-analysis). The smart shopping cart would use "local identification", as it would use the identity of the items in the cart to locally decide what other products to suggest to the user. Note that it does not matter whether this decision process is actually done on the shopping cart itself or wirelessly via a remote system, as long as the tracked tags are not correlated to other carts or shelves. A smart check-out station would need to declare "person tracking" again, in case a consumer loyalty card is scanned at the point of sale.

4.4   Collection Limitation by Appropriate Tag Selection

The first of the fair information principles requires data collectors to limit the amount of data they collect to what is absolutely necessary (today, the EU directive makes this a legal requirement in most European countries). Consequently, rather than asking *any* tag present to respond to a reader query and then filtering out the tags of interest on the application level, we want readers to limit their initial query to target only relevant tags in the first place, thus realizing the collection limitation principle already at the protocol level.

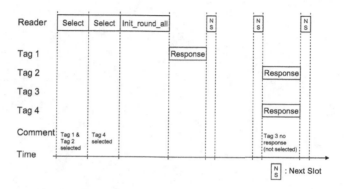

Fig. 5. *The modified inventory process.* The reader first selects a tag population, before initiating a round of tag replies by issuing the modified `Init_round_all` command. Previously selected tags (tag 1, 2 and 4) respond in a randomly chosen slot

As an example of how this would work in practice, let us look at the frequently considered usage scenario of a supermarket smart shelf, whose purpose is to detect whether it is stocked with sufficient supplies of a particular item. Instead of issuing indiscriminate read commands, which might also pick up tags in the clothing of nearby shoppers, the shelf reader will target only tags of products stacked on the shelf, such as a particular brand of razor blades. Optionally, the shelf reader could occasionally run a separate request that targets *all* of the supermarket's products in order to detect misplaced items.

To implement this functionality in our reader-to-tag-protocol, we make use of a similar mechanism that is typically used to singularize a particular tag from a set of tags in range (e.g., the Group-Select and Group-Unselect commands in ISO 18000 Part 6 Type B). However, instead of using a selection mask to facilitate and potentially speed up the inventory process, we are using selection masks to restrict tag ID collection by the reader to relevant tags for privacy reasons.

Once tags appear in the range of a reader and get energized, they initially begin in an "unselected" state. Unselected tags will need to be explicitly selected before replying to any inventory, read or write command from the reader. Tags become selected only after receiving a select mask that matches their data in

tion channel is available (e.g., wireless LAN or GSM), the watchdog tag can additionally translate the data transmitted over the RFID channel into a more expressive format, as shown in figure 8. Of course, any such lookup would require an appropriate backend infrastructure, e.g., the ONS architecture developed by the Auto-ID Center [13]. In addition, providing the reader location in a human readable format allows for a simple, manual detection of reader ID spoofs. More sophisticated watchdog tags featuring an integrated location system could potentially detect reader ID spoofing automatically.

The above screen shots were taken from our initial watchdog prototype, which serves as our design test bed for our protocol extension. Built on top of a standard Windows CE PDA, it uses the built-in wireless LAN to retrieve human readable descriptions. While we are currently working on a separate antenna design that allows us to interface our PDA directly with the RFID reader's communication channel, we so far have been simulating the complete RFID protocol over the wireless LAN as well (with a PC posing as a virtual RFID reader).

6   Discussion and Future Work

Even with our proposed protocol extensions, unauthorized read attempts by readers not conforming to our specification will still be possible. While consumers carrying a watchdog tag might be able to actively jam or block the tag-to-reader communication [11], for example based on user preferences regarding the reader's ID (e.g., following an online lookup), the average consumer would still need to resort to explicitly disabling her tags in order to completely prevent misuse. However, even without any additional devices, the required selection mechanism at the protocol level supports the core principle of *collection limitation*, while the compulsory identification string facilitates the principles of *openness* and *accountability*, thus providing the same level of protection as today's compulsory forms, signs, and placards announcing the privacy policy of the data collector. While they might be ignored in the routine of our everyday, their presence forms an important legal lever once a dispute over the proper use of personal data arises.

Our proposed protocol extensions are easily realized even with today's readers, as they only require updates to the reader's firmware, since the physical layer remains unaltered. While tags would require changes to their logic, these should be straightforward to implement, as the physical layer is not affected and only slight alterations to the medium access layer and the command set would be necessary. Our extensions do, however, affect the performance of an RFID system. The addition of the RPID, purpose code, and collection type require the additional transmission of 130 bits. At a data transfer rate of 30 kBit/s, typical for reader-to-tag signalling of systems operating in the UHF band, it prolongs the execution time of any command by 4.3 ms. This delay is thus comparable to the time it takes for a single tag to reply with its ID, assuming symmetrical data transfer rates. In modern RFID systems that typically read several dozens, if not hundreds of tags at a time, loosing a single tag slot thus seems negligible.

For an RFID system that features a slow data transfer rate, e.g., 1.6 kBit/s as specified in ISO 15693 (HF), the delay is more significant, approximately 80 ms. However, in many situations such a delay would be outweighted by the shortened reply times, as the `Select` command allows the reader to ignore tag IDs that are of no interest to the application in the first place. Newly arriving tags in the read range will have to wait for the next select command before they can be inventoried by a reader.

Future tags might also be able to incorporate basic cryptographic functionalities, thus facilitating a national or even supra-national (e.g., EU-wide) certification system for IDs, as well as allowing tags to thwart an imposter's attempt to "steal" the identification string of a valid reader (thus supporting the FIP principle *security*). To this end, companies would need to register their identification strings with the corresponding authorities, which would use their private keys to sign the submitted ID. Tags would be pre-programmed with the certification agencies public key and could therefore verify the validity of the registration in real-time. In order to prevent replay attacks from rogue readers, not only the ID of a reader, but also the public key of its owner would be signed by the agency (and subsequently transmitted to the tags), which would use this public key for all subsequent communication with the reader. Unauthorized readers would also need the real owner's private key in order to decipher tag IDs. Even though certificate revocation will not work with this scheme, the damage due to unrevokable certificates seems negligible, given the ability of consumer interest groups or concerned citizens to use watchdog tags with online lookup capabilities to detect misuse. Also, certified reader IDs could allow tags to implement the resurrecting duckling model proposed by Stajano [17], where tags would only respond to a "mother" reader, but ignore requests from all others. Instead of killing tags at checkout [3], stores would transfer their "mother" rights to the customer's reader, thus allowing for a safe post-sales RFID usage. Additionally, such "mother" readers could inhibit replies by "its" tags for non-desired purposes and intentions by unknown readers by programming the tags accordingly.

7 Conclusion

The work presented in this paper helps to build future privacy-aware RFID standards that are not only optimized for performance and low cost, but also satisfy the fair information principles. The key idea of our approach is to augment the communication protocol between RFID readers and tags with a feature set that identifies the reader to provide *openness* and *accountability*, enables RFID operators to disclose a *purpose specification* and collection type, and supports a selection mechanism to facilitate the principle of *collection limitation*. In concert with a watchdog tag or a similar device, selective jamming can support the principle of explicit *consent*, while the integration of readers into an overarching privacy-infrastructure such as "pawS" [12] would allow the enforcement of the *use limitation, data quality,* and *participation* principles. Its simplicity provides for a readily available, practical solution to many of today's RFID privacy concerns, while the possible integration of the watchdog tag functionality into future mobile phones might even make the detection of an RFID reader, its policy, and location in the future as easy as detecting the signal strength and operator IDs on a mobile phone today.

References

1. Resolution on Radio Frequency Identification. 25th International Conference of Data Protection and Privacy Commissioners, Nov. 2003.
2. R. Agrawal, J. Kiernan, R. Srikant, and Y. Xu. Implementing P3P Using Database Technology. In *Proceedings of the IEEE 19th International Conference on Data Engineering*, pages 595–606, Bangalor, India, Mar. 2003. Computer Society, IEEE Press.
3. Auto-ID Center. *Draft protocol specification for a 900 MHz Class 0 Radio Frequency Identification Tag*, 2003.
4. L. Cranor, M. Langheinrich, M. Marchiori, and J. Reagle. The Platform for Privacy Preferences 1.0 (P3P1.0) Specification. W3C Candidate Recommendation, Dec. 2000.
5. EPCglobal. EPC Tag Data Specification 1.1, Nov. 2003.
6. European Commission. Directive 95/46/EC of the European Parliament and of the Council of 24 October 1995 on the protection of individuals with regard to the processing of personal data and on the free movement of such data, Nov. 1995.
7. K. Finkenzeller. *RFID Handbook: Fundamentals and Applications in Contactless Smart Cards and Identification*. John Wiley & Sons, Ltd, 2003.
8. S. L. Garfinkel. Adopting Fair Information Practices in Low-Cost RFID Systems. Privacy Workshop at the International Conference on Ubiquitous Computing 2002 (Ubicomp2002), Sept. 2002.
9. A. Gershman and A. Fano. *A wireless world: The Internet sheds its chains.*
10. International Organization for Standardization. ISO/IEC 18000: Information technology automatic identification and data capture techniques - Radio frequency identification for item management air interface, 2003.
11. A. Juels and R. L. Rivest. The blocker tag: Selective blocking of RFID tags for consumer privacy. In *10th Annual ACM CCS 2003*, May 2003.
12. M. Langheinrich. A privacy awareness system for ubiquitous computing environments. In G. Borriello and L. Holmquist, editors, *4th International Conference on Ubiquitous Computing (UbiComp2002)*, LNCS 2498, pages 237–245. Springer, 2002.
13. M. Mealling. *Auto-ID Object Name Service (ONS) 1.0*, 2003.
14. Organisation for Economic Co-operation and Development (OECD). Recommendation of the Council Concerning Guidelines Governing the Protection of Privacy and Transborder Flows of Personal Data, Sept. 1980.
15. Privacy Rights Clearinghouse. Position statement on the use of RFID on consumer products.
16. S. E. Sarma, S. A. Weis, and D. W. Engels. RFID Systems and Security and Privacy Implications. In *Workshop on Cryptographic Hardware and Embedded Systems*, LNCS 2523, pages 454–470, Redwood Shores, CA, Aug. 2003. Springer.
17. F. Stajano. *Security for ubiquitous computing*. John Wiley & Sons, Ltd, 2002.

18. D. Wan. Magic medicine cabinet: A situated portal for consumer healthcare. In *Proceedings of the International Symposium on Handheld and Ubiquitous Computing (HUC'99)*, LNCS 1707, Karlsruhe, Germany, Sept. 1999. Springer.

19. M. Weiser, R. Gold, and J. Brown. The origins of ubiquitous computing research at PARC in the late 1980s. In *IBM Systems Journal*, pages 693–696, 1999.

Towards a Comprehensive Integration and Application Platform for Large-Scale Sensor Networks

Asuman Suenbuel, Joachim Schaper, and Thomas Odenwald

SAP Research Labs, LLC,
3475 Deer Creek Road, Palo Alto, CA, 94304
{Asuman.Suenbuel, Joachim.Schaper, Thomas.Odenwald}@sap.com

Abstract. This paper presents a study that has been performed in order to combine the strength of two emerging technologies: Smart Items and Enterprise Architectures. Smart Items are physical objects with sensing, computing and communication capabilities based on RFID techniques. Enterprise services are generic services that can be tailored to an industry's or a company's specific needs. Examples include accounting, health care, financing, supply chain management, oil and gas, consumer goods, automotive industry and many other domains. However, bringing these two emerging technologies together is not obvious and may become quite cumbersome. There are challenging modeling issues that need to be addressed. In this article, we will present our overall approach to discuss solutions for these challenging questions. We will then demonstrate our concepts along a case study that we have performed on the UC Berkeley sensor boards, (so called motes) for the domain of container security.

Keywords: Sensor Networks, Component Based System, Generic Code Generation, Ubiquitous Weaving.

1 Introduction

The current trend in software engineering shows that there is a strong divergence away from traditional computing: while the emphasis of traditional computing involves communicating protocols, e.g., over networks whose topology is more or less pre-determined, its more future-oriented counterpart is a collection of mostly mobile, tiny devices equipped with sensors and radio to interact with its physical environment and to communicate with each other. This paradigm is often referred to as ubiquitous computing, sensor networks, or to some degree also the so-called RFID systems. Certain computational behaviors of these devices are well comparable to biology; e.g. colonies of termites, ants or bees. Each individual's "computations" consist of a collection of more primitive tasks; the combination of these tasks has the potential to offer more computational power than a single individual "processor" could provide. In biology, this would correspond, for instance, to the ability of ants finding a food source by following certain pheromone trails marked by other ants and to build anthills, which would be impossible for an individual ant.

H. Murakami et al. (Eds.): UCS 2004, LNCS 3598, pp. 232–244, 2005.

Designing and implementing new business applications for using swarm like networks require significantly different software engineering approaches than those ones used for traditional programs running on a single PC [7].

In this paper, we want to address some key issues arising from the challenges imposed by the task of developing efficient and reliable software applications using RFID and/or AUTO-ID devices in general and sensor network devices in particular. These key questions are:

- How to integrate the wireless sensor hardware units into business service modeling? This includes issues dealing with the appropriate modeling of the transition between hardware and software model and with flexibility issues in case hardware and/or software units are changing.
- How to enhance modeling techniques for enterprise architectures in order to master the increased model complexity introduced by the new technology?
- How to maintain safety-critical properties at design and runtime in the presence of dynamically changing enterprise service components?

The paper is organized as follows: In Section 2, we will briefly introduce the main characteristic of the hardware platform that we are using for evaluation purposes. We give a brief overview about SAP's NetWeaver Platform.

Section 3 discusses the introduced design challenges and proposes integration and application solutions. Our ultimate goal is to add functionality to the NetWeaver Platform, so that it will be able to deal with any kind of ubiquitous settings.

In Section 4, we illustrate along a case study our concepts. Section 5 discusses the broad impact of this technology and our current activities, gives a summary, and outlines future research and development directions.

2 State of the Art in Sensor Networks and Business Process Modeling

2.1 UC Berkeley Motes

Motes are small hardware devices (2x2x2cm), developed by UC Berkeley, Electrical Engineering and Computer Science Department. The overall philosophy behind the motes project was, that MEMS devices are more and more becoming cheaper and physically smaller. This technology curve and the biological motivation to build ant or termite like colonies led to the development of motes and a series of motes families. Like in biology, if the computing capability of these distributed devices is combined, one could come up with exciting possibilities. In fact, one could imagine tagging many of real-world objects with this kind of technology, which would open new perspectives [3, 11].

Both, the hardware and software is evolving continuously, the ultimate goal is to reduce the physical size literally down to a dust particle and improving certain bottlenecks caused by the hardware or getting faster and cheaper.

We have performed our studies using mica motes. Such a device consists of 4 MHz 8-bit CPU, 128KB instruction memory, 4KB RAM, 4 Mbit flash, and an

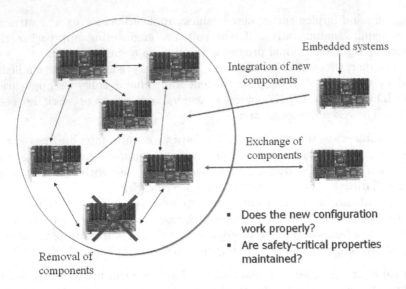

Embedded systems

Integration of new components

Exchange of components

Removal of components

- Does the new configuration work properly?
- Are safety-critical properties maintained?

Fig. 1. UC Berkeley Motes

SPI interface. Motes communicate with each other via radio signals. If a group of them are put near each other, they may automatically form a network. Motes can be operated with 2AA batteries; each communication or computation causes cost, which leads to shortage of physical resources. Motes are heavily resource constrained; they vary widely in terms of network connectivity, available power, available sensors, and reliability of sensor data. It typically takes a larger number of motes in order to reliably process certain kinds of information, e.g., detecting a moving target, triggering alarms etc. A mote by itself is almost worthless, but a network of communicating motes can perform complex tasks by sensing environment information, which can be used for triggering actions for monitoring and/or reacting on certain events.

2.2   SAP NetWeaver Platform

The SAP NetWeaver technology by itself is an integration and development platform for enterprise software [5,12]. At the same time, it is the technical foundation for almost all SAP solutions. We will not discuss the NetWeaver Platform in detail; we will only provide enough information that the reader becomes comfortable with our concepts of using this platform in the context of smart items. Our ultimate goal is reaching the status, where we are able to model and generate code to forward any kind of business logic to the 'smart-item', and the other way around, that data from the 'smart items' are sent back to the platform . Our research results will ultimately contribute to an extension of the current existing SAP NetWeaver Platform. It will provide the possibility to deal with any kind of 'smart items', making the technology platform 'ubiquitous'.

As a brief introductory, the individual components provide abstract services e.g. to ensure that employees have the information and functions that they require to perform their work as quickly and as efficiently as possible, (e.g. comparable to an automated workflow management system) It provides services to people integration, information integration and process integration needs, all based on SAP's Web Application Server. It ensures that services run on heterogeneous systems.

The Application Platform component supports application developments, such as web services in an open development environment by providing an application server. These are just examples to get an idea what SAP NetWeaver provides; again, the above described examples are just to get an idea what the SAP NetWeaver is intended to be.

3   SAP NetWeaver as Ubiquitous Application and Integration Platform

So far, we have briefly introduced the sensor networks and have introduced basic NetWeaver concepts. From now on, our research agenda will be to show how to benefit from these two emerging technologies by applying SAP's open, flexible NetWeaver infrastructure to sensor networks. We will start our discussion targeting one of the most challenging issues for achieving this goal: how can wireless sensor hardware units be integrated into business service modeling?

The general picture and the hardware/software interplay among the motes can briefly be described as follows: The motes communicate with each other, exchange data and are also able to communicate with control services as part of an enterprise system. The general idea is to enable the integration of information collected by the sensor and Auto-ID devices into the overall scheme of the enterprise system. In order to do that, we have to come up with a scheme that transparently provides access to the technical data of the sensor hardware in order to be able to process it in the enterprise system.

From a technical point of view, we deal with different kind of services and architectural abstractions on the sensor network level. First of all, we have the embedded system, the motes, which are running a specific operating system, in our case UC Berkeleys TinyOS. Motes application specific services run on top of TinyOS. The following list contains a first categorization of services that are provided by applications running on sensor network devices:

1. Network embedded services,
2. Business services/application specific services, (AUTO-ID Infrastructure)
3. Device controlling services

The operating systems services are usually part of the embedded system design and are directly provided by embedded system developers. In a concrete application setting, these services are "weaved" into an application that runs on the network embedded system.

3.1 Designing a Service Layer Architecture for Smart Items

Based on these facts, we are now able to introduce the general architecture as shown in Figure 2. As shown in that figure, we have identified four different layers of services that we are going to present in more detail in the sequel.

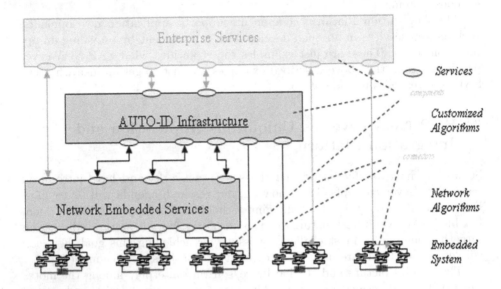

Fig. 2. Enterprise Architecture for Smart Items

Embedded System Level. At a single node level, the embedded system consists of the physical hardware, meaning the sensor or Auto-Id device. We are especially interested in those that are equipped with sensors and the ability to communicate with each other using radio signals as discussed in Section 2.1. There are several sub-layers that can be identified on the embedded system level:

- The so-called hardware abstraction layer provides services which enable analog to digital conversion, e.g. for sensor readings.
- On top of this layer we have the operating system layer providing for services like scheduler, higher-level access to hardware-level functionality (hardware clock control, radio message data format etc.)

Especially in wireless sensor networks it is quite important that the underlying building blocks are kept flexible. This means the ability to exchange program logic with less effort and most importantly to follow a 'plug-and-play' system development paradigm. The component-based modeling and implementation techniques can be used to achieve this goal; the operating system for the motes has already provided a component-based implementation language (Nesc), which enables the flexibility of the component-based approach on the implementation level. We are going to take this concept one step further by using the component-based technology not only for implementation purposes, but also and especially for the more abstract design levels, so that we already at the service specification are able exploit the flexibility of the component-based approach. First experiments in this respect have already been conducted and have been reported in [1, 7, 8, and 11].

Network Embedded Services. The network embedded services are comparable to traditional middleware services, although fundamental differences exist. The common thing is that the network embedded services, as traditional middleware services - as, for instance, introduced in the CORBA standard provide an abstraction layer above the services exported by the individual physical nodes. The main differences are given by the fact, that traditional middleware are by far too complex and require too many resources, that are not available on the minimally equipped sensor and Auto-Id devices. In order to have, for instance, a CORBA service in place for a network, usually all nodes participating in the network must have a local ORB (Object request Broker) service running, which consumes by far more resources that current sensor devices are able to provide given their constraints concerning processing power and unit measurements. For that reason, we need to develop specific middleware services; traditional algorithms from various disciplines within computer science need to be revised in order to be ready for their use within the embedded systems network context. Example for network embedded services include group membership and partial membership services, information caching, clock synchronization services, team formation services, localization and local routing services, feedback control and resource management. Middleware services abstract from issues like real-time, node failure, and specific hardware characteristics; the implementation of the network embedded services handles this kind of events and reacts to them according to the implemented service.

AUTO-ID Infrastructure: Business Services/Application Specific Services

An application-specific service is one that precisely satisfies the functional and performance requirements of an application or class of applications. We already discussed in Section 2 that the resources on sensor networks are very limited compared to traditional computing devices. This is one of the major reasons, why the introduction of a "Business Services/Application Specific Services Layer" seems to be inevitable. This layer provides customized services. Application domains, such as multimedia, databases, and parallel computing, require different services with different requirements concerning performance and functionality. Existing embedded system services provide fixed interfaces and implementations to system services and resources. This makes them inappropriate for applications whose resource demands and usage patterns are poorly matched by the services provided.

The entire RFID/AUTO-ID Infrastructure enables system services to be defined in an application-specific fashion through an extensible core. It offers fine-grained control over a machine's logical and physical resources to applications through run-time adaptation of the system to application requirements.

The key to application-specific services is an adaptable "kernel/controller" that enables system resources to be efficiently and safely managed by the application. By efficient, we mean that capable applications execute faster and with less programming complexity than when using a more conventional platform.

Contemporary embedded system design methods in commercial and research environments often provide interfaces that are inadequate for use by application-specific services. By inadequate, we mean that one of the following statements can be made about the embedded system: there are no interfaces through which application-specific services can exercise direct control over the logical and physical resources, or some interfaces for resource management exist, but they are clumsy, or inefficient, or both, or all applications have unconstrained access to resources, providing good performance when programs are well- behaved, but poor system stability when they are not. In the first case, applications must suffer with whatever interfaces and abstractions are provided by the embedded system. In the second case, the right abstraction can be realized, but at an intolerable performance cost. Finally, in the third case, any abstraction can be realized for a single program, but isolation between programs is not possible. In all three cases, a mismatch between the interfaces exported by the embedded system design and those required by an application-specific service make such services infeasible.

Enterprise Services. In the 'ubiquitous' SAP NetWeaver approach, the technology plattform is used as an integration and development platform as described in Section 3.1. 3.1 The information originating from the sensor and Auto-Id devices is processed and forwarded to the respective business applications configured for the overall business solution. This is especially useful for processes using large amount of physical resources. The data from these devices is transparently used in the same way as any other piece of information - for instance data from a customer and/or product database - so that the sensor devices are seamlessly integrated in the overall enterprise system.

3.2   Modeling and Design Principles

As already mentioned earlier, a component-based approach is used throughout the design and implementation process of 'ubiquitous' NetWeaver applications. In the following we will present some of the key ideas of this and other concepts used in the development process.

Flexibility

As the component-based modeling is used on all design levels, from business application layer to the hardware level, components connect directly to the hardware level, which makes it easy to not only exchange software components much more easily, but also experiment with different kind of hardware and use the hardware abstraction layer as the common service interface. Another example - which is depicted in the Figure 3 below - is the use of generic, more high-level components and connect them with concrete hardware abstraction components in order to provide for a variety of different configurations.

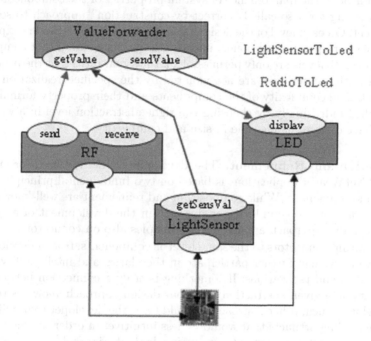

Fig. 3. Use Of Generic High-Level Components

The Figure illustrates this using a generic component "ValueForwarder", which is designed to simply listen to incoming sensor readings and send them to whatever is connected to its output port. Using different kinds of configuration - expressed using different colors in the picture - several functionalities can be achieved by simply connecting different hardware-level components to the import interfaces of the generic component.

Service Modeling Principles. The integration of wireless sensor network services adds another level of complexity to business application modeling. It is therefore crucial to provide concepts for the representation of component structures on different abstraction levels, allow flexible ways of representing semantics information about the components, and possibilities to verify and/or validate the development steps.

The use of identical design principles on all levels of the development process is crucial for a successful and efficient completion of a design. A basic principle that is going to be used in the context of the 'ubiquitous' SAP NetWeaver is the one of abstraction and refinement. This leads to a dramatic reduce in complexity of the models at all design levels and increases the effectiveness of the final implementation process. Following this principle also enables another important aspect: the maintenance of system properties of the components at all levels, providing for a so-called "correct-by-construction" approach to software development. On each level of the design process, desired properties are expressed in terms of the respective component specification; refinement of that component on more concrete levels are only permissible, if they guarantee that the properties expressed in the upper level are not violated by the specified realization of the component. The complexity of the components and their property formulas can be controlled individually by choosing the right abstraction level in a way that these artifact remain manageable in size and complexity.

Composition and Refinement. The development method used for creating new SAP NetWeaver applications is based on two fundamental principles: composition and refinement. While composition and refinement are well-known techniques to conquer the complexity arising within the development of a systems components, our approach applies these principles also on connectors.

By elevating connectors to the same level as components, from a development point of view, we can further participate in the clarity and intelligibility of the design models and realizations: If something is truly a connection between two components on a given abstraction level, our design approach allows us to actually model it as such; other approaches would force the developer to use different kinds of modeling artifacts that would be less intuitive. In order to illustrate the principle of connector refinement, lets have a look at Figure 4.

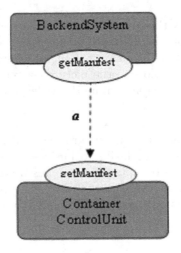

Fig. 4. Connector Refinement

Assuming we want to model the connection between a control unit of a shipment container (see also the case study in the following section) and the application component using an import service getManifest to request information about the contents of a container. On the depicted abstract representation of this situation, an abstract connector a is used to model the situation. In reality, the realization of these connections is even on an architectural level more complicated, but the general relationship between the components is much better comprehended using this abstract representation. The more concrete model depicted in Figure 5 shows a possible refinement of the abstract connector a:

we assume that the controlunit actively stores its manifest at some buffer component, and that the application component gets the requested information from that buffer component. This buffer-solution is conceivable, for always getting the last known information from the container, even if the radio communication is broken at the time of the request.

Maintaining Safety-critical System Properties. Especially in setting where security and safety issues are important, we want to make sure that critical system properties that are expressed on higher-level modeling levels are maintained throughout the refinement process within the development steps. We therefore use a scheme that requires providing the following information for each component:

- information concerning the provided and required properties for the export and import services of the component,
- information concerning constraints imposed on potential clients of the provided export services, and
- information concerning the way the imported services are being used in the body of the component (import structure)

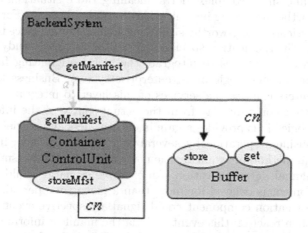

Fig. 5. Abstract Connector Representation

With this information it is possible to schematically check whether a given connection between an export service of one component with an import service of another component is permissible or not. This check can be done in different ways, depending on the stringency of the specification format used: if the above mentioned information is given using completely mathematical formalizations, this check can be carried out automatically by using state-of-the-art theorem prover systems; if the properties are expressed of a given connection involves more human interaction and evaluation.

3.3 Case Study: Container Security

We will now further illustrate our approach using a case study in the area of shipment container security. The idea is that the containers are equipped with sensor devices that enable electronic access to information about a containers location, its manifest, and historical data like loading/unloading date, time and location. In particular, the sensor devices in the container act as an intrusion detection mechanism by providing the functionality of an electronic seal, which uses different kind of sensor information in order to detect any kind of tampering attempt. Moreover, the sensors will also be used in appropriate settings to detect hazardous situations. A typical example is given in a situation, in which chemicals that are harmless on their own but in combination would yield dangerous materials, are loaded adjacent to each other either in the same container or in neighboring containers certain sensors could detect this and trigger an alarm. The underlying architecture of such a container security alert system is shown in Figure 4-1. It resembles the general architecture presented earlier by instantiating the layers with more concrete services and components: at the hardware level, we deal with sensor devices that are located inside or attached to the containers themselves; the network services layer is in this case the abstraction layer that provides access to container services, such as manifests, location information, and more complex alerts, meaning those situations that are only detected by further analyzing incoming hardware- level events. For the detection of more sophisticated alert-worthy situations artificial intelligence techniques can be employed. The application specific services for this case study is given by a layer that provides services to integrate the alerts originating from the lower levels into the business logic of an enterprise system. Business logic designers and implementers can use the services of this layer to integrate the alerts and information that come directly from the actual source of the information into the business logic. This provides a gain in effectiveness and efficiency concerning the overall business operation by several orders of magnitude, if compared to the traditional method of acquiring the now automatically transmitted information using manual data acquisition. An example scenario would be as follows: In case a shipment is delayed for more than a given time period, the container alert and information component could signal a respective event. The business logic would then react on this event and via the manifest information acquired using the respective service of the container alert and information component determine further reactions in the supply chain based on overall business process information. An example would be to trigger a search for alternative ways of delivering certain products to customers depending on information available in the enterprise backend system as, for instance, the customer profile, service contract, customer relationship information. Other scenarios involving the direct access to business logic and processes include the immediate reaction to any kind of unforeseen event that has been signaled using the information collected by the sensor device attached to the shipment containers.

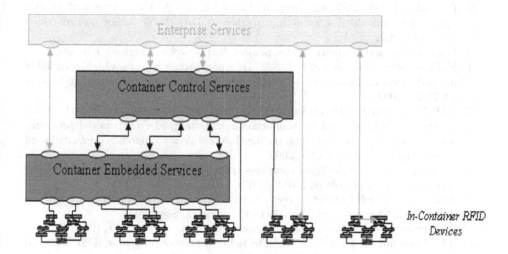

Fig. 6. Container Security Business Alert Architecture

4   Concluding Remarks

The results presented in this paper are part of the work, that has been done in the RFID/smart items group at SAP Labs in Palo Alto. We have taken a first step in addressing the integration of sensor data with SAP's NetWeaver platform, an integration and application platform for enterprise software. We have suggested different layers and outlined the concepts for the AUTO-ID infrastructure, network embedded services and enterprise services. We have discussed three key questions arising in the emerging context of enterprise software and sensor networks. Those three challenges deal with the integration of wireless sensor networks into business service modeling, enhancing modeling techniques to master the increased model complexity introduced by the new technology and maintaining the safety-critical properties at design and runtime in the presence of dynamically changing enterprise service components. We have done some studies in the area of container security; parts of this study have been used in this paper in order to present our concepts. We will further experiment with ubiquitous computing and smart items. Our ultimate goal will be to provide enterprise services as an AUTO-ID product to almost any kind of ubiquitous settings.

References

[1] Matthias Anlauff and Asuman Suenbuel.: Deriving evolutionary software for real-time embedded networks, Integrated Design & Process Technology, Proceedings of the IDPT 2003, Austin,Texas, Dec. 2003
[2] D. Culler, J. Hill, P.Buonadonna, R. Szewczyk, and A. Woo, A network-centric approach to embedded software for tiny devices, DARPA Workshop on Embedded Software, 2002.
[3] David Culler and students, Motes project, http://webs.cs.berkeley.edu/tos/.
[4] K. Srinivasan F. Sultan and L. Iftode, Transport layer support for highly-available network service, International Conference on Distributed Computing System (ICDCS), 2002.
[5] SAP NetWeaver For Dummies, ISBN: 0-7645- 6883-3 Format, April 2004
[6] A. Paul S. Adhikari and U. Ramachandran, Dstampede: Distributed programming system for ubiquitous computing, International Conference on Distributed Computing System (ICDCS), 2002.
[7] Asuman Suenbuel, Specifying components for NEST applications, Integrated Design & Process Technology, IDPT, 2002.
[8] Asuman Suenbuel, Correct by construction components,or: Would Nasreddin use components? Keynote, 28. EuroMicro Proceedings, Sept. 2003
[9] SAP Innovative Solutions to Businesses www.sap.com/company/press/
[10] SAP Launches First RFID Solution to Help Customers Automate RFID-Enabled Business Processes, www.sap.com/company/press
[11] Feng Zhao and Leonidas J. Guibas (eds.), Information processing in sensor networks, 2nd International Workshop, IPSN, 2003, Palo Alto, CA, USA, April 22-23, 2003
[12] SAP Alliance to Address the Challenges Faced by Food and Beverage Companies www.sap.com/company/press/ In a technical sense referring to client/server relationships between components

Inexpensive and Automatic Calibration for Acceleration Sensors

Albert Krohn, Michael Beigl, Christian Decker, Uwe Kochendörfer,
Philip Robinson, and Tobias Zimmer

Telecooperation Office (TecO),
Universität Karlsruhe

Abstract. In this paper, we present two methods for calibration of acceleration sensors that are inexpensive, in-situ, require minimum user interaction and are targeted to a broad set of acceleration sensor applications and devices. We overcome the necessity of orthogonal axes alignment by extending existing calibration methods with a non-orthogonal axes model. Our non-orthogonal method can furthermore be used to enable automatic calibration for 1- or 2-axes accelerometers or realize a simultaneous mass-calibration of sensors with minimum effort. The influence of noise to the presented calibration methods is analysed.

1 Introduction

Calibration is an important issue in sensor based systems as it is the only way to ensure a predictable quality of delivered information. Traditionally, calibration is done in a process during production time. The process is very costly and sometimes requires manual steps which makes it difficult to lower costs at this point. Recalibration is necessary after some time for most sensor systems and can often only be done at particular sites and hence incurs additional high costs. Ubiquitous computing environments differ in many aspects from traditional sensing settings. Ubiquitous Computing devices are used as peripheral devices disappearing from the user's awareness. Therefore it can be said that the majority of Ubiquitous Computing devices will be factually and metaphorically invisible [1]. As a consequence, users tend to ignore intense device administration, even though operational conditions may be extremely rigorous, such that errors due to neglected recalibration accumulate. Furthermore, the circumstances of device deployment in Ubiquitous Computing environments typically sees them embedded into other objects, hindering access and opportunity to perform mechanical recalibration. The amount of computational devices deployed is also envisioned to be on a higher scale in comparison to traditional sensor systems. We refer to hundreds of devices spread in the environment, comparable to the random distribution of low costs, everyday objects and consumer electronics to date. This introduces new challenges for management and maintenance especially for the calibration and recalibration processes.

In research, this development has already started with the instrumentation of everyday objects such as cups [2]. In order to allow embedding, the devices

H. Murakami et al. (Eds.): UCS 2004, LNCS 3598, pp. 245–258, 2005.

must be very small, priced in the cent range and absolutely maintenance free. Costly calibration including high priced hardware is not an option for these applications. Calibration has to be done in-situ without user intervention and additionally has to be done under the assumption that the sensor technology is cheap. A widely used sensor technology in Ubicomp is the MEMS-type acceleration sensor. The sensors are small and quite accurate. Various platforms and applications that incorporates them have been developed. Examples are Lancaster's DIY Smart-Its [3], TecO's particle computers [4],the WearPen and TiltPad [5]. Additionally, companies like Crossbow [6] and Silicon Designs [7] offer products for easy integration of accelerometers in other products even for 3-axial acceleration measurements.

Fig. 1. 3-Axes accelerometer built out of 1-axis sensors © Silicon Designs [7]

However, calibration is necessary, especially if acceleration sensors are used collaboratively. For example, if a 2-axes acceleration sensor device and a second 1-or 2-axes acceleration sensor device are used together in one system - e.g. attached to the same object - both devices can spontaneously form a 3-axes acceleration sensor device. Many of the mentioned platforms build their 3-axes acceleration sensors out of two 2-axes acceleration sensors that are orthogonally mounted. One example is the mentioned design from Silicon Designs. Figure 1 [7] shows how three 1-axis sensors are mechanically combined to a three-dimensional acceleration sensor.

In this paper we present a method that allows us to calibrate 3-axes accelerometers simply and simultaneously. It also makes it possible to combine several 1- or 2-axes accelerometers and to form a cheap 3-axes acceleration sensor on the fly and then calibrate the underlying 1- or 2-axes sensors. Such calibration can be done in parallel for many combined 3-axes sensors:

Hundreds of these sensor devices can be calibrated simultaneously by just putting them into one box and calibrating them all with only some measurements in different orientations of the box. During the measurements, the 1- and 2-dimensional sensors would build 3-axes accelerometers by virtually combining them to 3D sensor systems. The main problem to deal with in these setting is that the axes of the combined sensors are not orthogonal but randomly oriented in the box. This problem is not restricted to simple and cheap sensors it is also a problem for most off-the-shelf 3 dimensional acceleration sensors. The axes of the sensors are often not perfectly aligned to 90 due to mechanical impreciseness. The model that is presented in section 4 presents a solution for such 3D sensor calibration of sensors that have non-orthogonal axes either if they are already assembled or are assembled on-the-fly to form a 3-axes acceleration sensor.

One approach for in-situ calibration of *3-axes* acceleration sensors involving the parameters *offset* and *scale* was introduced by Lukowicz et al. in [8]. They proposed a method for the calibration that needs only some random measurements in different orientations taking advantage of the earth's gravity field.

Our paper focuses on in-situ calibration methods especially regarding noise in the measurements and tilted (non-orthogonal) accelerometer systems. We will extend the current approaches in order to take care not only of offset and scale within the calibration, but also of the *orthogonality* of the axes. The characteristic of in-situ calibration will be kept.

The paper proceeds with a short overview of calibration methods involving only offset and scale. Section 3 investigates the influence of measurement noise and tilted axes on the methods. Section 4 deals with non-orthogonal axes and gives an extension of the traditional approaches. Implementation consideration are covered in section 5 before we conclude in section 6.

2   State of the Art Calibration

In many applications there is a need for a calibrated acceleration measurement, but many sensors - especially MEMS types - are not calibrated after production. Instead the sensor have a sensitivity s and an offset o on each of their axes which lead to measurements that do not represent the actual physical value. Before presenting the two most important calibration techniques, we define some expression used throughout the paper:

- the physical acceleration is named as $x = (x, y, z)^T$. It is measured in multiples of the earth's gravity g
- the measurement offsets of the axes of sensors are named o_x, o_y, o_z and the scalings s_x, s_y, s_z, whereas a perfect system would have $o = 0$ and $s = 1$
- the values measured by an uncalibrated, *orthogonal* 3D acceleration sensor are named $u = (u, v, w)^T$; uncalibrated means here that offset and scaling errors are still present in the measurements
- the values measured by a *calibrated, non-orthogonal* 3D acceleration sensor are named $r = (r, s, t)^T$; calibrated means here that offset and scaling errors have been discovered and the measurements are corrected accordingly
- the interrelationship between measurements and real physical values in an orthogonal system is for x-axis: $x = (u - o_x)/s_x$;. For the y- and z-axis: the according equations.

2.1   Rotational Calibration

The method is described in [9] and determines the offset and the scale factor for each axis separately. Hereby, an axis (e.g. the x-axis) of the acceleration sensor is oriented to the earth's gravity centre and kept stationary. It is exposed to 1g and rotated and exposed to -1g. The measured values (in g) in both positions are $u_{max,x}$ and $u_{min,x}$. Solving the equation system

$$1 = \frac{u_{max,x} - o_x}{s_x}$$

$$-1 = \frac{u_{min,x} - o_x}{s_x}$$

will result in the offset o_x and scale factor s_x for this axis:

$$o_x = \frac{u_{max,x} + u_{min,x}}{2} \tag{1}$$

$$s_x = \frac{u_{max,x} - u_{min,x}}{2} \tag{2}$$

In order to find u_{max} and u_{min} the rotation has to be carried out very slowly to minimize the effect of dynamic acceleration components. The accuracy of the method relies significantly on the accuracy of the alignment.

2.2   Automatic Calibration

Another method for calibration of 3-axes accelerometers has been presented in [8]. It does not require a certain series of pre-defined positions like the method explained above and is therefore very practical in mobile settings. It can perform a calibration in-situ after a complete device has been assembled. It is also suitable for fast mass-calibration as the sensor virtually calibrates itself. The idea is to use the earth's gravity force as a known static acceleration on a 3-axes accelerometer when a sensor has no dynamic component applied on it. Is this state of being stationary detected the following equation (see [8], page 2) is valid:

$$|\boldsymbol{x}| = \sqrt{(x^2 + y^2 + z^2)} = 1 \tag{3}$$

With the according offsets and scale errors of the accelerometers, equation (3) extends to:

$$((u - o_x)/s_x)^2 + ((v - o_y)/s_y)^2 + \\ +((w - o_z)/s_z)^2) = 1 \tag{4}$$

With equation (4) the six unknown calibration variables $(o_x, o_y, o_z, s_x, s_y, s_z)$ can be solved when creating a six lined equation system using six earth's gravity vectors measured in different orientations of the sensor. The six necessary measurements should be significantly different from each other to guarantee a stable convergence of the non-linear solver. Additionally, it must be assured, that all three axes are *perfectly aligned to be orthogonal*, otherwise the precondition for the algorithm is violated and the results will be errorneous.

2.3   Concerns Using the Presented Calibration Methods

When calibrating acceleration sensors in MEMS technology we generally experience the problem of noise introduced in the measurement. Noise can have different reasons like thermal noise, quantization noise or noise introduced by A/D conversion. Noise during the calibration corrupts the measurements and therefore results in imprecise calibration. It is necessary to have a quantitative insight of the influence of noise to a calibration process.

Further, the calibration of the axes' angles is *not* addressed in either calibration method. A complete calibration of a 3D accelerometer includes as well the calibration of the axes' angles to 90 to be able to calculate the physical acceleration x from the measured value u. Some settings (mentioned in section 1) show that it's necessary to provide calibration methods for tilted axes. Furthermore, the axes' angles calibration is of special interest for the automatic calibration method as the orthogonality is the precondition for the validity of equation (3). With titled axes, the automatic calibration method will not work!

3   Influence of Noise

It is impossible to avoid errors on the calibration due to noise during the calibration process. To figure out what negative influence on the calibration results must be expected from a known noise level, we simulated different noise levels with an even distribution and a maximum of 5, 10, 20 and 50 mg and applied them on virtual measurements before using them in the two calibration procedures. Figures 2 and 3 show the accumulative error distribution of the

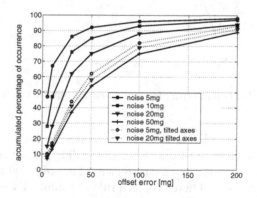

Fig. 2. Offset errors for simulated automatic calibration

calibration parameter offset using the two presented calibration methods. The offset errors are shown in absolute error, the scaling errors in Figures 4 and 5 relatively. Reading out from Figure 2 with parameter $noise = 20mg$ at abscissa $offseterror = 50mg$ gives the value 75. That means that statistically for 75% of

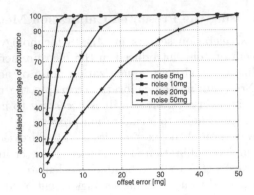

Fig. 3. Offsets errrors for simulated rotational calibration

the calibrations that have a 20mg noise level, the offset error in the results of the calibration will be less or equal 50mg. The 75% can be regarded as the statistical trust level of the offset error being less or equal 50mg in the calibration when applying 20mg of noise on the measurement.

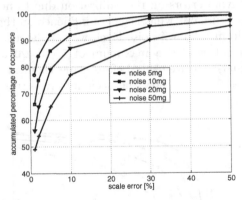

Fig. 4. Scaling errors for simulated automatic calibration

A quick example should show how the Figures 2 and 3 for the offset errors can be compared to Figures 4 and 5 for the scaling errors: An error of 10% in scaling would cause an error in a measurement of approx. 100mg when stationary pointing towards ground. Therefore, as a rule of thumb, 1% error in scaling can be compared to 10mg in offset error. The graphics are useful when a certain target accuracy is desired. Then, one can read out what the (mean) necessary input accuracy should be. For example, a desired target accuracy of 50mg in offset and 5% in scale with a trust level of 95% would require a noise level around 5mg using the automatic calibration.

When comparing e.g. the 10mg noise curves of Figure 2 and 3, one can see that the 95% confidence level for rotational method gives an offset error of around 100mg where the rotational method reaches 8mg! On the first sight, the rotational method would be the clear winner. But the result needs to be interpreted in a broader context. The solver of the non-linear equation array causes additional errors on the automatic calibration. And the noise model on the rotational algorithm does *not* include the errors that occur when the sensor was not measured in it's minimum and maximum but slightly off to these points. In [8] the authors gain a significant improvement in accuracy by averaging a series of results of one sensor.

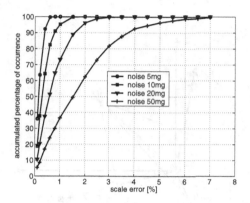

Fig. 5. Scaling errors for simulated rotational calibration

4 Non-orthogonal Axes

As already mentioned, the calibration of axes is not supported by either presented calibration method. For the rotational calibration, the axes are calibrated independently and the offset and scaling calibration is not negatively affected by angular displacement. For this reason, we propose an extension of the rotational algorithm in section 4.2 to calibrate possible axes displacements as a second step after the standard offset and scaling calibration.

For the automatic calibration method, it is a necessary precondition that the axes are orthogonal. We simulated some cases, where the angle was off by 5. These curves can be found as dotted lines in Figure 2. The error is significantly worse than without angular displacement, which motivates the extension of the algorithm to be able to deal with non-orthogonal systems.

4.1 Model of the Tilted Accelerometer Axes

The idea of the extension of the known equations and algorithms to be used with non-orthogonal angles reflects the wish to have three perfectly aligned accelerometers in a bundle. As this is not always the case, a mathematical conversion can simulate a perfectly aligned sensor array by calculating the *virtual orthogonal* values from the measured and *tilted* values. For this conversion, the off-axis angles of the acceleration sensor must be known. Figure 6 shows a euclidean coordinate space $\{x, y, z\}$ representing an ideal acceleration sensor array. For simplicity and w.l.o.g. we assume that the offset and scaling errors are not present and therefore only model the direct relationship between the tilted measurements r and the real physical acceleration x. Later, we can include the offset and scaling errors to formulate an expression including all negative influences. A vector a would be exactly measured with its three components x, y and z. But as the axes are not orthogonal, the values measured by the acceleration sensors (r, s, t) do not represent the correct 3D acceleration applied on the sensor.

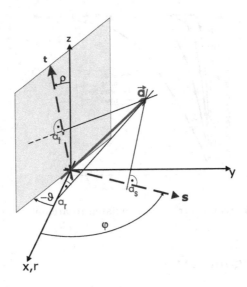

Fig. 6. Tilted Axes of accelerometers

The axes of the accelerometers have three levels of freedom named as φ, ρ and ϑ. For simplicity, we assume a sensible setting where the three accelerometer axes are close to the desired euclidean axes x, y and z and span an R^3 vector space. The axis of the accelerometers are named r, s and t. W.l.o.g, the r-Axis will be defined equal to the x-Axis. Then secondly, the s-Axis will lie in the x-y-plane and therefore only have one degree of freedom: the angle between r-Axis $(x - Axis)$ and s-Axis named φ. The tilted t-Axis has two degrees of freedom: ρ and ϑ. The ϑ is the angle between the positive x-Axis and a virtual plane that contains the z-Axis and the t-Axis. The ρ defines the angle between t- and z-Axis. It is defined in positive x direction if $\vartheta = 0$.

For the model, the first necessary formulas are the unit vectors of the new r, s- and t-axes. They are (in the euclidean system):

$$e_r = \begin{pmatrix} 1 \\ 0 \\ 0 \end{pmatrix}, \qquad e_s = \begin{pmatrix} \cos \varphi \\ \sin \varphi \\ 0 \end{pmatrix},$$

$$e_t = \begin{pmatrix} \cos\vartheta \cdot \sin\rho \\ \sin\vartheta \cdot \sin\rho \\ \cos\vartheta \end{pmatrix} \quad (5)$$

Generally, the measurement that a one-axis acceleration sensor derives from an arbitrary acceleration vector is the acceleration vector fraction, which is parallel to the acceleration sensor axis. Therefore, an arbitrary acceleration sensor like the a in figure 6 needs to be projected in an orthogonal manner on the r, s- and t-axis in order to find out what the according sensors would measure. The measurements are named a_r, a_s, a_t. Notice that this projection is different from a coordinate space transformation where the vector a would be decomposed in the directions parallel to the three axis. The projection from a on the s-axis is not parallel to the $r - t$-plane but orthogonal to the s-axis!

Therefore, the next step is the projection of a on the three axes r, s and t. The auxiliary plane

$$E : e_s \circ (x - a) = 0$$

is intersected with the auxiliary even

$$g : x = \lambda e_s$$

resulting in

$$\lambda = e_s \cdot a.$$

This defines the orthogonal projection vector of a on the s-axis being

$$(e_s \cdot a) \cdot e_s$$

and therefore its length being the measurement of an acceleration sensor pointing in e_s-direction measuring an arbitrary vector $a = (x, y, z)^T$. The length of this vector

$$s = |(e_s \cdot a) \cdot e_s| = e_s \cdot a =$$
$$v = \qquad x \cos\varphi + a \sin\varphi \quad (6)$$

Doing so equally for the w-axis results is

$$t = \qquad |(e_t \cdot a) \cdot e_t| = e_t \cdot a =$$
$$= x \cos\vartheta \cdot \sin\rho + y \sin\vartheta \cdot \sin\rho + z \cos\rho \quad (7)$$

The solution for the r-axis is trivial:

$$r = x \quad (8)$$

The three expressions (6),(7),(8) define the measurements of the acceleration sensor carrying the tilt angles φ, ϑ and ρ. If a measurement is gathered with such a sensor, the virtual values in an ideal orthogonal system could be calculated by inversing the expression for r, s and t. This results in:

$$x = \qquad r \quad (9)$$
$$y = \qquad \frac{s - r \cos\varphi}{\sin\varphi} \quad (10)$$
$$z = \frac{t}{\cos\rho} - r \cos\vartheta \tan\rho - (s - r \cos\varphi)\frac{\sin\vartheta}{\sin\varphi} \tan\rho \quad (11)$$

Now, an interrelationship between the tilt angles of the axes φ, ϑ, ρ, the measurements $(r, s, t)^T$ and the real physical acceleration $(x, y, z)^T$ has been found.

4.2   Using the Non-orthogonal Axes Model

The results from the previous section can generally be used in two ways: Firstly, they enable the automatic calibration model to be used in settings where the axes are not orthogonal. To do so, the expressions (9), (10), (11) can simply be put in place of the measurements u and in equation (4) to solve for the - now nine - unknown variables (three angles, three offsets, three scalings). It is therefore possible to extend the automatic calibration method to systems with non-orthogonal axes. Doing so, the simplified model of (9), (10) and (11) without scaling and offset errors is extended to a model including both the tilted axes and the offset and scaling errors.

Secondly, the results can be used to extend the rotational calibration to a complete calibration including the axes' angles. The rotational calibration method itself is not vulnerable to non-orthogonal axes systems as it calibrates the axes independently through the use of the minimal and maximal values. But it does not provide an easy way to also calibrate a possible axes angle displacement. For this reason, we extend the rotational calibration method after its completion (the offset and scaling are calibrated) with three steps to calibrate a possible axes angular displacement. For the following equations, the vector r is - like above - the measurement vector *including* the correction in scale and offset but *not including* the angular correction. The angle calibration process is as follows:

1. position the 3D sensor that the measurements $r = s = 0$. As the r, s, x and y-axis all lie in the same plane (see figure 6), the real physical values are $x = y = 0, z = g$. With (7):

$$t = z \cos \rho \Leftrightarrow \rho = \arccos(\frac{t}{g}) \qquad (12)$$

2. position the 3D sensor that the r-measurement is maximized. Then the real acceleration $x = (g, 0, 0)^T$, because x and r have been defined to be parallel. In (6):

$$r = g \cos \varphi \Leftrightarrow \varphi = \arccos(\frac{r}{g}) \qquad (13)$$

3. in the same position, but using equation (7) we get:

$$t = g \cos \vartheta \sin \rho \Leftrightarrow \vartheta = \arccos(\frac{t}{\sin \rho}) \qquad (14)$$

With these simple calculations, the three tilt angles can be calculated using only one extra position for the sensor (the position with u being maximized is anyway necessary for the offset and scaling calibration). It is important to notice that the angle calibration for the rotational calibration has to take place after the calibration for offset and scaling has been finished as we need both x and r for the calibration of the angles.

5   Implementation Considerations

Both previously presented calibration approaches are investigated for implementation on our particle computer platform [4]. On the sensor boards we are using two ADXL210 accelerometers mounted orthogonal to each other for a 3D accelerometer. Usually this mounting is done manually, which denies an accurate positioning of the sensors to each other. In the discussion we assume that data from the ADXL is provided in the gravity unit g. Sampling the raw data from the ADXL and converting them in g values can be done very quickly and with a manageable complexity [9].

5.1   Rotational Calibration

The complexity of this method can be directly derived from the equations (1) and (2). For each axis one has to compute scale and offset by just one addition and one division operation. Latter can be replaced by a right shift by one. The angles φ, ρ and ϑ are computed by applying the arccosine function.

5.2   Automatic Calibration

This calibration method requires solving a non-linear equation system with nine unknown variables. Standard mathematical literature proposes the Newton's method for this problem:

$$F'(\underline{x}_n)\underline{\delta} = -F(\underline{x}_n), \quad \underline{x}_{n+1} = \underline{x}_n + \underline{\delta} \tag{15}$$

Hereby, $F(\underline{x}_n)$ represents all nine equations written as a (9x1) vector, $\underline{x}_n = (o_x, o_y, o_z, s_x, s_y, s_z, \vartheta, \varphi, \rho)^T$ is the calibration's solution vector and $F'(\underline{x}_n)$ is the (9x9) Jacobi matrix of all partial derivations of $F(\underline{x}_n)$. The method works in 2 steps, which are iterated to produce better approximations in each step:

1. solve the linear equation system (LES) (15) for an auxiliary variable δ
2. compute next iteration solution by $\underline{x}_{n+1} = \underline{x}_n + \underline{\delta}$

In the first iteration an appropriate vector $\underline{x}_0$ as start value has to be selected. Further, nine measurements of 3-axis acceleration values $(m_x, m_y, m_z)^T$ gathered from nine different positions are neccessary for the computation of $F(\underline{x}_n)$ and $F'(\underline{x}_n)$. The following operations are necessary per iteration:

1. For compilation of LES: 121 additions, 163 multiplications, 80 divisions, and 7 trigonometric operations. The Gauss algorithm solving this LES needs additional 292 additions and 321 multiplication operations.
2. For $\underline{x}_{n+1}$ computation: 9 addition operations

Newton's method implies further constrains one has to take care of. If using an inappropriate start value, then Newton's method can get stuck in an infinite loop without producing improved approximations. One solution is a solver variation called damped Newton's method. Hereby, an additional contraction factor is introduced. As a result, the contraction speed of the method will slow down.

Math literature publishes strategies for selecting this factor optimal. However, the damped Newton's method adds additional complexity for computing this factor. In order to keep the overall computing effort low, the number of iterations should be kept low. However, to achieve a reasonable accuracy the stop criterion has to be carefully selected. Usually, the computation is aborted, if $|x_{n+1} - x_n| \leq \epsilon(\epsilon > 0)$, where x_n is the approximated null after n steps, ϵ is the accuracy requirement, and $|\,|$ is the euclidian distance. A reasonable result is often achieved in less then 10 iterations if the method's convergence order is 2. However, the damped Newton's method will converge only with linear speed implying more iterations.

5.3   PC Versus Microcontroller

Currently, we have implemented the automatic calibration method only on a PC receiving the measured acceleration sensor values from the particle computer sensor board (Figure 7).

Fig. 7. Particle sensor board

The PC implementation of the automatic calibration cooperates with the particle computer. Latter delivers the measurements for the Newton's method as g values from all three axes. Thereby the microcontroller already ensures that all measurements are taken in stationary situations. The values are given in $[mg]$ units. The challenge for the implementation on the PIC18f6720 microcontroller of the particle computer is the effort needed to achieve accuracy and speed. Although addition and multiplication are done on this processor in hardware, the internal registers only support 8bit integer operation. But, for automatic calibration floating point operation is mandatory. This implies more effort for each mathematical operation. Furthermore, this also adds a certain extra memory usage. In our experience the code size for arbitrary arithmetic functions increases significantly when going from integer to floating point or even including trigonometric functions. Table 1 summarizes this observation with an arbitrary small algorithm. All numbers are in bytes.

As an alternative to the more complex, unsupervised in-situ calibration we implemented a supervised calibration method that is able to run on small microcomputer systems. The rotational calibration we used here is significantly less complex than the automatic calibration and therefore consumes less memory and computing power resources. Using this method we do not rely anymore on the availability of a PC based backend program that was used to do the computational part of the calibration process in the automatic calibration method.

Table 1. Memory usage of math functions [in bytes]

	Integer	Float
ROM	234	1292
RAM	13	50

We implemented the rotational calibration with a very convenient user interface: the user needs only to roll the sensor board over each axes (x,y,z) until the respective LED is switching off. He is not requested to perform the movement in each of the axes in a certain way, so also inexperienced users can perform the calibration task. We studied the procedure with three users so far. They where shown how to handle the sensor boards and were then requested to calibrate the sensor systems about 10 times without help. All of the users were able to handle the task and all calibrations were done successfully. The achieved accuracy with this method was extremely precise and the calibrated sensors delivered values with deviation from the actual physical values that are in the order of the noise level of the hardware.

6   Conclusion and Future Work

In this paper, we presented two methods for the calibration of acceleration sensors with minimum user interaction. We extended the traditional methods with the capability to work with *non-orthogonal* axes to meet more practical requirements in real world settings especially for Ubiquitous and Pervasive Computing. We implemented and tested both methods. The methods are now able to handle settings with cheap sensors that have non-orthogonal axes and do not need any (expensive) additional equipment or complicated procedure for calibration.

While the automatic calibration runs completely unsupervised but requires some computing resources the rotational calibration is capable to run on small 8 bit microprocessors with limited resources. Both methods allow to calibrate cheap acceleration sensors in a convenient way without any additional equipment. They are also able to combine three 1-dimensional or two 2-dimensional acceleration sensors to a 3-dimensional sensor on the fly. Another possible use of the methods is mass-calibration of hundreds of sensors, as the calibration can be done in parallel. We have shown throughout the paper - backed up by practical experiments - that the results of the calibration is very good (in the order of the noise level of the hardware). Nevertheless, we are continuing our work to eliminate the remaining error sources. We identified that the solver for the non-linear equation is a major source for the errors in the calibration results and will look into customized solutions for this problem in the future.

Acknowledgements

The work presented in this paper was partially funded by the European Community through the project *CoBIs* (Collaborative Business Items) under contract no. 4270 and by the Ministry of Economic Affairs of the Netherlands through the project *Smart Surroundings* under contract no. 03060.

References

1. Mark Weiser. The computer of the 21st century. *Scientific American*, 265(3):94–104, September 1991.
2. Michael Beigl, Hans-Werner Gellersen, and Albrecht Schmidt. Mediacups: Experience with design and use of computer-augmented everyday objects. *Computer Networks, Special Issue on Pervasive Computing*, 35(4):401–409, March 2001.
3. *http://ubicomp.lancs.ac.uk/smart-its/*, accessed: 4/2004.
4. *http://particle.teco.edu*, accessed: 10/2004.
5. A. D. Cheok, K. G. Kumar, and S. Prince. Micro-accelerometer based hardware interfaces for wearable computer mixed reality applications. In *Sixth International Symposium on Wearable Computers (ISWC)*, Seattle, Washington, USA, 2002.
6. *Crossbow. http://www.xbow.com/*, accessed: 4/2004.
7. *Silicon Designs, Inc. http://www.silicondesigns.com/*, accessed: 4/2004.
8. Paul Lukowicz, Holger Junker, and Gerhard Trster. Automatic calibration of body worn acceleration sensors. In *Proceedings of the second international Pervasive Computing conference*, Vienna, Austria, 2004.
9. H. Weinberg. Using the adxl202 duty cycle output. iMEMS Technologies/Applications AN-604, Analog Devices, 1998.

Dependable Coding of Fiducial Tags

Andrew C. Rice[1], Christopher B. Cain[2], and John K. Fawcett[1]

[1] Laboratory for Communication Engineering*,
Department of Engineering, University of Cambridge, Cambridge, CB2 1PZ
[2] Department of Pure Mathematics and Mathematical Statistics,
Centre for Mathematical Sciences, University of Cambridge, CB3 0WB

Abstract. Fiducial tags can be recognised successfully and decoded by computer vision systems in order to produce location information. We term a system dependable if its observable results are predictable and repeatable. The dependability of such a vision system is fundamentally dependent on the scheme used to encode data on the tag. We show that the rotational symmetry common to many tag designs requires particular consideration in order to understand the performance of the coding schemes when errors occur. We develop an abstract representation of tags carrying symbolic data which allows existing information coding techniques to achieve robust codes. An error-correcting coding scheme is presented for carrying arbitrary symbolic data in a dependable vision system.

1 Introduction

High precision location information is an excellent source of context for many ubiquitous applications. Unfortunately, the sensing systems required to source such information are expensive to build, deploy and maintain—GPS is an example of this. Location systems that can derive information from commodity components such as WaveLAN or Bluetooth understandably fall short of the level of precision provided by more specialised, expensive systems.

Vision systems are an exception. They can be constructed from commodity components and yet have the potential to provide highly accurate information (c.f. photogrammetry). Modern cameras and CCD arrays can provide good quality images[1], whilst distortion caused by lensing systems[2] can be corrected to accuracies better than 0.01 pixels[3]. Fiducial tags are often used as markers to simplify the image recognition process. They present particular features to allow the application of faster processing algorithms and more robust recognition than for unconstrained vision systems.

Recently, researchers have begun to acknowledge the importance of reliability for ubiquitous computing[4]. The new users of context-aware systems will not have technical backgrounds or in-depth understanding of sensing systems and

---

* Now the Digital Technology Group, Computer Laboratory, University of Cambridge.

H. Murakami et al. (Eds.): UCS 2004, LNCS 3598, pp. 259–274, 2005.

yet must be convinced to trust these systems to assist in their tasks. The system must display predictable behaviour upon which users will base their mental models of the system. A system is considered *dependable* its observable results are predictable and repeatable.

In order to ensure that a location system is as dependable as possible we must ensure that every algorithm and process used within the system is robust and that the errors inherent within the system are understood. Identity is as a primary source of context useful to ubiquitous computing[5]. The robustness of identity information for vision systems relates to the mechanism used for encoding information identifier on the fiducial tag.

Squares and circles are common choices of fiducial shape for vision systems. Each of these shapes displays rotational symmetry that reduces the expected difference between each unique payload. We present a classification of coding systems for black and white fiducial tags and suggest a suitable design separation between tags and coding schemes so each can be considered in isolation. In particular, the importance of cyclic codes is demonstrated when considering the rotational symmetry of planar tags. Finally, we present new, robust coding schemes for encoding symbolic data as the tag payload.

2 Template-Based Codes

A template code encodes an identifier as a pattern that is decoded by searching a database of possible patterns for the closest match. ARToolKit[6] uses a set of manually-chosen patterns encoded onto a square tag. The imaged tag is compared, after perspective correction, using an auto-correlation co-efficient with a database of all issued patterns. The four-fold rotational symmetry of the tag is accommodated by comparing the template in all four corresponding rotations. The designers encourage users to select tag designs with strong asymmetric features. The purported advantage of this method is that the tag designs can be selected to have semantic meaning for the users of the system as any image can be used. However, the ad hoc selection for tag templates means that the system cannot guarantee good separation of the targets.

Owen *et al.* present a scheme for selecting a set of greyscale (asymmetric) templates with maximum auto-correlation distance[7]. This process creates approximately 200 maximally separated tags, but the tags no longer have semantic meaning for a human reader. Figure 1 shows an example template from AR-ToolKit and one using the maximum separation scheme.

Template schemes present a number of problems for a dependable vision system. Firstly, an analysis of the set of templates must be performed to verify that the auto-correlation between any pair of patterns is small and so incremental deployment is difficult. Secondly, perspective projection combined with the limited resolution of CCD cameras will introduce distortion into the imaged template affecting the correlation co-efficient; current schemes for template selection do not take this into account. Thirdly, noise produced by the image acquisition phase (e.g. dark current) will introduce additional distortion to the templates.

Fig. 1. A sample template from the ARToolKit distribution (left) and from the maximum distance set (right)

Finally, wide-scale deployment of a vision system will require a large address space that cannot be provided with this mechanism. For example, in our lab of approximately 40 people we have 206 tagged items—already exceeding the limit of the maximum distance method.

3   Symbolic Codes

A more promising approach for coding data on tags is a symbolic method. The tag is divided up into data cells, each of which is capable of storing a symbol. This approach presents a number of potential advantages over template-based codes: we expect to be able to achieve a substantially larger address space and error detecting or error correcting codes give the ability to detect or recover from image noise. If human interpretation of the tags is required a tag design could easily include human readable text or icons in addition to the machine readable coding.

Readers of symbolic tags should expect both single bit and burst errors. A bit error could occur due to the image being sampled at incorrect points or due to noise from the CCD array. Partial occlusions of the tags or complex lighting conditions will cause burst errors and an entire sequence of symbols will be misread. We assume that these errors are equally likely to occur across the whole tag.

The current generation of symbolic tags does not take full advantage of the error handling potential of symbolic codes due to the rotational symmetry of the tags. For example, TRIP[8] uses circular tags with two rings of data split into sectors. Each sector stores one of four possible symbols (each ring within the sector stores a binary value). The symbol corresponding to a completely black sector is reserved for a synchronisation sector. The remaining tag consists of two checksum sectors and the payload encoded as a base 3 number (because the fourth symbol is reserved for synchronisation). Despite the (weak) error detection properties of the checksum the code is limited by the unprotected synchronisation sector. As a result this scheme can only ever guarantee to detect one bit of error; two bits of error suffice to fool the system into starting decoding from the wrong sector. Whether or not this invalid reading will pass the checksum depends on the data that was encoded.

The Matrix Tag system[9] uses square tags to carry arbitrary payloads with CRCs appended on the ends. This approach lacks robustness because the tag has four-fold rotational symmetry. Thus, rotated tags read as permutations of the original code. We have no analytical way to determine whether or not these permutations will contain a valid CRC.

Zhong *et al.* present a square tag which carries 5 bits of data protected by a block sum code check or 6 bits of data protected by a Hamming code[10]. The four corner bits are used for orientation to ensure that the correct code can be read from the tag. Unfortunately, the block code does not protect these orientation bits and so two bits of error in the image can result in the system reading a rotated tag from the wrong orientation and thus returning an invalid code. The Hamming distance of this code should thus be considered to be only two bits until it can be proven that no two codes are rotationally self-similar.

Cho and Neumann encode data on their multi-ring circular tags using *solid* rings chosen from n colours[11]. Assuming these colours can be reliably identified by the system, the method has the potential to be robust because the code can be read radially at any position. However, the amount of data that can be stored on the tag is small due to the large amount of redundancy. Also, an additional error correcting code would be needed if error correction capability was required.

4   Rotational Invariance

The rotational symmetry of tags means that permutations of the codes can be read. Some current code designs attempt to resolve this problem by introducing anchor points in to the code (such as TRIP's synchronisation sectors or Zhong's orientation bits) but fail to protect these data when protecting the payload. Other systems have relied on the error detection capabilities of the coding scheme to additionally detect rotations of the tag data. The chance of collisions due to this approach cannot be analysed with existing information coding theory.

Cyclic codes present a solution to the rotational symmetry problem. One property of a cyclic code is that any rotation of a valid codeword is also a valid codeword. If we arrange data coded with a cyclic code in such a way that rotations of the tag correspond to rotations of the sampled data (rather than general permutations) then we can be assured that the error detecting or error correcting capabilities of the code will be unaffected. This separates the code from tag design details and enables a mathematical analysis of code capability. To see that this is true consider the following scenario. Suppose the minimum distance of the original code is d and given a valid codeword we introduce an error in less than d places. If the resulting word is equal to the rotation of some codeword then it itself must be a codeword (all rotations of codewords are codewords!). This contradicts the fact that the original code had minimum distance d.

We shall use the term *rotational invariance* for reading a code from a tag such that all symmetric rotations of the tag correspond to rotations of the code. It is straightforward to arrange to read a circular tag in a rotationally invariant

Fig. 2. A circular tag can be read in a rotationally invariant manner (left) or a non-invariant manner (right)

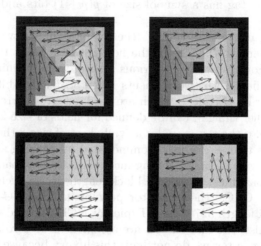

Fig. 3. A square tag can be read in a rotationally invariant manner (each reading could start in any of the four corners). Tags with an odd number of cells must sacrifice the central cell

manner (Figure 2). Arranging to read a square tag in this manner is less geometrically intuitive. For example, the immediately-appealing raster approach produces a different permutation of the code depending on the starting corner. A scheme that reads the tag as four triangular sections achieves rotational invariance (Figure 3) but if the code grid contains an odd number of data cells then the central cell cannot be used.

If we apply a cyclic code to a tag in a rotationally invariant manner we know that the error detecting or error correcting properties of the code will not be affected by the rotational symmetry of the tag. However, this presents an additional problem because the system will be unable to select the correct code from the set of possibilities read from the tag. Each possibility will appear as a valid codeword (after applying any applicable error correction routine). One approach is to select the particular rotation which has a smaller value than every other possibility. This means that for each value coded onto a tag there will be a number of additional codewords which also decode to the same value. We call codes exhibiting this property *symbolic identifier* codes—the code cannot store arbitrary data (without using a non-systematic code).

We can characterise a tag's data-carrying capability in terms of two variables: **Symbol Size** is the number of bits allocated to storing each symbol. If the tag is rotated by one place and the code re-sampled, the new value should be identical to the previous value after a rotation through *symbol size* bits; **Payload Size** is number of symbols the tag can store.

A circular tag with m rings and n sectors thus has a symbol size of m bits and a payload size n. A $2p \times 2p$ square tag laid out using the rotational invariant scheme in Figure 3 has symbol size of p^2 bits and payload size 4 whereas a $(2p + 1) \times (2p + 1)$ tag has symbol size of $p(p + 1)$ bits and payload size of 4 symbols.

We can also parameterise coding schemes in a similar way. The number of symbols corresponds to the size of the field used to define the polynomials in the cyclic code. For example, the various generator polynomials for a CRC are defined over the field with two elements (symbol size is 1-bit). Reed Solomon codes (a subset of BCH codes), which are used for error correction on CDs and DVDs (among other things), can be defined for fields of size 256 (symbol size is 8 bits). Of course, if the tag provides a symbol set of size 8 then codes requiring a symbol size less than 8 can be accommodated by packing additional symbols into each sector (with a corresponding increase in the payload size).

The payload size must equal the block length of the cyclic code. This precludes the use of CRCs: the generator polynomial for CRC-CCITT (a 16 bit CRC) has a block length 32767 bits. Typically, a CRC is used with much smaller messages than this—the unused bits are assumed to be zero and not transmitted. For a symmetric tag we do not have this luxury because we must transmit the zeros as well in order for all rotations of the code to be valid codewords. A circular tag carrying CRC-CCITT data would need 151 rings and 217 sectors!

5   Robust Data Coding Schemes

We have identified the concept of rotational invariance, that allows robust application of cyclic codes to symmetric tags. This exposes the ambiguity introduced into the coding system and hence reduces the codes to carrying only identifiers which can then be used for a database lookup, rather than symbolic data. Furthermore, we have shown that existing techniques that use synchronisation sectors or orientation bits to anchor the code are not capable of coping with more than 1 bit of error. It is possible to design synchronisation sectors that can withstand more than one bit of error at the expense of a reduced payload. We now present some additional coding schemes that allow tags to carry arbitrary data robustly.

5.1   Simple Parity Code

A bit string with parity at the end fulfils our criteria for a rotationally invariant code: every rotation of the coded data should also have valid parity. To generate a code we take a tag with payload size p and symbol size s and encode $s(p-1)$ bits and an additional parity symbol. This is an example of a code that can only encode an identifier because the decoded message must be rotated round until the minimal value is found. However, it achieves the same minimum hamming distance as the TRIP code and the Hamming code scheme by Zhong *et al.* and can store considerably more data.

5.2 Independent Chunk Code

Given a tag with a large *symbol size*, each symbol is considered as a separate codeword which is protected by an error detecting or error correcting code. The first bit of each symbol is used to anchor the code: the first bit of the first symbol is set and the first bit of every other symbol is unset. For example, a square tag of size 8 × 8 has a symbol size of 16 and a payload size of 4 symbols. We can encode a 44-bit payload in four 11-bit chunks. Each symbol on the tag contains one chunk, one orientation bit, and a 4-bit CRC (Figure 4). This code is at least as strong as the 4-bit CRC used for each symbol, if the designer required stronger error detection or error correction then a different code can be used for each symbol. In the cases where errors occur evenly over the tag rather than concentrated in one sector this code should be rather stronger than a single CRC-4. The orientation bits are included in the CRC-4 for additional reliability. The drawbacks of using this code is that 4 bits of every symbol are used to get the same Hamming distance as traditional use of a single 4-bit CRC. Additionally a further bit is required per symbol to orient the code. The advantage of this encoding method is that the code need not have rotational invariance and so a truncated CRC is permissible.

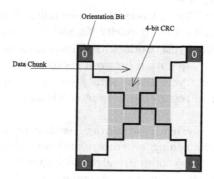

Fig. 4. The Independent Chunk Code operates on a tag with large symbols, each of which contains an orientation bit and some error protection

5.3 Structured Cyclic Code

Our third scheme is a more conventional cyclic code with additional structure that encodes the amount of rotation that the code has undergone. The full details are presented in Appendix A. A generator polynomial f is chosen that will produce a code with the desired error detecting or error correcting capabilities.

The target tag has a symbol size s and a payload size n. An auxiliary generator polynomial h, dependent on f, is then found and a primitive polynomial ω is found from h. These parameters are fixed for a particular instance of this coding scheme and so the computational costs of finding them is not a run-time issue.

We encode a message m of $n - \deg(f) - \deg(h)$ symbols and an arbitrary number α, $0 \le \alpha < (2^{s \deg(h)} - 1)/n$ by careful choice of a check polynomial c based on ω, α, m, h and f. The data (α, m) are encoded as $X^r m + c$ i.e. the message m is left-shifted by r symbols and the check polynomial c is written into the low bits. This will be a valid codeword for the generator polynomial f and so traditional error correction routines from the literature[12] can be applied. The additional structure imposed on our check polynomial c further provides a means of recovering the amount of rotation the code has undergone (in addition to α).

6 Evaluation

We used a test system to evaluate the performance of our new cyclic coding schemes. A circular tag with 5 rings and 31 sectors was used to carry a payload encoded with each of the new schemes.

- **TRIP.** Adaption of the original coding technique used in the TRIP system: 1 synchronisation sector followed by 2 checksum sectors and 28 payload sectors encoded base 31.
- **SPC.** Simple Parity Code: 154 payload cells (not sectors) followed by 1 parity cell encoded base 2.
- **ICC.** Independent Chunk Code: 31 independent chunks (one per symbol) containing 1 orientation bit, 1 parity bit and 3 bits of payload;
- **SCC-1.** Structured Cyclic Code with f chosen as in a Reed-Solomon code giving 3 symbols of separation between codewords.
- **SCC-2.** Structured Cyclic Code with f chosen as in a Reed-Solomon code giving 11 symbols of separation between codewords.

Figure 5 shows the system reading tags, each carrying the same value, encoded with each of the coding schemes mentioned above. The data carrying capabilities of each of these codes are given in Figure 6.

An OpenGL test harness was used to render tags fully facing the camera at a distance 2 times the tag width and 1000 trials per code with each coding scheme were run. Gaussian noise (mean 0 and standard deviation 53) was injected into the images and the target tags decoded. We define three possible results from each test run.

- **Successful Read.** The payload on the tag is decoded and the returned code matches the value encoded (a true positive).
- **Failed Read.** The payload on the tag fails to decode and so the system fails to recognise a tag.

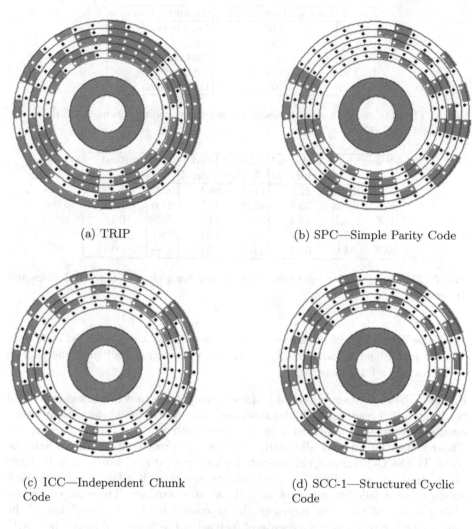

(a) TRIP

(b) SPC—Simple Parity Code

(c) ICC—Independent Chunk
Code

(d) SCC-1—Structured Cyclic
Code

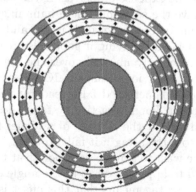

(e) SCC-2—Structured Cyclic
Code

Fig. 5. Examples of the system decoding each of the evaluated code types. The tags (faded to grey) have been sampled at the points shown

Name	Message Length (bits)	Hamming Distance
TRIP	139	2 symbols
SPC	154	2 bits
ICC	93	2 bits per symbol
SCC-1	141	3 symbols
SCC-2	101	11 symbols

Fig. 6. The data carrying capabilities of the evaluated coding schemes. 155 data cells are available on the tag

Name	Successful Read		Failed Read		False Read	
	%	Normalised	%	Normalised	%	Normalised
TRIP	24.0	21.5	74.0	66.4	2.00	1.79
SPC	31.0	30.8	46.0	45.7	23.0	22.9
ICC	27.1	16.3	72.6	43.6	0.300	0.18
SCC-1	55.7	50.7	6.20	5.64	38.1	34.7
SCC-2	94.0	61.3	6.00	3.91	$< \frac{1}{10}$	0

Fig. 7. The success, failed, and false reading rates for a circular tag with 5 rings and 31 sectors

– **False Read.** The payload on the tag is decoded but the returned code does not match the encoded value, i.e. the error detection built into the code is defeated (a false positive).

Figure 7 shows the percentage of frames for each code that contained successful readings, failed readings and false readings. Normalised values for these percentages are obtained by multiplying by the proportion of the utilised address space. The results confirm that allocating more bits to error control strengthens the code. The SCC-2 shows a particularly high successful read rate due to its large error-correcting capability. This redundancy also gives it a false read rate small enough that it failed to manifest itself in our 1000 samples. The error correction ability of the SCC-1 code increases the successful read rate above that of the non-correcting codes at the expense of increasing the false read rate. The TRIP, SPC, and ICC codes have the same minimum hamming distance. However, the noise was evenly distributed across the whole image and so the ICC code's parity bits acted mostly independently giving it good false read rate. The TRIP code distributes the code particularly unevenly over the tag, this manifests itself in the code's more variable behaviour than the ICC code—it shows an increased successful read rate *and* an increased false read rate even though there is no attempted error correction. For interactive systems, designers might choose to minimise the false read rate at the expense of a higher failed read rate because users can be expected to retry a tag if it fails to read.

For a circular tag we wish to sample data points at the centre of each sector. To achieve this we need to apply an offset to the angle of each sector. However, the symmetry of a circular tag means that this offset is unknown. One scheme for achieving a reliable reading is to attempt to read the code n times from the

Parity Bit

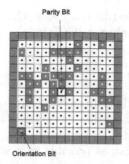

Orientation Bit

Fig. 8. A square tag carrying data with the ICC coding scheme. The tag (faded to grey) has been sampled at the points shown. One symbol, including its orientation bit and parity bit, has been highlighted

Name	Successful Read		Failed Read		False Read	
	%	Normalised	%	Normalised	%	Normalised
TRIP(square)	12.6	9.5475	83.4	63.12917	4	3.027778
SPC(square)	27.4	27.4083	44	43.69444	28.6	28.40139
ICC(square)	24	22.6667	70.5	66.58333	5.5	5.194444

Fig. 9. The successful, failed, and false reading rates for the evaluated coding schemes on a square tag of size 12×12

tag at intervals of $1/n$ sectors. The system can then select the correct reading by looking for duplicate readings. From a viewpoint of coding robustness this acts similarly to a repetition code: the same bit error must be present in two or more of the readings in order for it to be considered as a valid code. In practice this reduces the false error rate almost to zero for each of the coding techniques. Of course, if the errors in the decoding are systematic—perhaps due to an occlusion or lighting conditions—this will not be as successful. Also, use of this method reduces the success rate of the code as well, especially for the error correcting codes.

A further experiment using the TRIP, SPC, and ICC tests was performed using a square tag of size 12×12 rather than a circular tag. The SCC codes cannot be applied to square tags due to the constraints imposed on the message size. The ICC code for a square (Figure 8) is rather more efficient than for a circular tag due to the increased symbol size. We expect the square tag to perform less well as compared to the circular tag because its payload area is smaller. Figure 9 shows the various decoding rates which bear out the same trends as for the circular tag. This provides some justification for our argument that code selection can be done in isolation from the actual tag design. The ICC(square) code presents a better normalised successful read rate than the TRIP(square) code which is contrary to the results for circular tags. This is because the ICC code is much more efficient for tags with large symbol sizes and so its success rate is boosted to acknowledge this. However, the increased symbol size means that there will be fewer parity bits embedded in the code—this is reflected by the increased false read rate for ICC(square) over ICC(circle).

7 Asymmetric Tags

Another approach is to introduce an asymmetric feature into the tag design thus permitting use of conventional coding systems. For example, Foxlin[13] presents a system that uses an off-centre eyelet for this purpose. This addition to the tag design should be as unintrusive as possible as it will reduce the size of the data carrying area of the tag. However, we must also ensure that the noise in the image does not cause us to mis-read the orientation of the tag.

In order to maximise the data carrying capability of the tag we require that the new feature and the data carrying code are equally resistant to image noise—correct choice of the tag orientation is useless if the code cannot be subsequently decoded. It is difficult to quantify the strength of the introduced asymmetric feature and so designers must err on the side of safety.

QR Codes are a popular 2-dimensional barcode that use a particular pattern on three corners to orient the tag. Four different levels of error correction are available of which level 'M' corresponds most closely to the level afforded by the SCC-2 code presented above. QR Codes are available in a number of sizes, the largest of which has a data area with dimensions 177×177. This size of tag can store 18648^1 bits which corresponds to a utilisation of 59.5% whereas the SCC-2 code has a utilisation of 64%. The primary reason for this is that the area occupied by the asymmetric features added to the QR Code is disproportionately large compared with the error correction capability of the error correcting code.

Use of symmetric tags and rotationally invariant codes is advantageous in this respect because the minimum amount of payload space is wasted in order to encode rotation information. Also, rotationally invariant tags result in the least possible complication of the computer vision aspect of the decoding. The system need only read the data from the tag rather than search for additional features before decoding the information.

8 Conclusion

A dependable location system requires robust, predictable behaviour for every element of its operation. The choice of coding scheme used to store data on a fiducial tag is an important aspect often overlooked. Template-based systems pose a particular risk because it is difficult to analyse the effects of image noise or perspective projection on the pattern. Current symbolic coding schemes have not fully appreciated the rotational ambiguity caused by symmetric tags and thus do not have quantifiable characteristics. Sentient Computing must be dependable in order to fulfil its potential. This requires rigorously understood coding schemes and this work provides useful, successful, and efficient examples.

---

[1] See http://www.denso-wave.com/qrcode/vertable4-e.html

Tag abstraction coupled with the principle of rotational invariance allows tags to utilise existing information coding techniques and makes the result amenable to rigorous mathematical analysis. This decomposition highlights a particular class of symbolic codes capable only of encoding identifiers due to the rotational ambiguity of the tags. For systems requiring arbitrary symbolic data we have presented a number of dependable coding schemes.

When selecting a suitable code for a tag design we may choose to optimise based on the message size, error handling capabilities, implementation difficulty or computational cost. The Structured Cyclic Coding scheme presented herein proves to be a good choice: it makes efficient use of the available payload space to carry a large message whilst still providing a large degree of error correction. It allows one to encode arbitrary data and requires the minimal amount of computer vision possible. Future work will be to document the extension this technique to apply to square tags as well as circles.

Another approach for dealing with rotational symmetry was to introduce asymmetric features to the tag to break the ambiguity. However, designing the additional features required less efficient that the approach suggested here due to the (unmeasurable) trade-off between feature size and tag capacity.

Acknowledgements

This work was supported by the EPSRC. Grateful thanks to Alastair Beresford and Andy Hopper for their support and guidance.

References

1. Shortis, M.R., Beyer, H.A.: Chapter 5. In: Close Range Photogrammetry and Machine Vision. Whittles Publishing (1996) 106–155
2. Brown, D.: Decentering distortion of lenses. Photogrammetric Engineering and Remote Sensing **32** (1966) 444–462
3. Heikklä, J., Silvén, O.: A four-step camera calibration procedure with implicit image correction. In: Computer Vision and Pattern Recognition. (1997) 1106–1113
4. Hightower, J., Borriello, G.: Real-time error in location modeling for ubiquitous computing. In: Location Modeling for Ubiquitous Computing—Ubicomp 2001 Workshop. (2001) 21–27
5. Dey, A.K., D.Abowd, G.: Towards a better understanding of context and context-awareness. In: Proceedings of the CHI 2000 Workshop on "The What, Who, Where, When, Why and How of Context-Awareness". (2000)
6. Billinghurst, M., Kato, H.: Collaborative mixed reality. In: Proceedings of the First International Symposium on Mixed Reality. (1999) 261–284
7. Owen, C.B., Xiao, F., Middlin, P.: What is the best fiducial? In: The First IEEE International Augmented Reality Toolkit Workshop. (2002) 98–105
8. de Ipiña, D.L., Mendonạ, P.R.S., Hopper, A.: TRIP: a low-cost vision-based location system for ubiquitous computing. Personal and Ubiquitous Computing **6** (2002) 206–219
9. Rekimoto, J.: Matrix: A realtime object identification and registration method for augmented reality. In: Proceedings of Asia Pacific Computer Human Interaction. (1998) 63–68

10. Zhong, X., Liu, P., Georganas, N.D., Boulanger, P.: Designing a vision-based collaborative augmented reality application for industrial training. it-Information Technology **45** (2003) 7–18
11. Cho, Y., Neumann, U.: Multiring fiducial systems for scalable fiducial-tracking augmented reality. PRESENCE: Teleoperators and Virtual Environments **10** (2001) 599–612
12. Berlekamp, E.R.: Algebraic Coding Theory. McGraw-Hill (1968)
13. Naimark, L., Foxlin, E.: Circular data matrix fiducial system and robust image processing for a wearable vision-inertial self-tracker. In: IEEE International Symposium on Mixed and Augmented Reality. (2002) 27–36
14. Pholig, S., Hellman, M.: An improved algorithm for computing logarithms over gf(p) and its cryptographic significance. IEEE Transactions on Information Theory **24** (1978) 106–110

A   Robust Data Coding Scheme for Symmetric Tags

We operate in the finite field of size $q = p^s$ where p is a prime number and s is an integer. Selecting $p = 2$ leads to a convenient and efficient implementation. However this is not possible in the case of SCC for a square tag (see later). Take a generator polynomial f for some cyclic code that has the desired error control properties. As in a normal cyclic code of length n we have $X^n - 1 = fg$ for some g and all valid codewords are multiples of f. Our tag must have rotational symmetry of order k dividing n. We then find h which is an irreducible factor of g. For reasonable choices of f, h can be chosen so that X has order n modulo h. Since h is irreducible, there exists a primitive polynomial ω whereby every non-zero value modulo h can be expressed as ω^z mod h for some z. The order of ω is $l = q^{\deg(h)} - 1$. Since X has order n modulo h, it is possible to choose ω such that $\omega^{\frac{l}{n}} \equiv X$ mod h.

Let $r = \deg(f) + \deg(h)$. We can now encode a number $\alpha < \frac{l}{k}$ and a polynomial m where $\deg(m) < n - r$ as follows. Define the check polynomial c where $\deg(c) < r$ by the conditions $c \equiv \omega^\alpha - X^r m$ mod h and $c \equiv -X^r m$ mod f (this can be done using the Chinese Remainder Theorem—see page 29 of [12]). We encode (α, m) as $c + X^r m$. This is a valid codeword since $c + X^r m \equiv X^r m - X^r m \equiv 0$ mod f.

The received codeword y, read from the tag, should be a valid codeword for the generator polynomial f. If not, existing techniques for error correction[12] can now be applied to find the nearest valid codeword. If a codeword represented by the polynomial y is rotated one place round then the polynomial corresponding to the new codeword is given by Xy mod $X^n - 1$. Proof: if y is given by $a_0 + a_1 X + \ldots + a_{n-1}X^{n-1}$ then $Xy = a_0 X + a_1 X^2 + \ldots + a_{n-1}X^n$ and the rotated codeword is represented by $a_{n-1} + a_0 X + a_1 X^2 + \ldots + a_{n-2}X^{n-1}$. We see that the difference of these last two expressions is $a_{n-1}(X^n - 1)$, a multiple of $X^n - 1$.

Thus, if the tag has been rotated t times then the (possibly corrected) codeword y read from the tag will have been multiplied by $X^{tn/k}$ so $y = X^{tn/k}(X^r m + c)$ mod $(X^n - 1)$.

We now show how to find t (and α). This can then be used to recover $X^r m + c$ and hence the stored value. Since h divides $X^n - 1$ we see that:

$$y \equiv X^{tn/k}(c + X^r m) \mod h$$
$$\equiv X^{tn/k}(\omega^\alpha - X^r m + X^r m) \mod h$$
$$\equiv X^{tn/k}\omega^\alpha \mod h \equiv \omega^{\alpha + tl/k} \mod h$$

Thus, if we find the unique z such that $0 \leq z < l$ and $y \equiv \omega^z \mod h$ then:

$$\alpha = z \mod \frac{l}{k}, t = \lfloor \frac{z}{l/k} \rfloor \tag{1}$$

Our original message m is the most significant $n-r$ coefficients of y after rotating it right by tn/k places (dividing by $X^{tn/k}$).

The task of finding z (solving a discrete logarithm) is potentially computationally expensive. However, in practice h is typically small enough to allow this to be solved using a lookup table. In particular, for Reed-Solomon codes $n = q - 1$, $\deg(h) = 1$ and so $l = n$ which is small. Even in less favourable circumstances l tends to have a large number of small factors and so even for large values of l (which bounds z), the discrete log can be found efficiently using the Pohlig-Hellman algorithm[14].

When this is applied to a circular tag with n sectors and m rings (so $q = 2^m$) this allows

$$\frac{l}{n} 2^{m(n - \deg(f) - \deg(h))}$$
$$= \frac{1}{n}(2^{m \deg(h)} - 1)2^{m(n - \deg(f) - \deg(h))}$$
$$= \frac{1}{n}(1 - 2^{-m \deg(h)})2^{m(n - \deg(f))}$$

messages to be encoded. We get one nth of the message space given by just using the cyclic code given by f. That is, we lose $\log n$ bits compared to using the simple scheme.

If we are to apply this scheme to square tags then since there is a rotational symmetry of order 4, the number of symbols in our code must be a multiple of 4. Unfortunately, there are no good cyclic codes where the length of the code and the size of the underlying field share a common factor. This precludes the use of fields of size 2^m in this case. Instead we are forced to use fields based on other prime numbers. As a concrete example we use a square tag of size $19 \times 19 = 361$ sectors. We use the prime $p = 61$ and our code will be the Reed-Solomon code of length 60 over the field $GF(61)$ of 61 elements. We encode an element of $GF(61)$ by using 6 sectors of our tag. There are $2^6 = 64$ possibilities for how to set each group of 6 sectors and so there will be 3 possibilities for each symbol which do not correspond to any valid encoding under this scheme. Now we can encode 60 symbols onto our 19×19 tag in the following manner.

As this is a Reed-Solomon code we will have $\deg(h) = 1$ so $l = 60$. However, a rotation of the tag in this situation will correspond to a rotation of the codeword by 15 symbols ie. multiplication by X^{15}. Thus our maximum value for α is 15. We are able to encode $15 \times 61^{60-\deg(f)-\deg(h)} = 15 \times 61^{59-\deg(f)}$ messages. This is $353.82 - 5.93 \deg(f)$ bits and is not far away from the $360 - 6 \deg(f)$ bits which could be achieved using a similar Reed-Solomon code over $GF(64)$ with a tag of known orientation. In fact, the amount of wasted bits is less than 2 percent of the tag area.

Suppose more generally that m is a field size such that $m = 2^k - d$ for some small value of d. If we were to use our scheme with a Reed-Solomon code of length $m - 1$ over the field $GF(m)$ then we would need $m - 1$ to be a multiple of 4 so we would have to restrict to those m which are congruent to 1 modulo 4. We would have $\deg(h) = 1$ and so the maximum value for α would be $(m-1)/4$ and we could encode

$$\frac{m-1}{4} m^{m-1-\deg(f)-\deg(h)} = \frac{m-1}{4} m^{m-2-\deg(f)} \tag{2}$$

messages. This is

$$\log(m-1) - \log 4 + (m - 2 - \deg(f)) \log m$$
$$\approx (m-1) \log m - 2 - \deg(f) \log m$$
$$= (m-1) \log(2^k - d) - 2 - \deg(f) \log m$$
$$= (m-1) \log((1 - d/2^k)2^k) - 2 - \deg(f) \log m$$
$$\approx (m-1)k - \frac{(m-1)d}{2^k \ln 2} - 2 - \deg(f) \log m$$
$$\approx (m-1)k - \frac{d}{\ln 2} - 2 - \deg(f) \log m$$

bits. The wastage of $d/\ln 2 + 2$ bits is quite bearable, however, there is no guarantee that the $(m-1)k$ sectors that are needed will fit efficiently into any $n \times n$ square. Figure 10 shows a few examples of varying sizes which do work quite well.

Tag Size	Field Size	Code Length (symbols)	Symbol Size (cells)	Payload Size (bits)	Utilisation
7×7	13	12	4	42.3	86.4%
12×12	29	28	5	134.0	93.06%
13×13	31	30	5	146.6	86.8%
19×19	61	60	6	353.8	98.01%
29×29	121	120	7	828.3	98.49%
44×44	241	240	8	1897.1	97.99%
68×68	509	508	9	4565.7	98.74%
101×101	1021	1020	10	10193.7	99.93%

Fig. 10. A selection of square tag sizes carrying efficient SCC codes

Author Index

Lecture Notes in Computer Science

For information about Vols. 1–3501

please contact your bookseller or Springer

Vol. 3548: K. Julisch, C. Kruegel (Eds.), Intrusion and Malware Detection and Vulnerability Assessment. X, 241 pages. 2005.

Vol. 3547: F. Bomarius, S. Komi-Sirviö (Eds.), Product Focused Software Process Improvement. XIII, 588 pages. 2005.

Vol. 3546: T. Kanade, A. Jain, N.K. Ratha (Eds.), Audio- and Video-Based Biometric Person Authentication. XX, 1134 pages. 2005.

Vol. 3544: T. Higashino (Ed.), Principles of Distributed Systems. XII, 460 pages. 2005.

Vol. 3543: L. Kutvonen, N. Alonistioti (Eds.), Distributed Applications and Interoperable Systems. XI, 235 pages. 2005.

Vol. 3542: H.H. Hoos, D.G. Mitchell (Eds.), Theory and Applications of Satisfiability Testing. XIII, 393 pages. 2005.

Vol. 3541: N.C. Oza, R. Polikar, J. Kittler, F. Roli (Eds.), Multiple Classifier Systems. XII, 430 pages. 2005.

Vol. 3540: H. Kalviainen, J. Parkkinen, A. Kaarna (Eds.), Image Analysis. XXII, 1270 pages. 2005.

Vol. 3539: K. Morik, J.-F. Boulicaut, A. Siebes (Eds.), Local Pattern Detection. XI, 233 pages. 2005. (Subseries LNAI).

Vol. 3538: L. Ardissono, P. Brna, A. Mitrovic (Eds.), User Modeling 2005. XVI, 533 pages. 2005. (Subseries LNAI).

Vol. 3537: A. Apostolico, M. Crochemore, K. Park (Eds.), Combinatorial Pattern Matching. XI, 444 pages. 2005.

Vol. 3536: G. Ciardo, P. Darondeau (Eds.), Applications and Theory of Petri Nets 2005. XI, 470 pages. 2005.

Vol. 3535: M. Steffen, G. Zavattaro (Eds.), Formal Methods for Open Object-Based Distributed Systems. X, 323 pages. 2005.

Vol. 3534: S. Spaccapietra, E. Zimányi (Eds.), Journal on Data Semantics III. XI, 213 pages. 2005.

Vol. 3533: M. Ali, F. Esposito (Eds.), Innovations in Applied Artificial Intelligence. XX, 858 pages. 2005. (Subseries LNAI).

Vol. 3532: A. Gómez-Pérez, J. Euzenat (Eds.), The Semantic Web: Research and Applications. XV, 728 pages. 2005.

Vol. 3531: J. Ioannidis, A. Keromytis, M. Yung (Eds.), Applied Cryptography and Network Security. XI, 530 pages. 2005.

Vol. 3530: A. Prinz, R. Reed, J. Reed (Eds.), SDL 2005: Model Driven. XI, 361 pages. 2005.

Vol. 3528: P.S. Szczepaniak, J. Kacprzyk, A. Niewiadomski (Eds.), Advances in Web Intelligence. XVII, 513 pages. 2005. (Subseries LNAI).

Vol. 3527: R. Morrison, F. Oquendo (Eds.), Software Architecture. XII, 263 pages. 2005.

Vol. 3526: S.B. Cooper, B. Löwe, L. Torenvliet (Eds.), New Computational Paradigms. XVII, 574 pages. 2005.

Vol. 3525: A.E. Abdallah, C.B. Jones, J.W. Sanders (Eds.), Communicating Sequential Processes. XIV, 321 pages. 2005.

Vol. 3524: R. Barták, M. Milano (Eds.), Integration of AI and OR Techniques in Constraint Programming for Combinatorial Optimization Problems. XI, 320 pages. 2005.

Vol. 3523: J.S. Marques, N. Pérez de la Blanca, P. Pina (Eds.), Pattern Recognition and Image Analysis, Part II. XXVI, 733 pages. 2005.

Vol. 3522: J.S. Marques, N. Pérez de la Blanca, P. Pina (Eds.), Pattern Recognition and Image Analysis, Part I. XXVI, 703 pages. 2005.

Vol. 3521: N. Megiddo, Y. Xu, B. Zhu (Eds.), Algorithmic Applications in Management. XIII, 484 pages. 2005.

Vol. 3520: O. Pastor, J. Falcão e Cunha (Eds.), Advanced Information Systems Engineering. XVI, 584 pages. 2005.

Vol. 3519: H. Li, P. J. Olver, G. Sommer (Eds.), Computer Algebra and Geometric Algebra with Applications. IX, 449 pages. 2005.

Vol. 3518: T.B. Ho, D. Cheung, H. Liu (Eds.), Advances in Knowledge Discovery and Data Mining. XXI, 864 pages. 2005. (Subseries LNAI).

Vol. 3517: H.S. Baird, D.P. Lopresti (Eds.), Human Interactive Proofs. IX, 143 pages. 2005.

Vol. 3516: V.S. Sunderam, G.D.v. Albada, P.M.A. Sloot, J.J. Dongarra (Eds.), Computational Science – ICCS 2005, Part III. LXIII, 1143 pages. 2005.

Vol. 3515: V.S. Sunderam, G.D.v. Albada, P.M.A. Sloot, J.J. Dongarra (Eds.), Computational Science – ICCS 2005, Part II. LXIII, 1101 pages. 2005.

Vol. 3514: V.S. Sunderam, G.D.v. Albada, P.M.A. Sloot, J.J. Dongarra (Eds.), Computational Science – ICCS 2005, Part I. LXIII, 1089 pages. 2005.

Vol. 3513: A. Montoyo, R. Muñoz, E. Métais (Eds.), Natural Language Processing and Information Systems. XII, 408 pages. 2005.

Vol. 3512: J. Cabestany, A. Prieto, F. Sandoval (Eds.), Computational Intelligence and Bioinspired Systems. XXV, 1260 pages. 2005.

Vol. 3511: U.K. Wiil (Ed.), Metainformatics. VIII, 221 pages. 2005.

Vol. 3510: T. Braun, G. Carle, Y. Koucheryavy, V. Tsaousidis (Eds.), Wired/Wireless Internet Communications. XIV, 366 pages. 2005.

Vol. 3509: M. Jünger, V. Kaibel (Eds.), Integer Programming and Combinatorial Optimization. XI, 484 pages. 2005.

Vol. 3508: P. Bresciani, P. Giorgini, B. Henderson-Sellers, G. Low, M. Winikoff (Eds.), Agent-Oriented Information Systems II. X, 227 pages. 2005. (Subseries LNAI).

Vol. 3507: F. Crestani, I. Ruthven (Eds.), Information Context: Nature, Impact, and Role. XIII, 253 pages. 2005.

Vol. 3506: C. Park, S. Chee (Eds.), Information Security and Cryptology – ICISC 2004. XIV, 490 pages. 2005.

Vol. 3505: V. Gorodetsky, J. Liu, V. A. Skormin (Eds.), Autonomous Intelligent Systems: Agents and Data Mining. XIII, 303 pages. 2005. (Subseries LNAI).

Vol. 3504: A.F. Frangi, P.I. Radeva, A. Santos, M. Hernandez (Eds.), Functional Imaging and Modeling of the Heart. XV, 489 pages. 2005.

Vol. 3503: S.E. Nikoletseas (Ed.), Experimental and Efficient Algorithms. XV, 624 pages. 2005.

Vol. 3502: F. Khendek, R. Dssouli (Eds.), Testing of Communicating Systems. X, 381 pages. 2005.